T0336028

Software Design by Example

The best way to learn design in any field is to study examples, and some of the best examples of software design come from the tools programmers use in their own work. ***Software Design by Example: A Tool-Based Introduction with JavaScript*** therefore builds small versions of the things programmers use in order to demystify them and give some insights into how experienced programmers think. From a file backup system and a testing framework to a regular expression matcher, a browser layout engine, and a very small compiler, we explore common design patterns, show how making code easier to test also makes it easier to re-use, and help readers understand how debuggers, profilers, package managers, and version control systems work so that they can use them more effectively.

This material can be used for self-paced study, in an undergraduate course on software design, or as the core of an intensive weeklong workshop for working programmers. Each chapter has a set of exercises ranging in size and difficulty from half a dozen lines to a full day's work. Readers should be familiar with the basics of modern JavaScript, but the more advanced features of the language are explained and illustrated as they are introduced.

All the written material in this project can be freely reused under the terms of the Creative Commons - Attribution license, while all of the software is made available under the terms of the Hippocratic License. All proceeds from sale of this book will go to support the Red Door Family Shelter in Toronto.

Features

- Teaches software design by showing programmers how to build the tools they use every day
- Each chapter includes exercises to help readers check and deepen their understanding
- All the example code can be downloaded, re-used, and modified under an open license

Greg Wilson has worked in industry and academia for 35 years, and is the author, co-author, or editor of several books, including *Beautiful Code, The Architecture of Open Source Applications, JavaScript for Data Science, Teaching Tech Together*, and *Research Software Engineering with Python*. He is the co-founder and first executive director of Software Carpentry and received ACM SIGSOFT's Influential Educator Award in 2020.

Software Design by Example

A Tool-Based Introduction with JavaScript

Greg Wilson

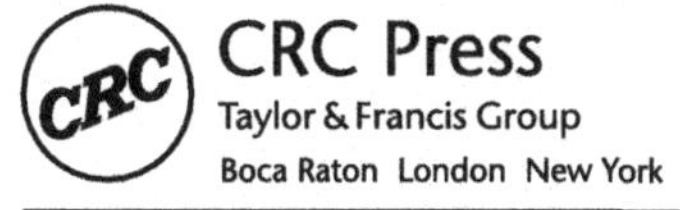

CRC Press is an imprint of the
Taylor & Francis Group, an **informa** business

First edition published 2023
by CRC Press
6000 Broken Sound Parkway NW, Suite 300, Boca Raton, FL 33487-2742

and by CRC Press
4 Park Square, Milton Park, Abingdon, Oxon, OX14 4RN

CRC Press is an imprint of Taylor & Francis Group, LLC

Library of Congress Cataloging-in-Publication Data

Names: Wilson, Greg, 1963- author.
Title: Software design by example : a tool-based introduction with JavaScript / Greg Wilson.
Description: First edition. | Boca Raton : C&H/CRC Press, 2023. | Includes bibliographical references and index.
Identifiers: LCCN 2022030475 (print) | LCCN 2022030476 (ebook) | ISBN 9781032399676 (hardback) | ISBN 9781032330235 (paperback) | ISBN 9781003317807 (ebook)
Subjects: LCSH: Software patterns. | Software architecture. | JavaScript (Compuer program language)
Classification: LCC QA76.76.P37 W55 2023 (print) | LCC QA76.76.P37 (ebook) | DDC 005.13/267--dc23/eng/20220906
LC record available at https://lccn.loc.gov/2022030475
LC ebook record available at https://lccn.loc.gov/2022030476

ISBN: 978-1-032-39967-6 (hbk)
ISBN: 978-1-032-33023-5 (pbk)
ISBN: 978-1-003-31780-7 (ebk)

DOI: 10.1201/9781003317807

Typeset in SFRM
by KnowledgeWorks Global Ltd.

Publisher's note: This book has been prepared from camera-ready copy provided by the authors.

Dedication

For Brian Kernighan,
who taught us all how to write about programming.

And for all the students who took part in CSC49X:
long may you run.

All royalties from sales of this book will go to support
the Red Door Family Shelter in Toronto.

Contents

1

Introduction

The best way to learn design is to study examples [Schon1984; Petre2016], and some of the best examples of software design come from the tools programmers use in their own work. In these lessons we build small versions of things like file backup systems, testing frameworks, regular expression matchers, and browser layout engines both to demystify them and to give some insights into how experienced programmers think. We draw inspiration from [Brown2011; Brown2012; Brown2016], Mary Rose Cook's[1] Gitlet[2], and the books that introduced the Unix philosophy to an entire generation of programmers [Kernighan1979; Kernighan1981; Kernighan1983; Kernighan1988].

All of the written material in this project can be freely reused under the terms of the Creative Commons - Attribution - NonCommercial license[3], while all of the software is made available under the terms of the Hippocratic License[4]. All proceeds from this project will go to support the Red Door Family Shelter[5].

1.1 Who is our audience?

Every lesson should be written with specific learners in mind. These three personas[6] describe ours:

- Aïsha started writing VB macros for Excel in an accounting course and never looked back. After spending three years doing front-end JavaScript work she now wants to learn how to build back-end applications. This material will fill in some gaps in her programming knowledge and teach her some common design patterns.
- Rupinder is studying computer science at college. He has learned a lot about the theory of algorithms, and while he uses Git and unit testing tools in his assignments, he doesn't feel he understands how they work. This material will give him a better understanding of those tools and of how to design new ones.
- Yim builds mobile apps for a living but also teaches two college courses: one on full-stack web development using JavaScript and Node and another titled "Software Design". They are happy with the former, but frustrated that so many books about the latter subject talk about it in the abstract and use examples that their students can't relate to. This material will fill those gaps and give them starting points for a wide variety of course assignments.

Like these three personas, readers should be able to:

- Write JavaScript programs using loops, arrays, functions, and classes.

[1]https://maryrosecook.com/
[2]http://gitlet.maryrosecook.com/
[3]https://creativecommons.org/licenses/by-nc/4.0/
[4]https://firstdonoharm.dev/
[5]https://www.reddoorshelter.ca/
[6]https://teachtogether.tech/en/index.html#s:process-personas

- Create static web pages using HTML and CSS.
- Install Node on their computer and run programs with it from the command line.
- Use Git[7] to save and share files. (It's OK not to know the more obscure commands[8].)
- Explain what a tree is and how to process one recursively. (This is the most complicated data structure and algorithm we *don't* explain.)

This book can be read on its own or used as a classroom resource. If you are looking for a project to do in a software design course, adding a tool to those covered here would be fun as well as educational. Please see Chapter 21 for more details.

1.2 What tools and ideas do we cover?

Programmers have invented a lot of tools[9] to make their lives easier. This volume focuses on a few that individual developers use while writing software; we hope future volumes will explore those used in the applications that programmers build.

Appendix E defines the terms we introduce in these lessons, which in turn define their scope:

- How to process a program like any other piece of text.
- How to turn a program into a data structure that can be analyzed and modified.
- What design patterns are and which ones are used most often.
- How programs are executed and how we can control and inspect their execution.
- How we can analyze programs' performance in order to make sensible design tradeoffs.
- How to find and run code modules on the fly.

[7]https://git-scm.com/
[8]https://git-man-page-generator.lokaltog.net/
[9]https://en.wikipedia.org/wiki/Programming_tool

1.3 How are these lessons laid out?

We display JavaScript source code like this:

```
for (const thing in collection) {
  console.log(thing)
}
```

Unix shell commands are shown like this:

```
for filename in *.dat
do
    cut -d , -f 10 $filename
done
```

and data and output like this:

```
Package,Releases
0,1
0-0,0
0-0-1,1
00print-lol,2
00smalinux,0
01changer,0
```

We occasionally wrap lines in source code in unnatural ways to make listings fit the printed page, and sometimes use ... to show where lines have been omitted. Where we need to break lines of output for the same reason, we end all but the last line with a single backslash \. The full listings are all available in our Git repository[10] and on our website[11].

Finally, we write functions as `functionName` rather than `functionName()`; the latter is more common, but people don't use `objectName{}` for objects or `arrayName[]` for arrays, and the empty parentheses makes it hard to tell whether we're talking about "the function itself" or "a call to the function with no parameters".

1.4 How did we get here?

In the early 2000s, the University of Toronto asked Greg Wilson[12] to teach an undergraduate course on software architecture. After delivering the course three times he told the university they should cancel it: between them, the dozen textbooks he had purchased with the phrase "software architecture" in their titles devoted a total of less than 30 pages to describing the designs of actual systems.

[10]https://github.com/gvwilson/sdxjs/
[11]https://stjs.tech/
[12]https://third-bit.com/

Frustrated by that, he and Andy Oram[13] persuaded some well-known programmers to contribute a chapter each to a collection called *Beautiful Code* [Oram2007], which went on to win the Jolt Award in 2007. Entries in the book described everything from figuring out whether three points are on a line to core components of Linux and the software for the Mars Rover, but the breadth that made them fun to read also meant they weren't particularly useful for teaching.

To fix that, Greg Wilson, Amy Brown[14], Tavish Armstrong[15], and Mike DiBernardo[16] edited a four-book series between 2011 and 2016 called *The Architecture of Open Source Applications*[17]. In the first two volumes, the creators of fifty open source projects described their systems' designs; the third book explored the performance of those systems, while in the fourth volume contributors built scale models of common tools as a way of demonstrating how those tools worked. These books were closer to what an instructor would need for an undergraduate class on software design, but still not quite right: the intended audience would probably not be familiar with many of the problem domains, and since each author used the programming language of their choice, much of the code would be hard to understand.

Software Tools in JavaScript is meant to address these shortcomings: all of the code is written in one language, and the examples are all tools that programmers use daily. Most of the programs are less than 60 lines long and the longest is less than 200; we believe each chapter can be covered in class in 1-2 hours, while the exercises range in difficulty from a few minutes to a couple of days.

1.5 How can people use and contribute to this material?

All of the written material on this site is made available under the Creative Commons - Attribution - NonCommercial 4.0 International license (CC-BY-NC-4.0), while the software is made available under the Hippocratic License. The first allows you to use and remix this material for non-commercial purposes, as-is or in adapted form, provided you cite its original source; the second allows you to use and remix the software on this site provided you do not violate international agreements governing human rights. Please see Appendix A for details.

If you would like to improve what we have or add new material, please see the Code of Conduct in Appendix B and the contributor guidelines in Appendix C. If you have questions or would like to use this material in a course, please file an issue in our GitHub repository[18] or send us email.

[13] http://www.praxagora.com/
[14] https://www.amyrhodabrown.com/
[15] http://tavisharmstrong.com/
[16] https://mikedebo.com/
[17] https://aosabook.org/
[18] https://github.com/gvwilson/sdxjs/

1.6 Who helped us?

I am grateful to the creators of diagrams.net[19], Emacs[20], ESLint[21], Glosario[22], GNU Make[23], LaTeX[24], Node[25], NPM[26], Standard JS[27], SVG Screenshot[28], WAVE[29], and all the other open source tools used in creating these lessons: if we all give a little, we all get a lot. I would also like to thank Darren McElligott, Evan Schultz, and Juanan Pereira for their feedback; any errors, omissions, or misunderstandings that remain are entirely my fault.

[19]https://www.diagrams.net/
[20]https://www.gnu.org/software/emacs/
[21]https://eslint.org/
[22]https://github.com/carpentries/glosario
[23]https://www.gnu.org/software/make/
[24]https://www.latex-project.org/
[25]https://nodejs.org/en/
[26]https://www.npmjs.com/
[27]https://standardjs.com/
[28]https://chrome.google.com/webstore/detail/svg-screenshot/nfakpcpmhhilkdpphcjgnokknpbpdllg
[29]https://wave.webaim.org/

2

Systems Programming

Terms defined: **anonymous function**, **asynchronous**, **Boolean**, **callback function**, **cognitive load**, **command-line argument**, **console**, **current working directory**, **destructuring assignment**, **edge case**, **filename extension**, **filesystem**, **filter**, **globbing**, **idiomatic**, **log message**, **path (in filesystem)**, **protocol**, **scope**, **single-threaded**, **string interpolation**

The biggest difference between JavaScript and most other programming languages is that many operations in JavaScript are **asynchronous**. Its designers didn't want browsers to freeze while waiting for data to arrive or for users to click on things, so operations that might be slow are implemented by describing now what to do later. And since anything that touches the hard drive is slow from a processor's point of view, Node[1] implements **filesystem** operations the same way.

> **How slow is slow?**
>
> [Gregg2020] used the analogy in Table 2.1 to show how long it takes a computer to do different things if we imagine that one CPU cycle is equivalent to one second.

Early JavaScript programs used **callback functions** to describe asynchronous operations, but as we're about to see, callbacks can be hard to understand even in small programs. In 2015, the language's developers standardized a higher-level tool called promises to make callbacks easier to manage, and more recently they have added new keywords called `async` and `await` to make it easier still. We need to understand all three layers in order to debug things when they go wrong, so this chapter explores callbacks, while Chapter 3 shows how promises and `async`/`await` work. This chapter also shows how to read and write files and directories with Node's standard libraries, because we're going to be doing that a lot.

Operation	Actual Time	Would Be...
1 CPU cycle	0.3 nsec	1 sec
Main memory access	120 nsec	6 min
Solid-state disk I/O	50-150 µsec	2-6 days
Rotational disk I/O	1-10 msec	1-12 months
Internet: San Francisco to New York	40 msec	4 years
Internet: San Francisco to Australia	183 msec	19 years
Physical system reboot	5 min	32,000 years

Table 2.1: Computer operation times at human scale.

[1]https://nodejs.org/en/

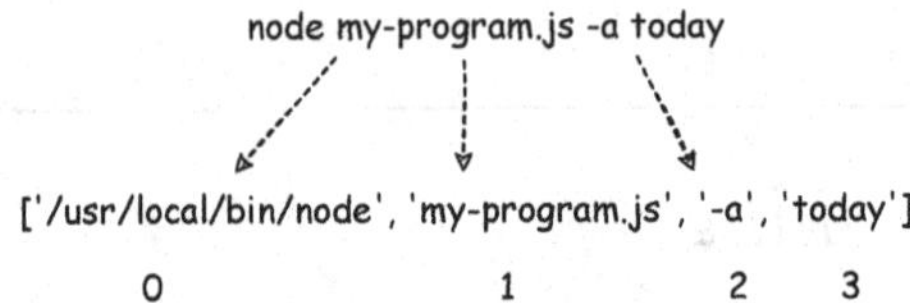

Figure 2.1: How Node stores command-line arguments in `process.argv`.

2.1 How can we list a directory?

To start, let's try listing the contents of a directory the way we would in Python[2] or Java[3]:

```
import fs from 'fs'

const srcDir = process.argv[2]
const results = fs.readdir(srcDir)
for (const name of results) {
  console.log(name)
}
```

We use `import` ***module*** `from 'source'` to load the library ***source*** and assign its contents to ***module***. After that, we can refer to things in the library using ***module.component*** just as we refer to things in any other object. We can use whatever name we want for the module, which allows us to give short nicknames to libraries with long names; we will take advantage of this in future chapters.

> **`require` versus `import`**
>
> In 2015, a new version of JavaScript called ES6 introduced the keyword `import` for importing modules. It improves on the older `require` function in several ways, but Node still uses `require` by default. To tell it to use `import`, we have added `"type": "module"` at the top level of our Node `package.json` file.

Our little program uses the `fs`[4] library which contains functions to create directories, read or delete files, etc. (Its name is short for "filesystem".) We tell the program what to list using **command-line arguments**, which Node automatically stores in an array called `process.argv`. The name of the program used to run our code is stored `process.argv[0]` (which in this case is `node`), while `process.argv[1]` is the name of our program (in this case `list-dir-wrong.js`). The rest of `process.argv` holds whatever arguments we gave at the command line when we ran the program, so `process.argv[2]` is the first argument after the name of our program (Figure 2.1).

[2]https://www.python.org/
[3]https://en.wikipedia.org/wiki/Java_(programming_language)
[4]https://nodejs.org/api/fs.html

If we run this program with the name of a directory as its argument, `fs.readdir` returns the names of the things in that directory as an array of strings. The program uses `for (const name of results)` to loop over the contents of that array. We could use `let` instead of `const`, but it's good practice to declare things as `const` wherever possible so that anyone reading the program knows the variable isn't actually going to vary—doing this reduces the **cognitive load** on people reading the program. Finally, `console.log` is JavaScript's equivalent of other languages' `print` command; its strange name comes from the fact that its original purpose was to create **log messages** in the browser **console**.

Unfortunately, our program doesn't work:

```
node list-dir-wrong.js .
```

```
node:internal/process/esm_loader:74
    internalBinding('errors').triggerUncaughtException(
                              ^

TypeError [ERR_INVALID_CALLBACK]: Callback must be a function. Received \
undefined
    at makeCallback (node:fs:181:3)
    at Object.readdir (node:fs:1030:14)
    at /u/stjs/systems-programming/list-dir-wrong.js:4:20
    at ModuleJob.run (node:internal/modules/esm/module_job:154:23)
    at async Loader.import (node:internal/modules/esm/loader:177:24)
    at async Object.loadESM (node:internal/process/esm_loader:68:5) {
  code: 'ERR_INVALID_CALLBACK'
}
```

The error message comes from something we didn't write whose source we would struggle to read. If we look for the name of our file (`list-dir-wrong.js`) we see the error occurred on line 4; everything above that is inside `fs.readdir`, while everything below it is Node loading and running our program.

The problem is that `fs.readdir` doesn't return anything. Instead, its documentation says that it needs a callback function that tells it what to do when data is available, so we need to explore those in order to make our program work.

A theorem

1. Every program contains at least one bug.
2. Every program can be made one line shorter.
3. Therefore, every program can be reduced to a single statement which is wrong.

— variously attributed

2.2 What is a callback function?

JavaScript uses a **single-threaded** programming model: as the introduction to this lesson said, it splits operations like file I/O into "please do this" and "do this when data is available". `fs.readdir` is the first part, but we need to write a function that specifies the second part.

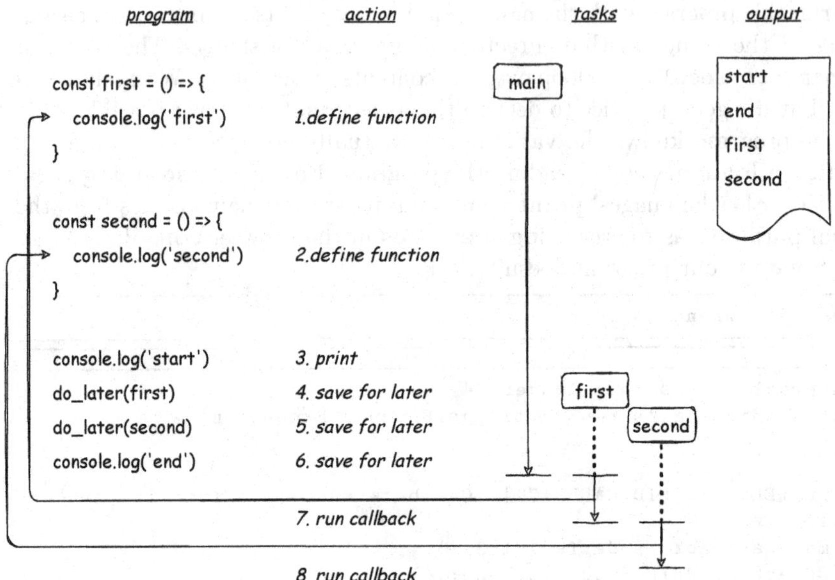

Figure 2.2: How JavaScript runs callback functions.

JavaScript saves a reference to this function and calls with a specific set of parameters when our data is ready (Figure 2.2). Those parameters defined a standard **protocol** for connecting to libraries, just like the USB standard allows us to plug hardware devices together.

This corrected program gives `fs.readdir` a callback function called `listContents`:

```
import fs from 'fs'

const listContents = (err, files) => {
  console.log('running callback')
  if (err) {
    console.error(err)
  } else {
    for (const name of files) {
      console.log(name)
    }
  }
}

const srcDir = process.argv[2]
fs.readdir(srcDir, listContents)
console.log('last line of program')
```

Node callbacks always get an error (if there is any) as their first argument and the result of a successful function call as their second. The function can tell the difference by checking to see if the error argument is `null`. If it is, the function lists the directory's contents with `console.log`, otherwise, it uses `console.error` to display the error message. Let's run the program with the **current working directory** (written as '.') as an argument:

```
node list-dir-function-defined.js .
```

```
last line of program
```

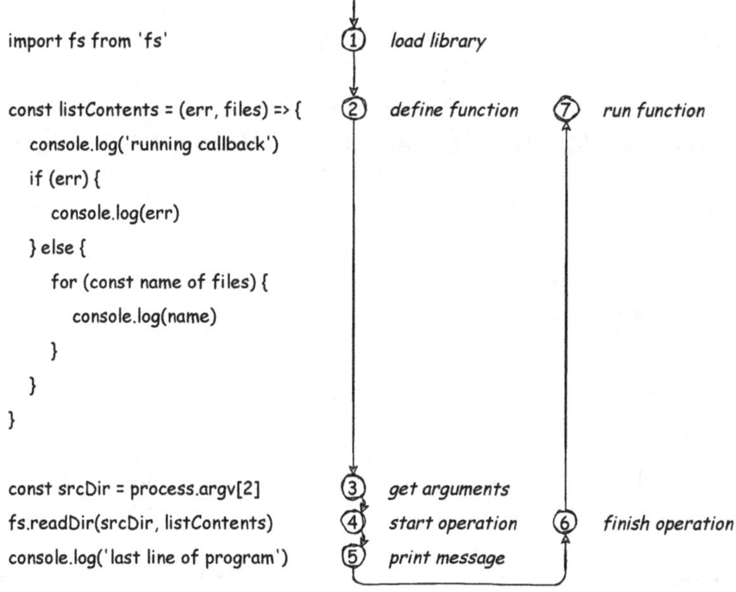

Figure 2.3: When JavaScript runs callback functions.

```
running callback
Makefile
copy-file-filtered.js
copy-file-unfiltered.js
...
x-trace-anonymous
x-trace-anonymous.md
x-trace-callback
x-trace-callback.md
x-where-is-node.md
```

Nothing that follows will make sense if we don't understand the order in which Node executes the statements in this program (Figure 2.3):

1. Execute the first line to load the `fs` library.
2. Define a function of two parameters and assign it to `listContents`. (Remember, a function is just another kind of data.)
3. Get the name of the directory from the command-line arguments.
4. Call `fs.readdir` to start a filesystem operation, telling it what directory we want to read and what function to call when data is available.
5. Print a message to show we're at the end of the file.
6. Wait until the filesystem operation finishes (this step is invisible).
7. Run the callback function, which prints the directory listing.

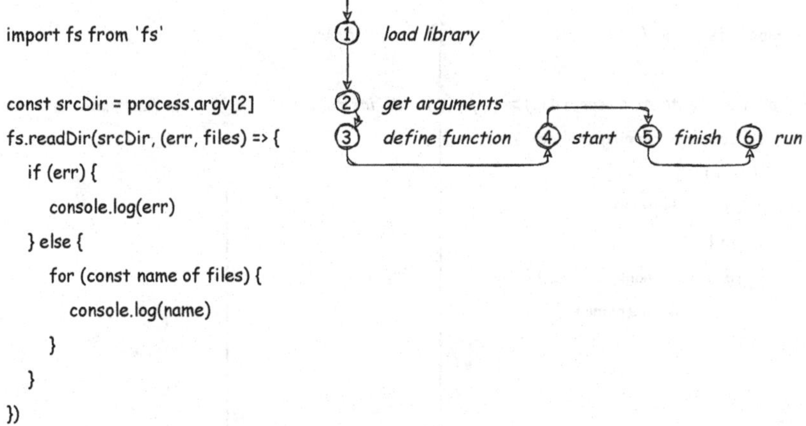

Figure 2.4: How and when JavaScript creates and runs anonymous callback functions.

2.3 What are anonymous functions?

Most JavaScript programmers wouldn't define the function `listContents` and then pass it as a callback. Instead, since the callback is only used in one place, it is more **idiomatic** to define it where it is needed as an **anonymous function**. This makes it easier to see what's going to happen when the operation completes, though it means the order of execution is quite different from the order of reading (Figure 2.4). Using an anonymous function gives us the final version of our program:

```
import fs from 'fs'

const srcDir = process.argv[2]
fs.readdir(srcDir, (err, files) => {
  if (err) {
    console.error(err)
  } else {
    for (const name of files) {
      console.log(name)
    }
  }
})
```

Functions are data

As we noted above, a function is just another kind of data. Instead of being made up of numbers, characters, or pixels, it is made up of instructions, but these are stored in memory like anything else. Defining a function on the fly is no different from defining an array in-place using `[1, 3, 5]`, and passing a function as an argument to another function is no different from passing an array. We are going to rely on this insight over and over again in the coming lessons.

Figure 2.5: Using `glob` patterns to match filenames.

2.4 How can we select a set of files?

Suppose we want to copy some files instead of listing a directory's contents. Depending on the situation we might want to copy only those files given on the command line or all files except some explicitly excluded. What we *don't* want to have to do is list the files one by one; instead, we want to be able to write patterns like `*.js`.

To find files that match patterns like that, we can use the `glob`[5] module. (To **glob** (short for "global") is an old Unix term for matching a set of files by name.) The `glob` module provides a function that takes a pattern and a callback and does something with every filename that matched the pattern:

```
import glob from 'glob'

glob('**/*.*', (err, files) => {
  if (err) {
    console.log(err)
  } else {
    for (const filename of files) {
      console.log(filename)
    }
  }
})
```

```
copy-file-filtered.js
copy-file-filtered.js.bck
copy-file-unfiltered.js
copy-file-unfiltered.js.bck
copy-file-unfiltered.out
...
x-trace-anonymous.md
x-trace-anonymous/trace.js
x-trace-callback.md
x-trace-callback/trace.js
x-where-is-node.md
```

The leading `**` means "recurse into subdirectories", while `*.*` means "any characters followed by '.' followed by any characters" (Figure 2.5). Names that don't match `*.*` won't be included, and by default, neither are names that start with a '.' character. This is another old Unix convention: files and directories whose names have a leading '.' usually contain configuration information for various programs, so most commands will leave them alone unless told to do otherwise.

This program works, but we probably don't want to copy editor backup files whose names end with `.bck`. We can get rid of them by **filtering** the list that `glob` returns:

[5] https://www.npmjs.com/package/glob

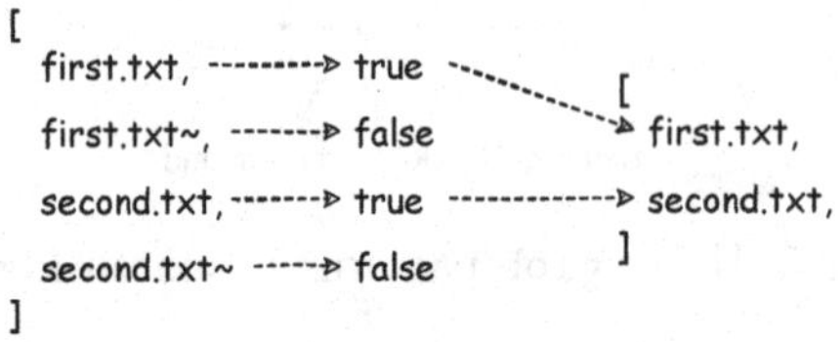

```
[
  first.txt,   --------> true  ----.      [
  first.txt~,  -------> false       '---> first.txt,
  second.txt,  -------> true  ------------> second.txt,
  second.txt~  -----> false                ]
]
```

Figure 2.6: Selecting array elements using `Array.filter`.

```
import glob from 'glob'

glob('**/*.*', (err, files) => {
  if (err) {
    console.log(err)
  } else {
    files = files.filter((f) => { return !f.endsWith('.bck') })
    for (const filename of files) {
      console.log(filename)
    }
  }
})
```

```
copy-file-filtered.js
copy-file-unfiltered.js
copy-file-unfiltered.out
copy-file-unfiltered.sh
copy-file-unfiltered.txt
...
x-trace-anonymous.md
x-trace-anonymous/trace.js
x-trace-callback.md
x-trace-callback/trace.js
x-where-is-node.md
```

`Array.filter` creates a new array containing all the items of the original array that pass a test (Figure 2.6). The test is specified as a callback function that `Array.filter` calls once once for each item. This function must return a **Boolean** that tells `Array.filter` whether to keep the item in the new array or not. `Array.filter` does not modify the original array, so we can filter our original list of filenames several times if we want to.

We can make our globbing program more idiomatic by removing the parentheses around the single parameter and writing just the expression we want the function to return:

```
import glob from 'glob'

glob('**/*.*', (err, files) => {
  if (err) {
    console.log(err)
  } else {
    files = files.filter(f => !f.endsWith('.bck'))
    for (const filename of files) {
      console.log(filename)
    }
  }
})
```

However, it turns out that `glob` will filter for us. According to its documentation, the function takes an `options` object full of key-value settings that control its behavior. This is another common pattern in Node libraries: rather than accepting a large number of rarely-used parameters, a function can take a single object full of settings.

If we use this, our program becomes:

```
import glob from 'glob'

glob('**/*.*', { ignore: '*.bck' }, (err, files) => {
  if (err) {
    console.log(err)
  } else {
    for (const filename of files) {
      console.log(filename)
    }
  }
})
```

Notice that we don't quote the key in the `options` object. The keys in objects are almost always strings, and if a string is simple enough that it won't confuse the parser, we don't need to put quotes around it. Here, "simple enough" means "looks like it could be a variable name", or equivalently "contains only letters, digits, and the underscore".

No one knows everything

We combined `glob.glob` and `Array.filter` in our functions for more than a year before someone pointed out the `ignore` option for `glob.glob`. This shows:

1. Life is short, so most of us find a way to solve the problem in front of us and re-use it rather than looking for something better.
2. Code reviews aren't just about finding bugs: they are also the most effective way to transfer knowledge between programmers. Even if someone is much more experienced than you, there's a good chance you might have stumbled over a better way to do something than the one they're using (see point #1 above).

To finish off our globbing program, let's specify a source directory on the command line and include that in the pattern:

```
import glob from 'glob'

const srcDir = process.argv[2]

glob(`${srcDir}/**/*.*`, { ignore: '*.bck' }, (err, files) => {
  if (err) {
    console.log(err)
  } else {
    for (const filename of files) {
      console.log(filename)
    }
  }
})
```

This program uses **string interpolation** to insert the value of `srcDir` into a string. The template string is written in back quotes, and JavaScript converts every expression written as `${expression}` to text. We could create the pattern by concatenating strings using `srcDir + '/**/*.*'`, but most programmers find interpolation easier to read.

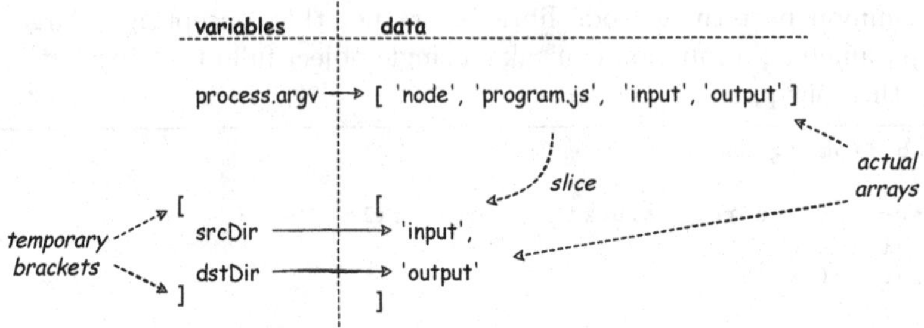

Figure 2.7: Assigning many values at once by destructuring.

2.5 How can we copy a set of files?

If we want to copy a set of files instead of just listing them we need a way to create the **paths** of the files we are going to create. If our program takes a second argument that specifies the desired output directory, we can construct the full output path by replacing the name of the source directory with that path:

```
import glob from 'glob'

const [srcDir, dstDir] = process.argv.slice(2)

glob(`${srcDir}/**/*.*`, { ignore: '*.bck' }, (err, files) => {
  if (err) {
    console.log(err)
  } else {
    for (const srcName of files) {
      const dstName = srcName.replace(srcDir, dstDir)
      console.log(srcName, dstName)
    }
  }
})
```

This program uses **destructuring assignment** to create two variables at once by unpacking the elements of an array (Figure 2.7). It only works if the array contains enough elements, i.e., if both a source and destination are given on the command line; we'll add a check for that in the exercises.

A more serious problem is that this program only works if the destination directory already exists: `fs` and equivalent libraries in other languages usually won't create directories for us automatically. The need to do this comes up so often that there is a function called `ensureDir` to do it:

```
import glob from 'glob'
import fs from 'fs-extra'
import path from 'path'

const [srcRoot, dstRoot] = process.argv.slice(2)

glob(`${srcRoot}/**/*.*`, { ignore: '*.bck' }, (err, files) => {
  if (err) {
    console.log(err)
  } else {
    for (const srcName of files) {
```

```
      const dstName = srcName.replace(srcRoot, dstRoot)
      const dstDir = path.dirname(dstName)
      fs.ensureDir(dstDir, (err) => {
        if (err) {
          console.error(err)
        }
      })
    }
  }
})
```

Notice that we import from `fs-extra` instead of `fs`; the `fs-extra`[6] module provides some useful utilities on top of `fs`. We also use `path`[7] to manipulate pathnames rather than concatenating or interpolating strings because there are a lot of tricky **edge cases** in pathnames that the authors of that module have figured out for us.

Using distinct names

We are now calling our command-line arguments `srcRoot` and `dstRoot` rather than `srcDir` and `dstDir`. We originally used `dstDir` as both the name of the top-level destination directory (from the command line) and the name of the particular output directory to create. This was legal, since every function creates a new **scope**, but hard for people to understand.

Our file copying program currently creates empty destination directories but doesn't actually copy any files. Let's use `fs.copy` to do that:

```
import glob from 'glob'
import fs from 'fs-extra'
import path from 'path'

const [srcRoot, dstRoot] = process.argv.slice(2)

glob(`${srcRoot}/**/*.*`, { ignore: '*.bck' }, (err, files) => {
  if (err) {
    console.log(err)
  } else {
    for (const srcName of files) {
      const dstName = srcName.replace(srcRoot, dstRoot)
      const dstDir = path.dirname(dstName)
      fs.ensureDir(dstDir, (err) => {
        if (err) {
          console.error(err)
        } else {
          fs.copy(srcName, dstName, (err) => {
            if (err) {
              console.error(err)
            }
          })
        }
      })
    }
  }
})
```

[6]https://www.npmjs.com/package/fs-extra
[7]https://nodejs.org/api/path.html

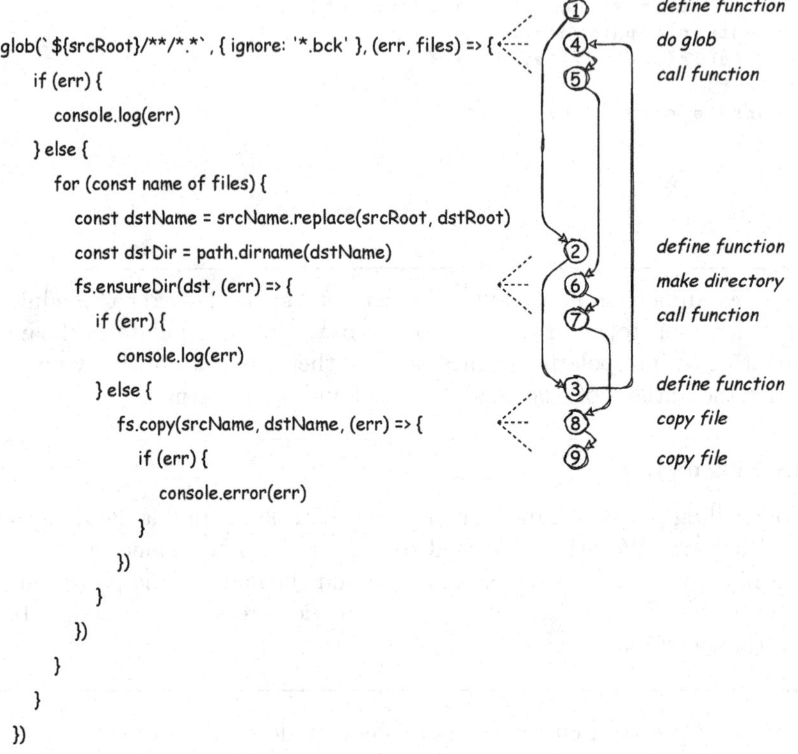
glob(`${srcRoot}/**/*.*`, { ignore: '*.bck' }, (err, files) => {
if (err) {
console.log(err)
} else {
for (const name of files) {
const dstName = srcName.replace(srcRoot, dstRoot)
const dstDir = path.dirname(dstName)
fs.ensureDir(dst, (err) => {
if (err) {
console.log(err)
} else {
fs.copy(srcName, dstName, (err) => {
if (err) {
console.error(err)
}
})
}
})
}
}
})
define function
do glob
call function
define function
make directory
call function
define function
copy file
copy file

Figure 2.8: Three levels of callback in the running example.

The program now has three levels of callback (Figure 2.8):

1. When `glob` has data, do things and then call `ensureDir`.
2. When `ensureDir` completes, copy a file.
3. When `copy` finishes, check the error status.

Our program looks like it should work, but if we try to copy everything in the directory containing these lessons we get an error message:

```
rm -rf /tmp/out
mkdir /tmp/out
node copy-file-unfiltered.js ../node_modules /tmp/out 2>&1 | head -n 6
```

```
[Error: ENOENT: no such file or directory, chmod \
'/tmp/out/@nodelib/fs.stat/README.md'] {
  errno: -2,
  code: 'ENOENT',
  syscall: 'chmod',
  path: '/tmp/out/@nodelib/fs.stat/README.md'
}
```

The problem is that `node_modules/fs.stat` and `node_modules/fs.walk` match our globbing expression, but are directories rather than files. To prevent our program from trying to use `fs.copy` on directories, we must use `fs.stat` to get the properties of the things glob gives us and then check if they are files. The name "stat" is short for "status", and since the status of something in the filesystem can be very complex, fs.stat returns an object with methods that can answer common questions[8].

Here's the final version of our file copying program:

```
import glob from 'glob'
import fs from 'fs-extra'
import path from 'path'

const [srcRoot, dstRoot] = process.argv.slice(2)

glob(`${srcRoot}/**/*.*`, { ignore: '*.bck' }, (err, files) => {
  if (err) {
    console.log(err)
  } else {
    for (const srcName of files) {
      fs.stat(srcName, (err, stats) => {
        if (err) {
          console.error(err)
        } else if (stats.isFile()) {
          const dstName = srcName.replace(srcRoot, dstRoot)
          const dstDir = path.dirname(dstName)
          fs.ensureDir(dstDir, (err) => {
            if (err) {
              console.error(err)
            } else {
              fs.copy(srcName, dstName, (err) => {
                if (err) {
                  console.error(err)
                }
              })
            }
          })
        }
      })
    }
  }
})
```

It works, but four levels of asynchronous callbacks is hard for humans to understand. Chapter 3 will introduce a pair of tools that make code like this easier to read.

2.6 Exercises

Where is Node?

Write a program called wherenode.js that prints the full path to the version of Node it is run with.

Tracing callbacks

In what order does the program below print messages?

[8] https://nodejs.org/api/fs.html#fs_class_fs_stats

```
const red = () => {
  console.log('RED')
}

const green = (func) => {
  console.log('GREEN')
  func()
}

const blue = (left, right) => {
  console.log('BLUE')
  left(right)
}

blue(green, red)
```

Tracing anonymous callbacks

In what order does the program below print messages?

```
const blue = (left, right) => {
  console.log('BLUE')
  left(right)
}

blue(
  (callback) => {
    console.log('GREEN')
    callback()
  },
  () => console.log('RED')
)
```

Checking arguments

Modify the file copying program to check that it has been given the right number of command-line arguments and to print a sensible error message (including a usage statement) if it hasn't.

Glob patterns

What filenames does each of the following glob patterns match?

- `results-[0123456789].csv`
- `results.(tsv|csv)`
- `results.dat?`
- `./results.data`

Filtering arrays

Fill in the blank in the code below so that the output matches the one shown. Note: you can compare strings in JavaScript using <, >=, and other operators, so that (for example) `person.personal > 'P'` is **true** if someone's personal name starts with a letter that comes after 'P' in the alphabet.

```
const people = [
  { personal: 'Jean', family: 'Jennings' },
  { personal: 'Marlyn', family: 'Wescoff' },
  { personal: 'Ruth', family: 'Lichterman' },
  { personal: 'Betty', family: 'Snyder' },
  { personal: 'Frances', family: 'Bilas' },
  { personal: 'Kay', family: 'McNulty' }
]

const result = people.filter(____ => ____)

console.log(result)
```

```
[
  { personal: 'Jean', family: 'Jennings' },
  { personal: 'Ruth', family: 'Lichterman' },
  { personal: 'Frances', family: 'Bilas' }
]
```

String interpolation

Fill in the code below so that it prints the message shown.

```
const people = [
  { personal: 'Christine', family: 'Darden' },
  { personal: 'Mary', family: 'Jackson' },
  { personal: 'Katherine', family: 'Johnson' },
  { personal: 'Dorothy', family: 'Vaughan' }
]

for (const person of people) {
  console.log(`$____, $____`)
}
```

```
Darden, Christine
Jackson, Mary
Johnson, Katherine
Vaughan, Dorothy
```

Destructuring assignment

What is assigned to each named variable in each statement below?

1. `const first = [10, 20, 30]`
2. `const [first, second] = [10, 20, 30]`
3. `const [first, second, third] = [10, 20, 30]`
4. `const [first, second, third, fourth] = [10, 20, 30]`
5. `const {left, right} = {left: 10, right: 30}`
6. `const {left, middle, right} = {left: 10, middle: 20, right: 30}`

Counting lines

Write a program called `lc` that counts and reports the number of lines in one or more files and the total number of lines, so that `lc a.txt b.txt` displays something like:

```
a.txt 475
b.txt 31
total 506
```

Renaming files

Write a program called `rename` that takes three or more command-line arguments:

1. A **filename extension** to match.
2. An extension to replace it with.
3. The names of one or more existing files.

When it runs, `rename` renames any files with the first extension to create files with the second extension, but will *not* overwrite an existing file. For example, suppose a directory contains `a.txt`, `b.txt`, and `b.bck`. The command:

```
rename .txt .bck a.txt b.txt
```

will rename `a.txt` to `a.bck`, but will *not* rename `b.txt` because `b.bck` already exists.

3

Asynchronous Programming

Terms defined: **call stack**, **character encoding**, **class**, **constructor**, **event loop**, **exception**, **fluent interface**, **method**, **method chaining**, **non-blocking execution**, **promise**, **promisification**, **protocol**, **UTF-8**

Callbacks work, but they are hard to read and debug, which means they only "work" in a limited sense. JavaScript's developers added **promises** to the language in 2015 to make callbacks easier to write and understand, and more recently they added the keywords `async` and `await` as well to make asynchronous programming easier still. To show how these work, we will create a **class** of our own called `Pledge` that provides the same core features as promises. Our explanation was inspired by Trey Huffine's[1] tutorial[2], and we encourage you to read that as well.

3.1 How can we manage asynchronous execution?

JavaScript is built around an **event loop**. Every task is represented by an entry in a queue; the event loop repeatedly takes a task from the front of the queue, runs it, and adds any new tasks that it creates to the back of the queue to run later. Only one task runs at a time; each has its own **call stack**, but objects can be shared between tasks (Figure 3.1).

Most tasks execute all the code available in the order it is written. For example, this one-line program uses `Array.forEach` to print each element of an array in turn:

```
[1000, 1500, 500].forEach(t => console.log(t))
```

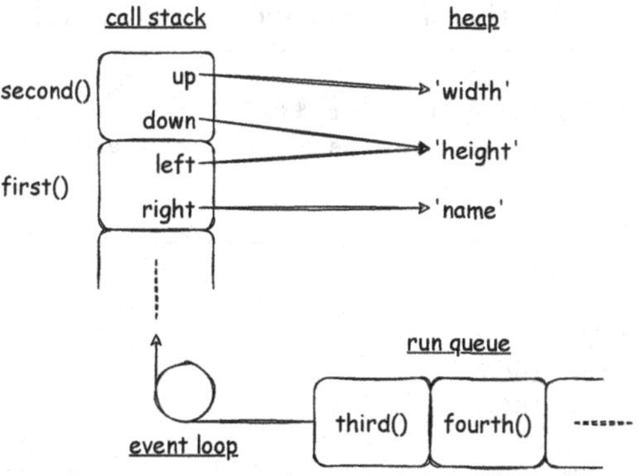

Figure 3.1: Using an event loop to manage concurrent tasks.

[1] https://medium.com/@treyhuffine

[2] https://levelup.gitconnected.com/understand-javascript-promises-by-building-a-promise-from-scratch-84c0fd855720

```
1000
1500
500
```

However, a handful of special built-in functions make Node[3] switch tasks or add new tasks to the run queue. For example, `setTimeout` tells Node to run a callback function after a certain number of milliseconds have passed. Its first argument is a callback function that takes no arguments, and its second is the delay. When `setTimeout` is called, Node sets the callback aside for the requested length of time, then adds it to the run queue. (This means the task runs *at least* the specified number of milliseconds later.)

Why zero arguments?

`setTimeout`'s requirement that callback functions take no arguments is another example of a **protocol**. One way to think about it is that protocols allow old code to use new code: whoever wrote `setTimeout` couldn't know what specific tasks we want to delay, so they specified a way to wrap up any task at all.

As the listing below shows, the original task can generate many new tasks before it completes, and those tasks can run in a different order than the order in which they were created (Figure 3.2).

```
[1000, 1500, 500].forEach(t => {
  console.log(`about to setTimeout for ${t}`)
  setTimeout(() => console.log(`inside timer handler for ${t}`), t)
})
```

```
about to setTimeout for 1000
about to setTimeout for 1500
about to setTimeout for 500
inside timer handler for 500
inside timer handler for 1000
inside timer handler for 1500
```

If we give `setTimeout` a delay of zero milliseconds, the new task can be run right away, but any other tasks that are waiting have a chance to run as well:

```
[1000, 1500, 500].forEach(t => {
  console.log(`about to setTimeout for ${t}`)
  setTimeout(() => console.log(`inside timer handler for ${t}`), 0)
})
```

```
about to setTimeout for 1000
about to setTimeout for 1500
about to setTimeout for 500
inside timer handler for 1000
inside timer handler for 1500
inside timer handler for 500
```

We can use this trick to build a generic **non-blocking function** that takes a callback defining a task and switches tasks if any others are available:

[3] https://nodejs.org/en/

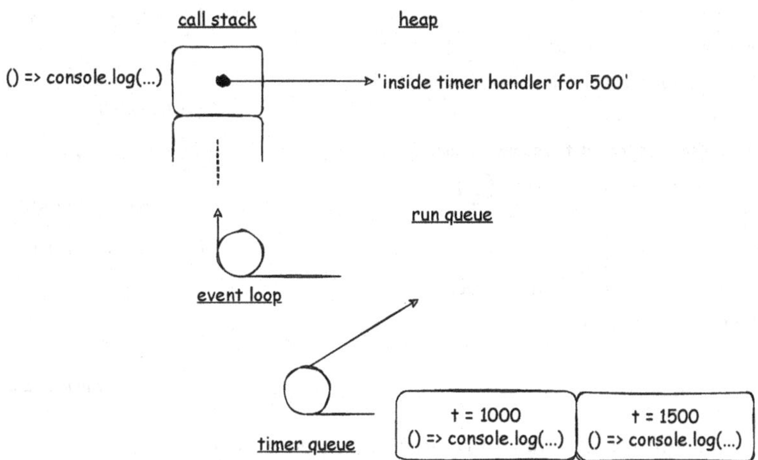

Figure 3.2: Using `setTimeout` to delay operations.

```
const nonBlocking = (callback) => {
  setTimeout(callback, 0)
}

[1000, 1500, 500].forEach(t => {
  console.log(`about to do nonBlocking for ${t}`)
  nonBlocking(() => console.log(`inside timer handler for ${t}`))
})
```

```
about to do nonBlocking for 1000
about to do nonBlocking for 1500
about to do nonBlocking for 500
inside timer handler for 1000
inside timer handler for 1500
inside timer handler for 500
```

Node's built-in function `setImmediate` does exactly what our `nonBlocking` function does: Node also has `process.nextTick`, which doesn't do quite the same thing—we'll explore the differences in the exercises.

```
[1000, 1500, 500].forEach(t => {
  console.log(`about to do setImmediate for ${t}`)
  setImmediate(() => console.log(`inside immediate handler for ${t}`))
})
```

```
about to do setImmediate for 1000
about to do setImmediate for 1500
about to do setImmediate for 500
inside immediate handler for 1000
inside immediate handler for 1500
inside immediate handler for 500
```

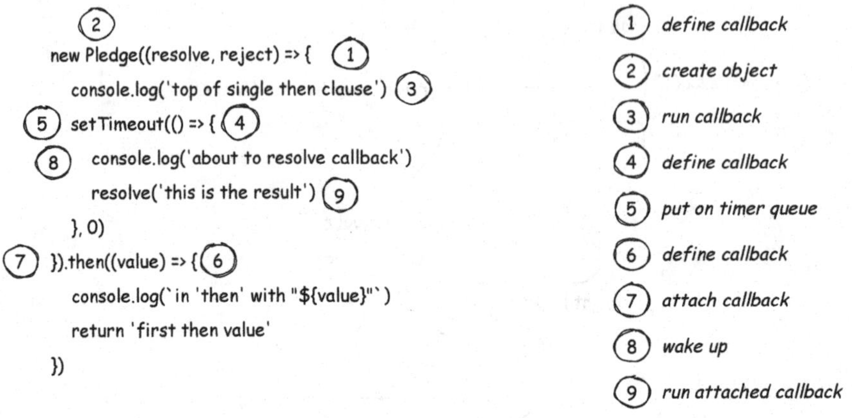

```
      (2)
new Pledge((resolve, reject) => { (1)
  console.log('top of single then clause') (3)
(5) setTimeout(() => { (4)
(8)   console.log('about to resolve callback')
      resolve('this is the result') (9)
  }, 0)
(7) }).then((value) => { (6)
  console.log(`in 'then' with "${value}"`)
  return 'first then value'
})
```

1. *define callback*
2. *create object*
3. *run callback*
4. *define callback*
5. *put on timer queue*
6. *define callback*
7. *attach callback*
8. *wake up*
9. *run attached callback*

Figure 3.3: Order of operations when a promise resolves.

3.2 How do promises work?

Before we start building our own promises, let's look at how we want them to work:

```
import Pledge from './pledge.js'

new Pledge((resolve, reject) => {
  console.log('top of a single then clause')
  setTimeout(() => {
    console.log('about to call resolve callback')
    resolve('this is the result')
  }, 0)
}).then((value) => {
  console.log(`in 'then' with "${value}"`)
  return 'first then value'
})
```

```
top of a single then clause
about to call resolve callback
in 'then' with "this is the result"
```

This short program creates a new `Pledge` with a callback that takes two other callbacks as arguments: `resolve` (which will run when everything worked) and `reject` (which will run when something went wrong). The top-level callback does the first part of what we want to do, i.e., whatever we want to run before we expect a delay; for demonstration purposes, we will use `setTimeout` with zero delay to switch tasks. Once this task resumes, we call the `resolve` callback to trigger whatever is supposed to happen after the delay.

Now look at the line with `then`. This is a **method** of the `Pledge` object we just created, and its job is to do whatever we want to do after the delay. The argument to `then` is yet another callback function; it will get the value passed to `resolve`, which is how the first part of the action communicates with the second (Figure 3.3).

In order to make this work, `Pledge`'s **constructor** must take a single function called `action`. This function must take two callbacks as arguments: what to do if the action completes successfully and what to do if it doesn't (i.e., how to handle errors). `Pledge` will provide these callbacks to the action at the right times.

`Pledge` also needs two methods: `then` to enable more actions and `catch` to handle errors. To simplify things just a little bit, we will allow users to **chain** as many `then`s as they want, but only allow one `catch`.

3.3 How can we chain operations together?

A **fluent interface** is a style of object-oriented programming in which the methods of an object return `this` so that method calls can be chained together. For example, if our class is:

```
class Fluent {
  constructor () {...}

  first (top) {
    ...do something with top...
    return this
  }

  second (left, right) {
    ...do something with left and right...
  }
}
```

then we can write:

```
  const f = new Fluent()
  f.first('hello').second('and', 'goodbye')
```

or even

```
  (new Fluent()).first('hello').second('and', 'goodbye')
```

`Array`'s fluent interface lets us write expressions like `Array.filter(...).map(...)` that are usually more readable than assigning intermediate results to temporary variables.

If the original action given to our `Pledge` completes successfully, the `Pledge` gives us a value by calling the `resolve` callback. We pass this value to the first `then`, pass the result of that `then` to the second one, and so on. If any of them fail and throw an **exception**, we pass that exception to the error handler. Putting it all together, the whole class looks like this:

```
class Pledge {
  constructor (action) {
    this.actionCallbacks = []
    this.errorCallback = () => {}
    action(this.onResolve.bind(this), this.onReject.bind(this))
  }

  then (thenHandler) {
    this.actionCallbacks.push(thenHandler)
    return this
  }

  catch (errorHandler) {
    this.errorCallback = errorHandler
    return this
  }
```

```
  onResolve (value) {
    let storedValue = value
    try {
      this.actionCallbacks.forEach((action) => {
        storedValue = action(storedValue)
      })
    } catch (err) {
      this.actionCallbacks = []
      this.onReject(err)
    }
  }

  onReject (err) {
    this.errorCallback(err)
  }
}

export default Pledge
```

Binding `this`

`Pledge`'s constructor makes two calls to a special function called `bind`. When we create an object `obj` and call a method `meth`, JavaScript sets the special variable `this` to `obj` inside `meth`. If we use a method as a callback, though, `this` isn't automatically set to the correct object. To convert the method to a plain old function with the right `this`, we have to use `bind`. The documentation[4] has more details and examples.

Let's create a `Pledge` and return a value:

```
import Pledge from './pledge.js'

new Pledge((resolve, reject) => {
  console.log('top of a single then clause')
}).then((value) => {
  console.log(`then with "${value}"`)
  return 'first then value'
})
```

```
top of a single then clause
```

Why didn't this work?

1. We can't use `return` with pledges because the call stack of the task that created the pledge is gone by the time the pledge executes. Instead, we must call `resolve` or `reject`.

2. We haven't done anything that defers execution, i.e., there is no call to `setTimeout`, `setImmediate`, or anything else that would switch tasks. Our original motivating example got this right.

This example shows how we can chain actions together:

```
import Pledge from './pledge.js'

new Pledge((resolve, reject) => {
```

[4]https://developer.mozilla.org/en-US/docs/Web/JavaScript/Reference/Global_objects/Function/bind

```
  console.log('top of action callback with double then and a catch')
  setTimeout(() => {
    console.log('about to call resolve callback')
    resolve('initial result')
    console.log('after resolve callback')
  }, 0)
  console.log('end of action callback')
}).then((value) => {
  console.log(`first then with "${value}"`)
  return 'first value'
}).then((value) => {
  console.log(`second then with "${value}"`)
  return 'second value'
})
```

```
top of action callback with double then and a catch
end of action callback
about to call resolve callback
first then with "initial result"
second then with "first value"
after resolve callback
```

Notice that inside each **then** we *do* use **return** because these clauses all run in a single task. As we will see in the next section, the full implementation of **Promise** allows us to run both normal code and delayed tasks inside **then** handlers.

Finally, in this example we explicitly signal a problem by calling **reject** to make sure our error handling does what it's supposed to:

```
import Pledge from './pledge.js'

new Pledge((resolve, reject) => {
  console.log('top of action callback with deliberate error')
  setTimeout(() => {
    console.log('about to reject on purpose')
    reject('error on purpose')
  }, 0)
}).then((value) => {
  console.log(`should not be here with "${value}"`)
}).catch((err) => {
  console.log(`in error handler with "${err}"`)
})
```

```
top of action callback with deliberate error
about to reject on purpose
in error handler with "error on purpose"
```

3.4 How are real promises different?

Let's rewrite our chained pledge with built-in promises:

```
new Promise((resolve, reject) => {
  console.log('top of action callback with double then and a catch')
  setTimeout(() => {
    console.log('about to call resolve callback')
```

```
    resolve('initial result')
    console.log('after resolve callback')
  }, 0)
  console.log('end of action callback')
}).then((value) => {
  console.log(`first then with "${value}"`)
  return 'first value'
}).then((value) => {
  console.log(`second then with "${value}"`)
  return 'second value'
})
```

```
top of action callback with double then and a catch
end of action callback
about to call resolve callback
after resolve callback
first then with "initial result"
second then with "first value"
```

It looks almost the same, but if we read the output carefully we can see that the callbacks run *after* the main program finishes. This is a signal that Node is delaying the execution of the code in the `then` handler.

A very common pattern is to return another promise from inside `then` so that the next `then` is called on the returned promise, not on the original promise (Figure 3.4). This is another way to implement a fluent interface: if a method of one object returns a second object, we can call a method of the second object immediately.

```
const delay = (message) => {
  return new Promise((resolve, reject) => {
    console.log(`constructing promise: ${message}`)
    setTimeout(() => {
      resolve(`resolving: ${message}`)
    }, 1)
  })
}

console.log('before')
delay('outer delay')
  .then((value) => {
    console.log(`first then: ${value}`)
    return delay('inner delay')
  }).then((value) => {
    console.log(`second then: ${value}`)
  })
console.log('after')
```

```
before
constructing promise: outer delay
after
first then: resolving: outer delay
constructing promise: inner delay
second then: resolving: inner delay
```

We therefore have three rules for chaining promises:

1. If our code can run synchronously, just put it in `then`.

2. If we want to use our own asynchronous function, it must create and return a promise.

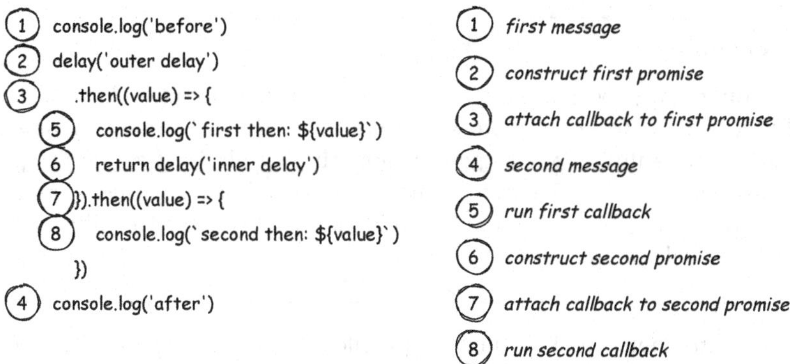

Figure 3.4: Chaining promises to make asynchronous operations depend on each other.

3. Finally, if we want to use a library function that relies on callbacks, we have to convert it to use promises. Doing this is called **promisification** (because programmers will rarely pass up an opportunity to add a bit of jargon to the world), and most functions in Node have already been promisified.

3.5 How can we build tools with promises?

Promises may seem more complex than callbacks right now, but that's because we're looking at how they work rather than at how to use them. To explore the latter subject, let's use promises to build a program to count the number of lines in a set of files. A few moments of search on NPM[5] turns up a promisified version of `fs-extra` called `fs-extra-promise`, so we will rely on it for file operations.

Our first step is to count the lines in a single file:

```
import fs from 'fs-extra-promise'

const filename = process.argv[2]

fs.readFileAsync(filename, { encoding: 'utf-8' })
  .then(data => {
    const length = data.split('\n').length - 1
    console.log(`${filename}: ${length}`)
  })
  .catch(err => {
    console.error(err.message)
  })
```

```
node count-lines-single-file.js count-lines-single-file.js
```

```
count-lines-single-file.js: 12
```

[5]https://www.npmjs.com/

Character encoding

A **character encoding** specifies how characters are stored as bytes. The most widely used is **UTF-8**, which stores characters common in Western European languages in a single byte and uses multi-byte sequences for other symbols. If we don't specify a character encoding, `fs.readFileAsync` gives us an array of bytes rather than a string of characters. We can tell we've made this mistake when we try to call a method of `String` and Node tells us we can't.

The next step is to count the lines in multiple files. We can use `glob-promise` to delay handling the output of `glob`, but we need some way to create a separate task to count the lines in each file and to wait until those line counts are available before exiting our program.

The tool we want is `Promise.all`, which waits until all of the promises in an array have completed. To make our program a little more readable, we will put the creation of the promise for each file in a separate function:

```
import glob from 'glob-promise'
import fs from 'fs-extra-promise'

const main = (srcDir) => {
  glob(`${srcDir}/**/*.*`)
    .then(files => Promise.all(files.map(f => lineCount(f))))
    .then(counts => counts.forEach(c => console.log(c)))
    .catch(err => console.log(err.message))
}

const lineCount = (filename) => {
  return new Promise((resolve, reject) => {
    fs.readFileAsync(filename, { encoding: 'utf-8' })
      .then(data => resolve(data.split('\n').length - 1))
      .catch(err => reject(err))
  })
}

const srcDir = process.argv[2]
main(srcDir)
```

```
node count-lines-globbed-files.js .
```

```
10
1
12
4
1
...
3
2
5
2
14
```

However, we want to display the names of the files whose lines we're counting along with the counts. To do this our `then` must return two values. We could put them in an array, but it's better practice to construct a temporary object with named fields (Figure 3.5). This approach allows us to add or rearrange fields without breaking code and also serves as a bit of documentation. With this change our line-counting program becomes:

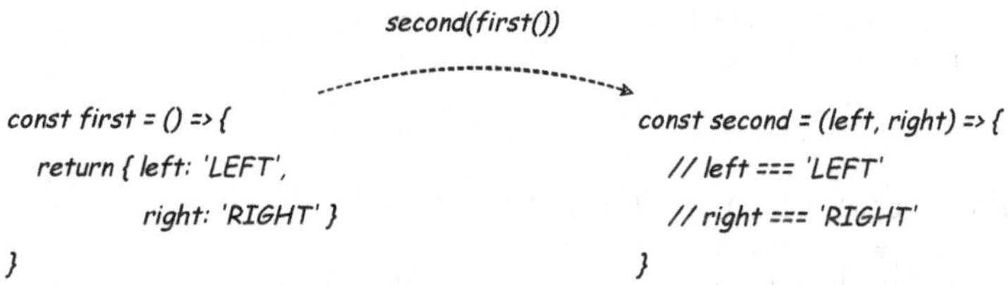

Figure 3.5: Creating temporary objects with named fields to carry values forward.

```
import glob from 'glob-promise'
import fs from 'fs-extra-promise'

const main = (srcDir) => {
  glob(`${srcDir}/**/*.*`)
    .then(files => Promise.all(files.map(f => lineCount(f))))
    .then(counts => counts.forEach(
      c => console.log(`${c.lines}: ${c.name}`)))
    .catch(err => console.log(err.message))
}

const lineCount = (filename) => {
  return new Promise((resolve, reject) => {
    fs.readFileAsync(filename, { encoding: 'utf-8' })
      .then(data => resolve({
        name: filename,
        lines: data.split('\n').length - 1
      }))
      .catch(err => reject(err))
  })
}

const srcDir = process.argv[2]
main(srcDir)
```

As in Chapter 2, this works until we run into a directory whose name name matches `*.*`, which we do when counting the lines in the contents of `node_modules`. The solution once again is to use `stat` to check if something is a file or not before trying to read it. And since `stat` returns an object that doesn't include the file's name, we create another temporary object to pass information down the chain of `then`s.

```
import glob from 'glob-promise'
import fs from 'fs-extra-promise'

const main = (srcDir) => {
  glob(`${srcDir}/**/*.*`)
    .then(files => Promise.all(files.map(f => statPair(f))))
    .then(files => files.filter(pair => pair.stats.isFile()))
    .then(files => files.map(pair => pair.filename))
    .then(files => Promise.all(files.map(f => lineCount(f))))
    .then(counts => counts.forEach(
      c => console.log(`${c.lines}: ${c.name}`)))
    .catch(err => console.log(err.message))
}

const statPair = (filename) => {
  return new Promise((resolve, reject) => {
    fs.statAsync(filename)
```

```
      .then(stats => resolve({ filename, stats }))
      .catch(err => reject(err))
  })
}

const lineCount = (filename) => {
  return new Promise((resolve, reject) => {
    fs.readFileAsync(filename, { encoding: 'utf-8' })
      .then(data => resolve({
        name: filename,
        lines: data.split('\n').length - 1
      }))
      .catch(err => reject(err))
  })
}

const srcDir = process.argv[2]
main(srcDir)
```

```
node count-lines-with-stat.js .
```

```
10: ./assign-immediately.js
1: ./assign-immediately.out
12: ./await-fs.js
4: ./await-fs.out
1: ./await-fs.sh
...
3: ./x-multiple-catch/example.js
2: ./x-multiple-catch/example.txt
5: ./x-trace-load.md
2: ./x-trace-load/config.yml
14: ./x-trace-load/example.js
```

This code is complex, but much simpler than it would be if we were using callbacks.

Lining things up

This code uses the expression `{filename, stats}` to create an object whose keys are `filename` and `stats`, and whose values are the values of the corresponding variables. Doing this makes the code easier to read, both because it's shorter but also because it signals that the value associated with the key `filename` is exactly the value of the variable with the same name.

3.6 How can we make this more readable?

Promises eliminate the deep nesting associated with callbacks of callbacks, but they are still hard to follow. The latest versions of JavaScript provide two new keywords `async` and `await` to flatten code further. `async` means "this function implicitly returns a promise", while `await` means "wait for a promise to resolve". This short program uses both keywords to print the first ten characters of a file:

```
import fs from 'fs-extra-promise'
```

```
const firstTenCharacters = async (filename) => {
  const text = await fs.readFileAsync(filename, 'utf-8')
  console.log(`inside, raw text is ${text.length} characters long`)
  return text.slice(0, 10)
}

console.log('about to call')
const result = firstTenCharacters(process.argv[2])
console.log(`function result has type ${result.constructor.name}`)
result.then(value => console.log(`outside, final result is "${value}"`))
```

```
about to call
function result has type Promise
inside, raw text is 24 characters long
outside, final result is "Begin at t"
```

Translating code

When Node sees `await` and `async` it silently converts the code to use promises with `then`, `resolve`, and `reject`; we will see how this works in Chapter 15. In order to provide a context for this transformation we must put `await` inside a function that is declared to be `async`: we can't simply write `await fs.statAsync(...)` at the top level of our program outside a function. This requirement is occasionally annoying, but since we should be putting our code in functions anyway it's hard to complain.

To see how much cleaner our code is with `await` and `async`, let's rewrite our line counting program to use them. First, we modify the two helper functions to look like they're waiting for results and returning them. They actually wrap their results in promises and return those, but Node now takes care of that for us:

```
const statPair = async (filename) => {
  const stats = await fs.statAsync(filename)
  return { filename, stats }
}

const lineCount = async (filename) => {
  const data = await fs.readFileAsync(filename, 'utf-8')
  return {
    filename,
    lines: data.split('\n').length - 1
  }
}
```

Next, we modify `main` to wait for things to complete. We must still use `Promise.all` to handle the promises that are counting lines for individual files, but the result is less cluttered than our previous version.

```
const main = async (srcDir) => {
  const files = await glob(`${srcDir}/**/*.*`)
  const pairs = await Promise.all(
    files.map(async filename => await statPair(filename))
  )
  const filtered = pairs
    .filter(pair => pair.stats.isFile())
    .map(pair => pair.filename)
  const counts = await Promise.all(
```

async function returnImmediately () {
try {
1
3
return Promise.reject(new Error('deliberate'))
} catch (err) {
2
console.log('caught exception')
}
}
1 create promise for later execution
2 check for error (none)
3 raise exception

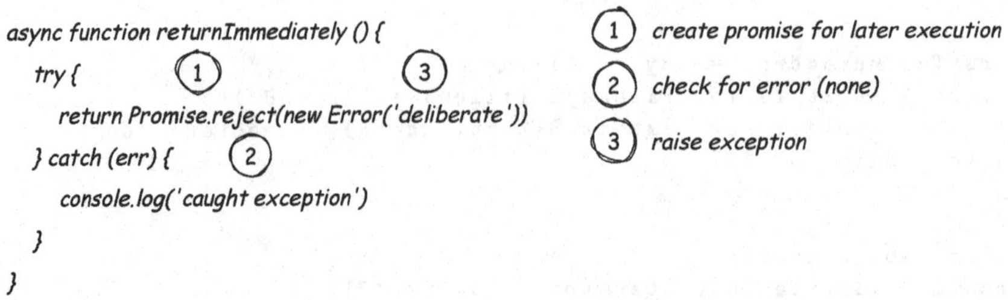

Figure 3.6: Wrong and right ways to handle errors in asynchronous code.

```
    filtered.map(async name => await lineCount(name))
  )
  counts.forEach(
    ({ filename, lines }) => console.log(`${lines}: ${filename}`)
  )
}

const srcDir = process.argv[2]
main(srcDir)
```

3.7 How can we handle errors with asynchronous code?

We created several intermediate variables in the line-counting program to make the steps clearer. Doing this also helps with error handling; to see how, we will build up an example in stages.

First, if we return a promise that fails without using `await`, then our main function will finish running before the error occurs, and our `try`/`catch` doesn't help us (Figure 3.6):

```
async function returnImmediately () {
  try {
    return Promise.reject(new Error('deliberate'))
  } catch (err) {
    console.log('caught exception')
  }
}

returnImmediately()
```

```
/u/stjs/async-programming/return-immediately.js:3
```

One solution to this problem is to be consistent and always return something. Because the function is declared `async`, the `Error` in the code below is automatically wrapped in a promise so we can use `.then` and `.catch` to handle it as before:

```
async function returnImmediately () {
  try {
    return Promise.reject(new Error('deliberate'))
  } catch (err) {
    return new Error('caught exception')
  }
}
```

```
const result = returnImmediately()
result.catch(err => console.log(`caller caught ${err}`))
```

```
caller caught Error: deliberate
```

If instead we **return await**, the function waits until the promise runs before returning. The promise is turned into an exception because it failed, and since we're inside the scope of our `try`/`catch` block, everything works as we want:

```
async function returnAwait () {
  try {
    return await Promise.reject(new Error('deliberate'))
  } catch (err) {
    console.log('caught exception')
  }
}

returnAwait()
```

```
caught exception
```

We prefer the second approach, but whichever you choose, please be consistent.

3.8 Exercises

Immediate versus next tick

What is the difference between `setImmediate` and `process.nextTick`? When would you use each one?

Tracing promise execution

1. What does this code print and why?

```
Promise.resolve('hello')
```

2. What does this code print and why?

```
Promise.resolve('hello').then(result => console.log(result))
```

3. What does this code print and why?

```
const p = new Promise((resolve, reject) => resolve('hello'))
  .then(result => console.log(result))
```

Hint: try each snippet of code interactively in the Node interpreter and as a command-line script.

Multiple catches

Suppose we create a promise that deliberately fails and then add two error handlers:

```
const oops = new Promise((resolve, reject) => reject(new Error('failure')))
oops.catch(err => console.log(err.message))
oops.catch(err => console.log(err.message))
```

When the code is run it produces:

```
failure
failure
```

1. Trace the order of operations: what is created and when is it executed?
2. What happens if we run these same lines interactively? Why do we see something different than what we see when we run this file from the command line?

Then after catch

Suppose we create a promise that deliberately fails and attach both `then` and `catch` to it:

```
new Promise((resolve, reject) => reject(new Error('failure')))
  .catch(err => console.log(err))
  .then(err => console.log(err))
```

When the code is run it produces:

```
Error: failure
    at /u/stjs/promises/catch-then/example.js:1:41
    at new Promise (<anonymous>)
    at Object.<anonymous> (/u/stjs/promises/catch-then/example.js:1:1)
    at Module._compile (internal/modules/cjs/loader.js:1151:30)
    at Object.Module._extensions..js \
 (internal/modules/cjs/loader.js:1171:10)
    at Module.load (internal/modules/cjs/loader.js:1000:32)
    at Function.Module._load (internal/modules/cjs/loader.js:899:14)
    at Function.executeUserEntryPoint [as runMain] \
 (internal/modules/run_main.js:71:12)
    at internal/main/run_main_module.js:17:47
undefined
```

1. Trace the order of execution.
2. Why is `undefined` printed at the end?

Head and tail

The Unix `head` command shows the first few lines of one or more files, while the `tail` command shows the last few. Write programs `head.js` and `tail.js` that do the same things using promises and `async`/`await`, so that:

```
node head.js 5 first.txt second.txt third.txt
```

prints the first five lines of each of the three files and:

```
node tail.js 5 first.txt second.txt third.txt
```

prints the last five lines of each file.

Histogram of line counts

Extend `count-lines-with-stat-async.js` to create a program `lh.js` that prints two columns of output: the number of lines in one or more files and the number of files that are that long. For example, if we run:

```
node lh.js promises/*.*
```

the output might be:

Length	Number of Files
1	7
3	3
4	3
6	7
8	2
12	2
13	1
15	1
17	2
20	1
24	1
35	2
37	3
38	1
171	1

Select matching lines

Using `async` and `await`, write a program called `match.js` that finds and prints lines containing a given string. For example:

```
node match.js Toronto first.txt second.txt third.txt
```

would print all of the lines from the three files that contain the word "Toronto".

Find lines in all files

Using `async` and `await`, write a program called `in-all.js` that finds and prints lines found in all of its input files. For example:

```
node in-all.js first.txt second.txt third.txt
```

will print those lines that occur in all three files.

Find differences between two files

Using `async` and `await`, write a program called `file-diff.js` that compares the lines in two files and shows which ones are only in the first file, which are only in the second, and which are in both. For example, if `left.txt` contains:

```
some
people
```

and `right.txt` contains:

```
write
some
code
```

then:

```
node file-diff.js left.txt right.txt
```

would print:

```
2 code
1 people
* some
2 write
```

where 1, 2, and * show whether lines are in only the first or second file or are in both. Note that the order of the lines in the file doesn't matter.

Hint: you may want to use the `Set` class to store lines.

Trace file loading

Suppose we are loading a YAML configuration file using the promisified version of the `fs` library. In what order do the print statements in this test program appear and why?

```
import fs from 'fs-extra-promise'
import yaml from 'js-yaml'

const test = async () => {
  const raw = await fs.readFileAsync('config.yml', 'utf-8')
  console.log('inside test, raw text', raw)
  const cooked = yaml.safeLoad(raw)
  console.log('inside test, cooked configuration', cooked)
  return cooked
}

const result = test()
console.log('outside test, result is', result.constructor.name)
result.then(something => console.log('outside test we have', something))
```

Any and all

1. Add a method `Pledge.any` that takes an array of pledges and as soon as one of the pledges in the array resolves, returns a single promise that resolves with the value from that pledge.

2. Add another method `Pledge.all` that takes an array of pledges and returns a single promise that resolves to an array containing the final values of all of those pledges.

   This article[6] may be helpful.

[6]https://2ality.com/2019/08/promise-combinators.html

4

Unit Testing

Terms defined: **absolute error**, **actual result (of test)**, **assertion**, **caching**, **defensive programming**, **design pattern**, **dynamic loading**, **error (in a test)**, **exception handler**, **expected result (of test)**, **exploratory programming**, **fail (a test)**, **fixture**, **global variable**, **introspection**, **lifecycle**, **pass (a test)**, **relative error**, **side effect**, **Singleton pattern**, **test runner**, **test subject**, **throw (exception)**, **unit test**

We have written many small programs in the previous two chapters, but haven't really tested any of them. That's OK for **exploratory programming**, but if our software is going to be used instead of just read, we should try to make sure it works.

A tool for writing and running **unit tests** is a good first step. Such a tool should:

- find files containing tests;
- find the tests in those files;
- run the tests;
- capture their results; and
- report each test's result and a summary of those results.

Our design is inspired by tools like Mocha[1] and Jest[2], which were in turn inspired by tools built for other languages from the 1980s onward [Meszaros2007; Tudose2020].

4.1 How should we structure unit testing?

As in other unit testing frameworks, each test will be a function of zero arguments so that the framework can run them all in the same way. Each test will create a **fixture** to be tested and use **assertions** to compare the **actual result** against the **expected result**. The outcome can be exactly one of:

- **Pass**: the **test subject** works as expected.
- **Fail**: something is wrong with the test subject.
- **Error**: something is wrong in the test itself, which means we don't know whether the test subject is working properly or not.

To make this work, we need some way to distinguish failing tests from broken ones. Our solution relies on the fact that exceptions are objects and that a program can use **introspection** to determine the class of an object. If a test **throws an exception** whose class is `assert.AssertionError`, then we will assume the exception came from one of the assertions we put in the test as a check (Figure 4.1). Any other kind of assertion indicates that the test itself contains an error.

[1]https://mochajs.org/
[2]https://jestjs.io/

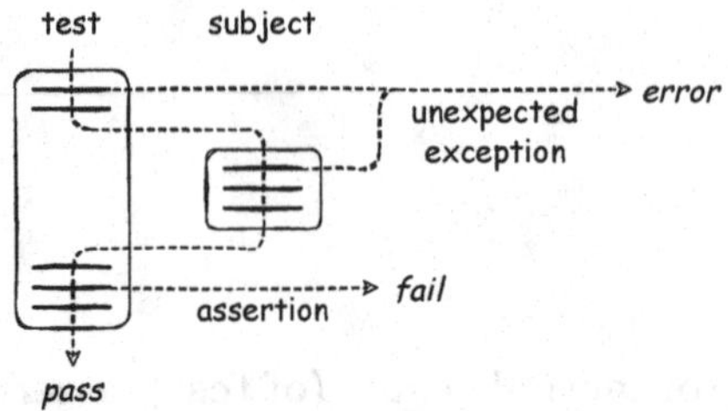

Figure 4.1: Running tests that can pass, fail, or contain errors.

4.2 How can we separate registration, execution, and reporting?

To start, let's use a handful of **global variables** to record tests and their results:

```
// State of tests.
const HopeTests = []
let HopePass = 0
let HopeFail = 0
let HopeError = 0
```

We don't run tests immediately because we want to wrap each one in our own **exception handler**. Instead, the function `hopeThat` saves a descriptive message and a callback function that implements a test in the `HopeTest` array.

```
// Record a single test for running later.
const hopeThat = (message, callback) => {
  HopeTests.push([message, callback])
}
```

Independence

Because we're appending tests to an array, they will be run in the order in which they are registered, but we shouldn't rely on that. Every unit test should work independently of every other so that an error or failure in an early test doesn't affect the result of a later one.

Finally, the function `main` runs all registered tests:

```
// Run all of the tests that have been asked for and report summary.
const main = () => {
  HopeTests.forEach(([message, test]) => {
    try {
      test()
      HopePass += 1
    } catch (e) {
      if (e instanceof assert.AssertionError) {
        HopeFail += 1
      } else {
        HopeError += 1
      }
    }
  })
```

```
  console.log(`pass ${HopePass}`)
  console.log(`fail ${HopeFail}`)
  console.log(`error ${HopeError}`)
}
```

If a test completes without an exception, it passes. If any of the **assert** calls inside the test raises an `AssertionError`, the test fails, and if it raises any other exception, it's an error. After all tests are run, **main** reports the number of results of each kind.

Let's try it out:

```
// Something to test (doesn't handle zero properly).
const sign = (value) => {
  if (value < 0) {
    return -1
  } else {
    return 1
  }
}

// These two should pass.
hopeThat('Sign of negative is -1', () => assert(sign(-3) === -1))
hopeThat('Sign of positive is 1', () => assert(sign(19) === 1))

// This one should fail.
hopeThat('Sign of zero is 0', () => assert(sign(0) === 0))

// This one is an error.
hopeThat('Sign misspelled is error', () => assert(sgn(1) === 1))

// Call the main driver.
main()
```

```
pass 2
fail 1
error 1
```

This simple "framework" does what it's supposed to, but:

1. It doesn't tell us which tests have passed or failed.
2. Those global variables should be consolidated somehow so that it's clear they belong together.
3. It doesn't discover tests on its own.
4. We don't have a way to test things that are supposed to raise `AssertionError`. Putting assertions into code to check that it is behaving correctly is called **defensive programming**; it's a good practice, but we should make sure those assertions are failing when they're supposed to, just as we should test our smoke detectors every once in a while.

4.3 How should we structure test registration?

The next version of our testing tool solves the first two problems in the original by putting the testing machinery in a class. It uses the **Singleton design pattern** to ensure that only one object of that class is ever created [Osmani2017]. Singletons are a way to manage global variables that belong together like the ones we're using to record tests and their results. As an extra benefit, if we decide later that we need several copies of those variables, we can just construct more instances of the class.

The file `hope.js` defines the class and exports one instance of it:

```
import assert from 'assert'
import caller from 'caller'

class Hope {
  constructor () {
    this.todo = []
    this.passes = []
    this.fails = []
    this.errors = []
  }

  test (comment, callback) {
    this.todo.push([`${caller()}::${comment}`, callback])
  }

  run () {
    this.todo.forEach(([comment, test]) => {
      try {
        test()
        this.passes.push(comment)
      } catch (e) {
        if (e instanceof assert.AssertionError) {
          this.fails.push(comment)
        } else {
          this.errors.push(comment)
        }
      }
    })
  }

}

export default new Hope()
```

This strategy relies on two things:

1. Node[3] executes the code in a JavaScript module as it loads it, which means that it runs `new Hope()` and exports the newly-created object.

2. Node **caches** modules so that a given module is only loaded once no matter how many times it is imported. This ensures that `new Hope()` really is only called once.

Once a program has imported `hope`, it can call `Hope.test` to record a test for later execution and `Hope.run` to execute all of the tests registered up until that point (Figure 4.2).

[3]https://nodejs.org/en/

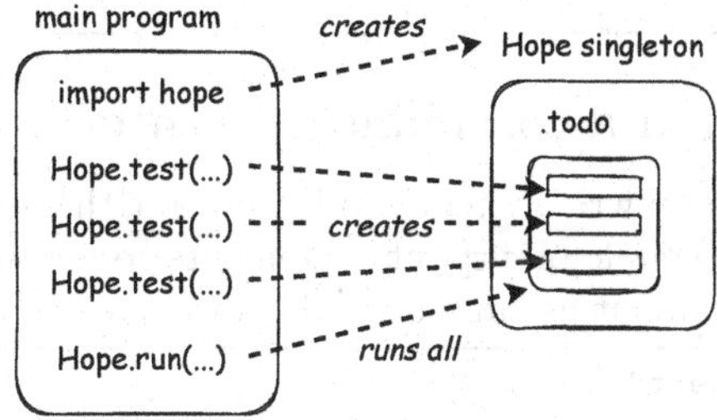

Figure 4.2: Creating a singleton, recording tests, and running them.

Finally, our `Hope` class can report results as both a terse one-line summary and as a detailed listing. It can also provide the titles and results of individual tests so that if someone wants to format them in a different way (e.g., as HTML) they can do so:

```
terse () {
  return this.cases()
    .map(([title, results]) => `${title}: ${results.length}`)
    .join(' ')
}

verbose () {
  let report = ''
  let prefix = ''
  for (const [title, results] of this.cases()) {
    report += `${prefix}${title}:`
    prefix = '\n'
    for (const r of results) {
      report += `${prefix}  ${r}`
    }
  }
  return report
}

cases () {
  return [
    ['passes', this.passes],
    ['fails', this.fails],
    ['errors', this.errors]]
}
```

Who's calling?

`Hope.test` uses the `caller`[4] module to get the name of the function that is registering a test. Reporting the test's name helps the user figure out where to start debugging; getting it via introspection rather than requiring the user to pass the function's name as a string reduces typing and guarantees that what we report is accurate. Programmers will often copy, paste, and modify tests; sooner or later (probably sooner) they will forget to modify the copy-and-pasted function name being passed into `Hope.test` and will then lose time trying to figure out why `test_this` is failing when the failure is actually in `test_that`.

[4]https://www.npmjs.com/package/caller

4.4 How can we build a command-line interface for testing?

Most programmers don't enjoy writing tests, so if we want them to do it, we have to make it as painless as possible. A couple of `import` statements to get `assert` and `hope` and then one function call per test is about as simple as we can make the tests themselves:

```
import assert from 'assert'
import hope from './hope.js'

hope.test('Sum of 1 and 2', () => assert((1 + 2) === 3))
```

But that just defines the tests—how will we find them so that we can run them? One option is to require people to `import` each of the files containing tests into another file:

```
// all-the-tests.js

import './test-add.js'
import './test-sub.js'
import './test-mul.js'
import './test-div.js'

Hope.run()
...
```

Here, `all-the-tests.js` imports other files so that they will register tests as a **side effect** via calls to `hope.test` and then calls `Hope.run` to execute them. It works, but sooner or later (probably sooner) someone will forget to import one of the test files.

A better strategy is to load test files **dynamically**. While `import` is usually written as a statement, it can also be used as an `async` function that takes a path as a parameter and loads the corresponding file. The program `pray.js` (shown below) does this; as before, loading files executes the code they contain, which registers tests as a side effect:

```
import minimist from 'minimist'
import glob from 'glob'
import hope from './hope.js'

const main = async (args) => {
  const options = parse(args)
  if (options.filenames.length === 0) {
    options.filenames = glob.sync(`${options.root}/**/test-*.js`)
  }
  for (const f of options.filenames) {
    await import(f)
  }
  hope.run()
  const result = (options.output === 'terse')
    ? hope.terse()
    : hope.verbose()
  console.log(result)
}


main(process.argv.slice(2))
```

By default, this program finds all files below the current working directory whose names match the pattern `test-*.js` and uses terse output. Since we may want to look for files somewhere else, or request verbose output, the program needs to handle command-line arguments.

The `minimist`[5] module does this in a way that is consistent with Unix conventions. Given command-line arguments *after* the program's name (i.e., from `process.argv[2]` onward), it looks for patterns like `-x something` and creates an object with flags as keys and values associated with them.

Filenames in `minimist`

If we use a command line like `pray.js -v something.js`, then `something.js` becomes the value of `-v`. To indicate that we want `something.js` added to the list of trailing filenames associated with the special key `_` (a single underscore), we have to write `pray.js -v -- something.js`. The double dash is a common Unix convention for signalling the end of parameters.

Our **test runner** is now complete, so we can try it out with some files containing tests that pass, fail, and contain errors:

```
node pray.js -v
```

```
passes:
  /u/stjs/unit-test/test-add.js::Sum of 1 and 2
  /u/stjs/unit-test/test-sub.js::Difference of 1 and 2
fails:
  /u/stjs/unit-test/test-div.js::Quotient of 1 and 0
  /u/stjs/unit-test/test-mul.js::Product of 1 and 2
errors:
  /u/stjs/unit-test/test-missing.js::Sum of x and 0
```

Infinity is allowed

`test-div.js` contains the line:

```
hope.test('Quotient of 1 and 0', () => assert((1 / 0) === 0))
```

This test counts as a failure rather than an error because the result of dividing by zero is the special value `Infinity` rather than an arithmetic error.

Loading modules dynamically so that they can register something for us to call later is a common pattern in many programming languages. Control flow goes back and forth between the framework and the module being loaded as this happens so we must specify the **lifecycle** of the loaded modules quite carefully. Figure 4.3 illustrates what happens when a pair of files `test-add.js` and `test-sub.js` are loaded by our framework:

1. `pray` loads `hope.js`.
2. Loading `hope.js` creates a single instance of the class `Hope`.
3. `pray` uses `glob` to find files with tests.
4. `pray` loads `test-add.js` using `import` as a function.
5. As `test-add.js` runs, it loads `hope.js`. Since `hope.js` is already loaded, this does not create a new instance of `Hope`.

[5]https://www.npmjs.com/package/minimist

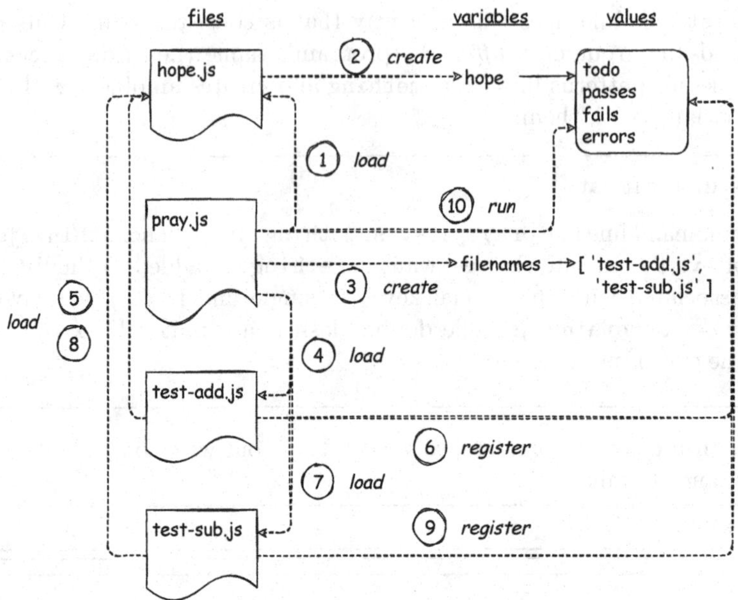

Figure 4.3: Lifecycle of dynamically-discovered unit tests.

6. `test-add.js` uses `hope.test` to register a test (which does not run yet).
7. `pray` then loads `test-sub.js`...
8. ...which loads `Hope`...
9. ...then registers a test.
10. `pray` can now ask the unique instance of `Hope` to run all of the tests, then get a report from the `Hope` singleton and display it.

4.5 Exercises

Asynchronous globbing

Modify `pray.js` to use the asynchronous version of `glob` rather than `glob.sync`.

Timing tests

Install the `microtime`[6] package and then modify the `dry-run.js` example so that it records and reports the execution times for tests.

[6]https://www.npmjs.com/package/microtime

Approximately equal

1. Write a function `assertApproxEqual` that does nothing if two values are within a certain tolerance of each other but throws an exception if they are not:

```
// throws exception
assertApproxEqual(1.0, 2.0, 0.01, 'Values are too far apart')

// does not throw
assertApproxEqual(1.0, 2.0, 10.0, 'Large margin of error')
```

2. Modify the function so that a default tolerance is used if none is specified:

```
// throws exception
assertApproxEqual(1.0, 2.0, 'Values are too far apart')

// does not throw
assertApproxEqual(1.0, 2.0, 'Large margin of error', 10.0)
```

3. Modify the function again so that it checks the **relative error** instead of the **absolute error**. (The relative error is the absolute value of the difference between the actual and expected value, divided by the absolute value.)

Rectangle overlay

A windowing application represents rectangles using objects with four values: `x` and `y` are the coordinates of the lower-left corner, while `w` and `h` are the width and height. All values are non-negative: the lower-left corner of the screen is at `(0, 0)` and the screen's size is `WIDTHxHEIGHT`.

1. Write tests to check that an object represents a valid rectangle.

2. The function `overlay(a, b)` takes two rectangles and returns either a new rectangle representing the region where they overlap or `null` if they do not overlap. Write tests to check that `overlay` is working correctly.

3. Do your tests assume that two rectangles that touch on an edge overlap or not? What about two rectangles that only touch at a single corner?

Selecting tests

Modify `pray.js` so that if the user provides `-s pattern` or `--select pattern` then the program only runs tests in files that contain the string `pattern` in their name.

Tagging tests

Modify `hope.js` so that users can optionally provide an array of strings to tag tests:

```
hope.test('Difference of 1 and 2',
          () => assert((1 - 2) === -1),
          ['math', 'fast'])
```

Then modify `pray.js` so that if users specify either `-t tagName` or `--tag tagName` only tests with that tag are run.

Mock objects

A mock object is a simplified replacement for part of a program whose behavior is easier to control and predict than the thing it is replacing. For example, we may want to test that our program does the right thing if an error occurs while reading a file. To do this, we write a function that wraps `fs.readFileSync`:

```
const mockReadFileSync = (filename, encoding = 'utf-8') => {
  return fs.readFileSync(filename, encoding)
}
```

and then modify it so that it throws an exception under our control. For example, if we define `MOCK_READ_FILE_CONTROL` like this:

```
const MOCK_READ_FILE_CONTROL = [false, false, true, false, true]
```

then the third and fifth calls to `mockReadFileSync` throw an exception instead of reading data, as do any calls after the fifth. Write this function.

Setup and teardown

Testing frameworks often allow programmers to specify a `setup` function that is to be run before each test and a corresponding `teardown` function that is to be run after each test. (`setup` usually re-creates complicated test fixtures, while `teardown` functions are sometimes needed to clean up after tests, e.g., to close database connections or delete temporary files.)

Modify the testing framework in this chapter so that if a file of tests contains something like this:

```
const createFixtures = () => {
  ...do something...
}

hope.setup(createFixtures)
```

then the function `createFixtures` will be called exactly once before each test in that file. Add a similar way to register a teardown function with `hope.teardown`.

Multiple tests

Add a method `hope.multiTest` that allows users to specify multiple test cases for a function at once. For example, this:

```
hope.multiTest('check all of these`, functionToTest, [
  [['arg1a', 'arg1b'], 'result1'],
  [['arg2a', 'arg2b'], 'result2'],
  [['arg3a', 'arg3b'], 'result3']
])
```

should be equivalent to this:

```
hope.test('check all of these 0',
  () => assert(functionToTest('arg1a', 'arg1b') === 'result1')
)
hope.test('check all of these 1',
  () => assert(functionToTest('arg2a', 'arg2b') === 'result2')
)
hope.test('check all of these 2',
  () => assert(functionToTest('arg3a', 'arg3b') === 'result3')
)
```

Assertions for sets and maps

1. Write functions `assertSetEqual` and `assertMapEqual` that check whether two instances of `Set` or two instances of `Map` are equal.

2. Write a function `assertArraySame` that checks whether two arrays have the same elements, even if those elements are in different orders.

Testing promises

Modify the unit testing framework to handle `async` functions, so that:

```
hope.test('delayed test', async () => {...})
```

does the right thing. (Note that you can use `typeof` to determine whether the object given to `hope.test` is a function or a promise.)

5

File Backup

Terms defined: **Application Programming Interface**, **collision**, **comma-separated values**, **Coordinated Universal Time**, **cryptographic hash function**, **data migration**, **handler**, **hash code**, **hash function**, **JavaScript Object Notation**, **mock object**, **pipe**, **race condition**, **SHA-1 hash**, **stream**, **streaming API**, **Time of check/time of use**, **timestamp**, **version control system**

Now that we can test software, we have something worth saving. A **version control system** like Git[1] keeps track of changes to files so that we can recover old versions if we want to. Its core is a way to archive files that:

1. records which versions of which files existed at the same time (so that we can go back to a consistent previous state), and

2. stores any particular version of a file only once, so that we don't waste disk space.

In this chapter we will build a tool for doing both tasks. It won't do everything Git does: in particular, it won't let us create and merge branches. If you would like to know how that works, please see Mary Rose Cook's[2] excellent Gitlet[3] project.

5.1 How can we uniquely identify files?

To avoid storing redundant copies of files, we need a way to tell when two files contain the same data. We can't rely on names because files can be renamed or moved over time; we could compare the files byte-by-byte, but a quicker way is to use a **hash function** that turns arbitrary data into a fixed-length string of bits (Figure 5.1).

A hash function always produces the same **hash code** for a given input. A **cryptographic hash function** has two extra properties:

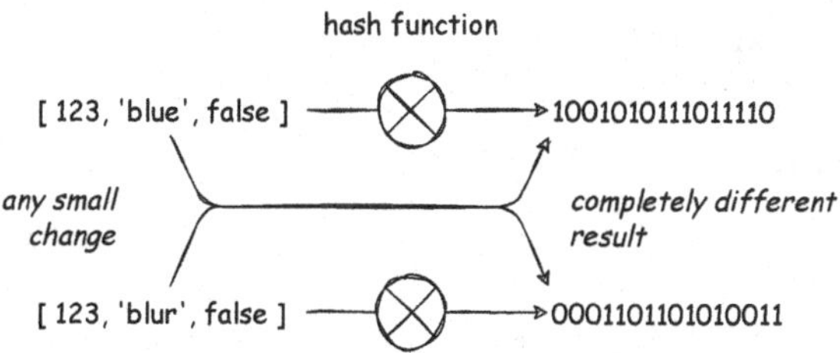

Figure 5.1: How hash functions speed up lookup.

[1] https://git-scm.com/
[2] https://maryrosecook.com/
[3] http://gitlet.maryrosecook.com/

1. The output depends on the entire input: changing even a single byte results in a different hash code.

2. The outputs look like random numbers: they are unpredictable and evenly distributed (i.e., the odds of getting any specific hash code are the same).

It's easy to write a bad hash function, but very hard to write one that qualifies as cryptographic. We will therefore use a library to calculate 160-bit **SHA-1** hashes for our files. These are not random enough to keep data secret from a patient, well-funded attacker, but that's not what we're using them for: we just want hashes that are random to make **collision** extremely unlikely.

The Birthday Problem

The odds that two people share a birthday are 1/365 (ignoring February 29). The odds that they *don't* are therefore 364/365. When we add a third person, the odds that they don't share a birthday with either of the preceding two people are 363/365, so the overall odds that nobody shares a birthday are $(365/365)\times(364/365)\times(363/365)$. If we keep calculating, there's a 50% chance of two people sharing a birthday in a group of just 23 people, and a 99.9% chance with 70 people.

We can use the same math to calculate how many files we need to hash before there's a 50% chance of a collision. Instead of 365, we use 2^{160} (the number of values that are 160 bits long), and after checking Wikipedia[4] and doing a few calculations with Wolfram Alpha[5], we calculate that we would need to have approximately 10^{24} files in order to have a 50% chance of a collision. We're willing to take that risk.

Node's[6] `crypto`[7] module provides tools to create a SHA-1 hash. To use them, we create an object that keeps track of the current state of the hashing calculations, tell it how we want to encode (or represent) the hash value, and then feed it some bytes. When we are done, we call its `.end` method and then use its `.read` method to get the final result:

```
import crypto from 'crypto'

// create a SHA1 hasher
const hash = crypto.createHash('sha1')

// encode as hex (rather than binary)
hash.setEncoding('hex')

// send it some text
const text = process.argv[2]
hash.write(text)

// signal end of text
hash.end()

// display the result
const sha1sum = hash.read()
console.log(`SHA1 of "${text}" is ${sha1sum}`)
```

[4]https://en.wikipedia.org/wiki/Birthday_problem#A_simple_exponentiation
[5]http://wolframalpha.com
[6]https://nodejs.org/en/
[7]https://nodejs.org/api/crypto.html

```
node hash-text.js something
```

```
SHA1 of "something" is 1af17e73721dbe0c40011b82ed4bb1a7dbe3ce29
```

Hashing a file instead of a fixed string is straightforward: we just read the file's contents and pass those characters to the hashing object:

```
import fs from 'fs'
import crypto from 'crypto'

const filename = process.argv[2]
const data = fs.readFileSync(filename, 'utf-8')

const hash = crypto.createHash('sha1').setEncoding('hex')
hash.write(data)
hash.end()
const sha1sum = hash.read()

console.log(`SHA1 of "${filename}" is ${sha1sum}`)
```

```
node hash-file.js hash-file.js
```

```
SHA1 of "hash-file.js" is c54c8ee3e576770d29ae2d0d73568e5a5c49eac0
```

However, it is more efficient to process the file as a **stream**:

```
import fs from 'fs'
import crypto from 'crypto'

const filename = process.argv[2]
const hash = crypto.createHash('sha1').setEncoding('hex')
fs.createReadStream(filename).pipe(hash)
hash.on('finish', () => {
  const final = hash.read()
  console.log('final', final)
})
console.log('program ends')
```

```
node hash-stream.js hash-stream.js
```

```
program ends
final dc9e6c231e243860dace2dbf52845b121062b60e
```

This kind of interface is called a **streaming API** because it is designed to process a stream of data one chunk at a time rather than requiring all of the data to be in memory at once. Many applications use streams so that programs don't have to read entire (possibly large) files into memory.

To start, this program asks the `fs` library to create a reading stream for a file and to **pipe** the data from that stream to the hashing object (Figure 5.2). It then tells the hashing object what to do when there is no more data by providing a **handler** for the "finish" event. This is called asynchronously: as the output shows, the main program ends before the task handling the end of data is scheduled and run. Most programs also provide a handler for "data" events to do something with each block of data as it comes in; the `hash` object in our program does that for us.

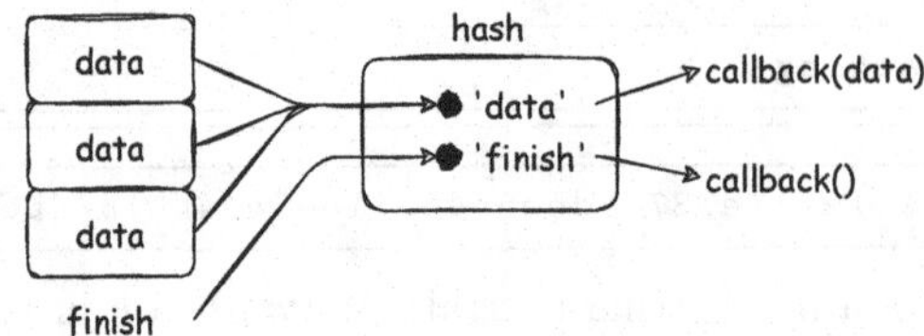

Figure 5.2: Processing files as streams of chunks.

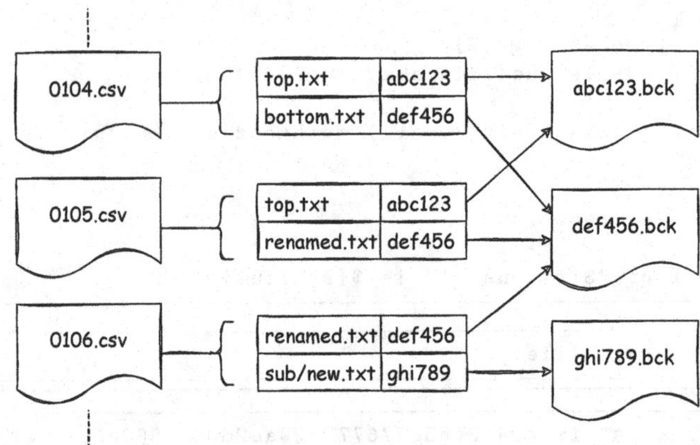

Figure 5.3: Organization of backup file storage.

5.2 How can we back up files?

Many files only change occasionally after they're created, or not at all. It would be wasteful for a version control system to make copies each time the user wanted to save a snapshot of a project, so instead our tool will copy each unique file to something like `abcd1234.bck`, where `abcd1234` is a hash of the file's contents. It will then store a data structure that records the filenames and hash keys for each snapshot. The hash keys tell it which unique files are part of the snapshot, while the filenames tell us what each file's contents were called when the snapshot was made (since files can be moved or renamed). To restore a particular snapshot, all we have to do is copy the saved `.bck` files back to where they were (Figure 5.3).

We can build the tools we need to do this using promises (Chapter 3). The main function creates a promise that uses the asynchronous version of `glob` to find files and then:

1. checks that entries in the list are actually files;
2. reads each file into memory; and
3. calculates hashes for those files.

```
import fs from 'fs-extra-promise'
import glob from 'glob-promise'
import crypto from 'crypto'

const hashExisting = (rootDir) => {
```

```
  const pattern = `${rootDir}/**/*`
  return new Promise((resolve, reject) => {
    glob(pattern, {})
      .then(matches => Promise.all(
        matches.map(path => statPath(path))))
      .then(pairs => pairs.filter(
        ([path, stat]) => stat.isFile()))
      .then(pairs => Promise.all(
        pairs.map(([path, stat]) => readPath(path))))
      .then(pairs => Promise.all(
        pairs.map(([path, content]) => hashPath(path, content))))
      .then(pairs => resolve(pairs))
      .catch(err => reject(err))
  })
}
```

This function uses `Promise.all` to wait for the operations on all of the files in the list to complete before going on to the next step. A different design would combine stat, read, and hash into a single step so that each file would be handled independently and use one `Promise.all` at the end to bring them all together.

The first two helper functions that `hashExisting` relies on wrap asynchronous operation in promises:

```
const statPath = (path) => {
  return new Promise((resolve, reject) => {
    fs.statAsync(path)
      .then(stat => resolve([path, stat]))
      .catch(err => reject(err))
  })
}

const readPath = (path) => {
  return new Promise((resolve, reject) => {
    fs.readFileAsync(path, 'utf-8')
      .then(content => resolve([path, content]))
      .catch(err => reject(err))
  })
}
```

The final helper function calculates the hash synchronously, but we can use `Promise.all` to wait on those operations finishing anyway:

```
const hashPath = (path, content) => {
  const hasher = crypto.createHash('sha1').setEncoding('hex')
  hasher.write(content)
  hasher.end()
  return [path, hasher.read()]
}
```

Let's try running it:

```
import hashExisting from './hash-existing-promise.js'

const root = process.argv[2]
hashExisting(root).then(pairs => pairs.forEach(
  ([path, hash]) => console.log(path, hash)
))
```

```
node run-hash-existing-promise.js . | fgrep -v test/ | fgrep -v '~'
```

```
./backup.js 11422489e11be3d8ff76278503457665f6152ebe
./check-existing-files.js 66b933cf9e792e9a9204171d04e0f8b530ec3f4f
./figures/hash-function.pdf 0eb82de379a95ee2be3f00b38c0102e2f2f8170e
./figures/hash-function.svg 563996575d581f2a08e3e954d7faba4d189d0773
./figures/mock-fs.pdf 0b3bba44e69122ee53bcc9d777c186c84b7c2ff2
...
./x-from-to.md f0f63b3576042dfc0050029ddfcccc3c42fe275d
./x-io-streams.md 1fb4d8b7785c5e7b2f1e29588e2ba28d101ced1a
./x-json-manifests.md 223e0e4167acc6d4d81b76ba1287b90234c95e22
./x-mock-hashes.md 580edfc0cb8eaca4f3700307002ae10ee97af8d2
./x-pre-commit.md b7d945af4554fc0f64b708fe735417bee8b33eef
```

The code we have written is clearer than it would be with callbacks (try rewriting it if you don't believe this) but the layer of promises around everything still obscures its meaning. The same operations are easier to read when written using **async** and **await**:

```
const statPath = async (path) => {
  const stat = await fs.statAsync(path)
  return [path, stat]
}

const readPath = async (path) => {
  const content = await fs.readFileAsync(path, 'utf-8')
  return [path, content]
}

const hashPath = (path, content) => {
  const hasher = crypto.createHash('sha1').setEncoding('hex')
  hasher.write(content)
  hasher.end()
  return [path, hasher.read()]
}

const hashExisting = async (rootDir) => {
  const pattern = `${rootDir}/**/*`
  const options = {}
  const matches = await glob(pattern, options)
  const stats = await Promise.all(matches.map(path => statPath(path)))
  const files = stats.filter(([path, stat]) => stat.isFile())
  const contents = await Promise.all(
    files.map(([path, stat]) => readPath(path)))
  const hashes = contents.map(
    ([path, content]) => hashPath(path, content))
  return hashes
}
```

This version creates and resolves exactly the same promises as the previous one, but those promises are created for us automatically by Node. To check that it works, let's run it for the same input files:

```
import hashExisting from './hash-existing-async.js'

const root = process.argv[2]
hashExisting(root).then(
  pairs => pairs.forEach(([path, hash]) => console.log(path, hash)))
```

```
node run-hash-existing-async.js . | fgrep -v test/ | fgrep -v '~'
```

```
./backup.js 11422489e11be3d8ff76278503457665f6152ebe
./check-existing-files.js 66b933cf9e792e9a9204171d04e0f8b530ec3f4f
./figures/hash-function.pdf 0eb82de379a95ee2be3f00b38c0102e2f2f8170e
./figures/hash-function.svg 563996575d581f2a08e3e954d7faba4d189d0773
./figures/mock-fs.pdf 0b3bba44e69122ee53bcc9d777c186c84b7c2ff2
...
./x-from-to.md f0f63b3576042dfc0050029ddfcccc3c42fe275d
./x-io-streams.md 1fb4d8b7785c5e7b2f1e29588e2ba28d101ced1a
./x-json-manifests.md 223e0e4167acc6d4d81b76ba1287b90234c95e22
./x-mock-hashes.md 580edfc0cb8eaca4f3700307002ae10ee97af8d2
./x-pre-commit.md b7d945af4554fc0f64b708fe735417bee8b33eef
```

5.3 How can we track which files have already been backed up?

The second part of our backup tool keeps track of which files have and haven't been backed up already. It stores backups in a directory that contains backup files like `abcd1234.bck` and files describing the contents of particular snapshots. The latter are named `ssssssssss.csv`, where `ssssssssss` is the **UTC timestamp** of the backup's creation and the `.csv` extension indicates that the file is formatted as **comma-separated values**. (We could store these files as **JSON**, but CSV is easier for people to read.)

Time of check/time of use

Our naming convention for index files will fail if we try to create more than one backup per second. This might seem very unlikely, but many faults and security holes are the result of programmers assuming things weren't going to happen.

We could try to avoid this problem by using a two-part naming scheme `ssssssss-a.csv`, `ssssssss-b.csv`, and so on, but this leads to a **race condition** called **time of check/time of use**. If two users run the backup tool at the same time, they will both see that there isn't a file (yet) with the current timestamp, so they will both try to create the first one.

```
import glob from 'glob-promise'
import path from 'path'

const findNew = async (rootDir, pathHashPairs) => {
  const hashToPath = pathHashPairs.reduce((obj, [path, hash]) => {
    obj[hash] = path
    return obj
  }, {})

  const pattern = `${rootDir}/*.bck`
  const options = {}
  const existingFiles = await glob(pattern, options)

  existingFiles.forEach(filename => {
    const stripped = path.basename(filename).replace(/\.bck$/, '')
    delete hashToPath[stripped]
  })
```

```
  return hashToPath
}

export default findNew
```

To test our program, let's manually create testing directories with manufactured (shortened) hashes:

```
tree test
```

```
test
├── bck-0-csv-0
├── bck-1-csv-1
│   ├── 0001.csv
│   └── abcd1234.bck
├── bck-4-csv-2
│   ├── 0001.csv
│   ├── 3028.csv
│   ├── 3456cdef.bck
│   ├── abcd1234.bck
│   └── bcde2345.bck
├── test-backup.js
├── test-find-mock.js
└── test-find.js

3 directories, 10 files
```

We use Mocha[8] to manage our tests. Every test is an `async` function; Mocha automatically waits for them all to complete before reporting results. To run them, we add the line:

```
"test": "mocha */test/test-*.js"
```

in the `scripts` section of our project's `package.json` file so that when we run `npm run test`, Mocha looks for files in `test` sub-directories of the directories holding our lessons.

Here are our first few tests:

```
import assert from 'assert'

import findNew from '../check-existing-files.js'

describe('pre-existing hashes and actual filesystem', () => {
  it('finds no pre-existing files when none given or exist', async () => {
    const expected = {}
    const actual = await findNew('file-backup/test/bck-0-csv-0', [])
    assert.deepStrictEqual(expected, actual,
      'Expected no files')
  })

  it('finds some files when one is given and none exist', async () => {
    const check = [['somefile.txt', '9876fedc']]
    const expected = { '9876fedc': 'somefile.txt' }
    const actual = await findNew('file-backup/test/bck-0-csv-0', check)
    assert.deepStrictEqual(expected, actual,
      'Expected one file')
  })

  it('finds nothing needs backup when there is a match', async () => {
    const check = [['alpha.js', 'abcd1234']]
```

[8]https://mochajs.org/

```
    const expected = {}
    const actual = await findNew('file-backup/test/bck-1-csv-1', check)
    assert.deepStrictEqual(expected, actual,
      'Expected no files')
  })

  it('finds something needs backup when there is a mismatch', async () => {
    const check = [['alpha.js', 'a1b2c3d4']]
    const expected = { a1b2c3d4: 'alpha.js' }
    const actual = await findNew('file-backup/test/bck-1-csv-1', check)
    assert.deepStrictEqual(expected, actual,
      'Expected one file')
  })

  it('finds mixed matches', async () => {
    const check = [
      ['matches.js', '3456cdef'],
      ['matches.txt', 'abcd1234'],
      ['mismatch.txt', '12345678']
    ]
    const expected = { 12345678: 'mismatch.txt' }
    const actual = await findNew('file-backup/test/bck-4-csv-2', check)
    assert.deepStrictEqual(expected, actual,
      'Expected one file')
  })
})
```

and here is Mocha's report:

```
> stjs@1.0.0 test
> mocha */test/test-*.js "-g" "pre-existing hashes"


  pre-existing hashes and actual filesystem
    ✓ finds no pre-existing files when none given or exist
    ✓ finds some files when one is given and none exist
    ✓ finds nothing needs backup when there is a match
    ✓ finds something needs backup when there is a mismatch
    ✓ finds mixed matches


  5 passing (16ms)
```

5.4 How can we test code that modifies files?

The final thing our tool needs to do is copy the files that need copying and create a new index file. The code itself will be relatively simple, but testing will be complicated by the fact that our tests will need to create directories and files before they run and then delete them afterward (so that they don't contaminate subsequent tests).

A better approach is to use a **mock object** instead of the real filesystem. A mock object has the same interface as the function, object, class, or library that it replaces, but is designed to be used solely for testing. Node's `mock-fs`[9] library provides the same functions as the `fs` library, but stores everything in memory (Figure 5.4). This prevents our tests from

[9]https://www.npmjs.com/package/mock-fs

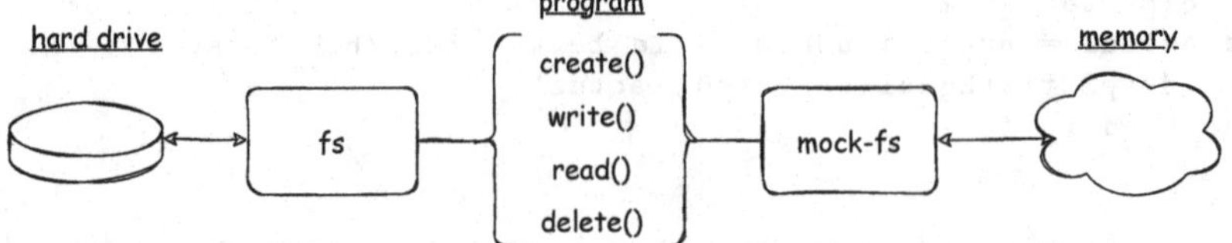

Figure 5.4: Using a mock filesystem to simplify testing.

accidentally disturbing the filesystem, and also makes tests much faster (since in-memory operations are thousands of times faster than operations that touch the disk).

We can create a mock filesystem by giving the library a JSON description of the files and what they should contain:

```
import assert from 'assert'
import mock from 'mock-fs'

import findNew from '../check-existing-files.js'

describe('checks for pre-existing hashes using mock filesystem', () => {
  beforeEach(() => {
    mock({
      'bck-0-csv-0': {},
      'bck-1-csv-1': {
        '0001.csv': 'alpha.js,abcd1234',
        'abcd1234.bck': 'alpha.js content'
      },
      'bck-4-csv-2': {
        '0001.csv': ['alpha.js,abcd1234',
          'beta.txt,bcde2345'].join('\n'),
        '3024.csv': ['alpha.js,abcd1234',
          'gamma.png,3456cdef',
          'subdir/renamed.txt,bcde2345'].join('\n'),
        '3456cdef.bck': 'gamma.png content',
        'abcd1234.bck': 'alpha content',
        'bcde2345.bck': 'beta.txt became subdir/renamed.txt'
      }
    })
  })

  afterEach(() => {
    mock.restore()
  })

})
```

Mocha automatically calls `beforeEach` before running each tests, and `afterEach` after each tests completes (which is yet another protocol). All of the tests stay exactly the same, and since `mock-fs` replaces the functions in the standard `fs` library with its own, nothing in our application needs to change either.

We are finally ready to write the program that actually backs up files:

```
import fs from 'fs-extra-promise'

import hashExisting from './hash-existing-async.js'
import findNew from './check-existing-files.js'

const backup = async (src, dst, timestamp = null) => {
```

```
  if (timestamp === null) {
    timestamp = Math.round((new Date()).getTime() / 1000)
  }
  timestamp = String(timestamp).padStart(10, '0')

  const existing = await hashExisting(src)
  const needToCopy = await findNew(dst, existing)
  await copyFiles(dst, needToCopy)
  await saveManifest(dst, timestamp, existing)
}

const copyFiles = async (dst, needToCopy) => {
  const promises = Object.keys(needToCopy).map(hash => {
    const srcPath = needToCopy[hash]
    const dstPath = `${dst}/${hash}.bck`
    fs.copyFileAsync(srcPath, dstPath)
  })
  return Promise.all(promises)
}

const saveManifest = async (dst, timestamp, pathHash) => {
  pathHash = pathHash.sort()
  const content = pathHash.map(
    ([path, hash]) => `${path},${hash}`).join('\n')
  const manifest = `${dst}/${timestamp}.csv`
  fs.writeFileAsync(manifest, content, 'utf-8')
}

export default backup
```

The tests for this are more complicated than tests we have written previously because we want to check with actual file hashes. Let's set up some fixtures to run tests on:

```
import backup from '../backup.js'

const hashString = (data) => {
  const hasher = crypto.createHash('sha1').setEncoding('hex')
  hasher.write(data)
  hasher.end()
  return hasher.read()
}

const Contents = {
  aaa: 'AAA',
  bbb: 'BBB',
  ccc: 'CCC'
}

const Hashes = Object.keys(Contents).reduce((obj, key) => {
  obj[key] = hashString(Contents[key])
  return obj
}, {})

const Fixture = {
  source: {
    'alpha.txt': Contents.aaa,
    'beta.txt': Contents.bbb,
    gamma: {
      'delta.txt': Contents.ccc
    }
  },
```

```
  backup: {}
}

const InitialBackups = Object.keys(Hashes).reduce((set, filename) => {
  set.add(`backup/${Hashes[filename]}.bck`)
  return set
}, new Set())
```

and then run some tests:

```
describe('check entire backup process', () => {
  beforeEach(() => {
    mock(Fixture)
  })

  afterEach(() => {
    mock.restore()
  })

  it('creates an initial CSV manifest', async () => {
    await backup('source', 'backup', 0)

    assert.strictEqual((await glob('backup/*')).length, 4,
      'Expected 4 files')

    const actualBackups = new Set(await glob('backup/*.bck'))
    assert.deepStrictEqual(actualBackups, InitialBackups,
      'Expected 3 backup files')

    const actualManifests = await glob('backup/*.csv')
    assert.deepStrictEqual(actualManifests, ['backup/0000000000.csv'],
      'Expected one manifest')
  })

  it('does not duplicate files unnecessarily', async () => {
    await backup('source', 'backup', 0)
    assert.strictEqual((await glob('backup/*')).length, 4,
      'Expected 4 files after first backup')

    await backup('source', 'backup', 1)
    assert.strictEqual((await glob('backup/*')).length, 5,
      'Expected 5 files after second backup')
    const actualBackups = new Set(await glob('backup/*.bck'))
    assert.deepStrictEqual(actualBackups, InitialBackups,
      'Expected 3 backup files after second backup')

    const actualManifests = (await glob('backup/*.csv')).sort()
    assert.deepStrictEqual(actualManifests,
      ['backup/0000000000.csv', 'backup/0000000001.csv'],
      'Expected two manifests')
  })

  it('adds a file as needed', async () => {
    await backup('source', 'backup', 0)
    assert.strictEqual((await glob('backup/*')).length, 4,
      'Expected 4 files after first backup')

    await fs.writeFileAsync('source/newfile.txt', 'NNN')
    const hashOfNewFile = hashString('NNN')

    await backup('source', 'backup', 1)
```

```
    assert.strictEqual((await glob('backup/*')).length, 6,
      'Expected 6 files after second backup')
    const expected = new Set(InitialBackups)
      .add(`backup/${hashOfNewFile}.bck`)
    const actualBackups = new Set(await glob('backup/*.bck'))
    assert.deepStrictEqual(actualBackups, expected,
      'Expected 4 backup files after second backup')

    const actualManifests = (await glob('backup/*.csv')).sort()
    assert.deepStrictEqual(actualManifests,
      ['backup/0000000000.csv', 'backup/0000000001.csv'],
      'Expected two manifests')
  })
})
```

```
> stjs@1.0.0 test
> mocha */test/test-*.js "-g" "check entire backup process"


  check entire backup process
    ✓ creates an initial CSV manifest
    ✓ does not duplicate files unnecessarily
    ✓ adds a file as needed


  3 passing (18ms)
```

Design for test

One of the best ways—maybe *the* best way—to evaluate software design is by thinking about testability [Feathers2004]. We were able to use a mock filesystem instead of a real one because the filesystem has a well-defined API that is provided to us in a single library, so replacing it is a matter of changing one thing in one place. If you have to change several parts of your code in order to test it, the code is telling you to consolidate those parts into one component.

5.5 Exercises

Odds of collision

If hashes were only 2 bits long, then the chances of collision with each successive file assuming no previous collision are:

Number of Files	Odds of Collision
1	0%
2	25%
3	50%
4	75%
5	100%

A colleague of yours says this means that if we hash four files, there's only a 75% chance of any collision occurring. What are the actual odds?

Streaming I/O

Write a small program using `fs.createReadStream` and `fs.createWriteStream` that copies a file piece-by-piece instead of reading it into memory and then writing it out again.

Sequencing backups

Modify the backup program so that manifests are numbered sequentially as `00000001.csv`, `00000002.csv`, and so on rather than being timestamped. Why doesn't this solve the time of check/time of use race condition mentioned earlier?

JSON manifests

1. Modify `backup.js` so that it can save JSON manifests as well as CSV manifests based on a command-line flag.
2. Write another program called `migrate.js` that converts a set of manifests from CSV to JSON. (The program's name comes from the term **data migration**.)
3. Modify `backup.js` programs so that each manifest stores the user name of the person who created it along with file hashes, and then modify `migrate.js` to transform old files into the new format.

Mock hashes

1. Modify the file backup program so that it uses a function called `ourHash` to hash files.
2. Create a replacement that returns some predictable value, such as the first few characters of the data.
3. Rewrite the tests to use this function.

How did you modify the main program so that the tests could control which hashing function is used?

Comparing manifests

Write a program `compare-manifests.js` that reads two manifest files and reports:

- Which files have the same names but different hashes (i.e., their contents have changed).
- Which files have the same hashes but different names (i.e., they have been renamed).
- Which files are in the first hash but neither their names nor their hashes are in the second (i.e., they have been deleted).
- Which files are in the second hash but neither their names nor their hashes are in the first (i.e., they have been added).

From one state to another

1. Write a program called `from-to.js` that takes the name of a directory and the name of a manifest file as its command-line arguments, then adds, removes, and/or renames files in the directory to restore the state described in the manifest. The program should only perform file operations when it needs to, e.g., it should not delete a file and re-add it if the contents have not changed.

2. Write some tests for `from-to.js` using Mocha and `mock-fs`.

File history

1. Write a program called `file-history.js` that takes the name of a file as a command-line argument and displays the history of that file by tracing it back in time through the available manifests.

2. Write tests for your program using Mocha and `mock-fs`.

Pre-commit hooks

Modify `backup.js` to load and run a function called `preCommit` from a file called `pre-commit.js` stored in the root directory of the files being backed up. If `preCommit` returns `true`, the backup proceeds; if it returns `false` or throws an exception, no backup is created.

6

Data Tables

Terms defined: **character encoding**, **column-major storage**, **data frame**, **fixed-width (of strings)**, **garbage collection**, **heterogeneous**, **homogeneous**, **immutable**, **index (in a database)**, **JavaScript Object Notation**, **join**, **pad (a string)**, **row-major storage**, **sparse matrix**, **SQL**, **tagged data**, **test harness**

Chapter 2 said that operations in memory are thousands of times faster than operations that touch the filesystem, but what about different in-memory operations—how do they compare with each other? Putting it another way, how can we tell which of several designs is going to be the most efficient?

The best answer is to conduct some experiments. To see how to do this, we will take a look at several ways to implement data tables with one or more named columns and zero or more rows. Each row has one value for each column, and all the values in a column have the same type (Figure 6.1). Data tables appear over and over again in programming, from spreadsheets and databases to the **data frames** in R's tidyverse[1] packages, Python's[2] Pandas[3] library, or the DataForge[4] library for JavaScript [Davis2018].

The key operations on data tables are those provided by **SQL**: filter, select, summarize, and join. These can be implemented in about 500 lines of code, but their performance depends on how the data table is stored.

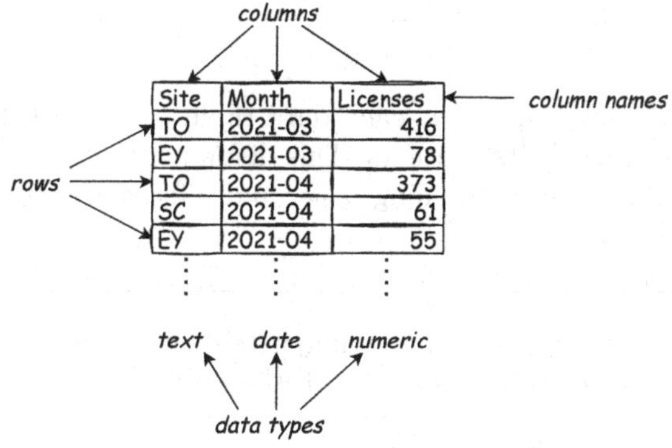

Figure 6.1: The structure of a data table.

[1]https://www.tidyverse.org/
[2]https://www.python.org/
[3]https://pandas.pydata.org/
[4]http://www.data-forge-js.com/

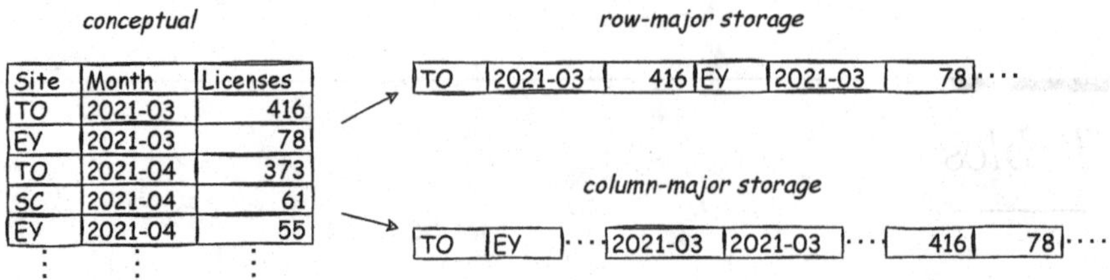

Figure 6.2: Row-major storage vs. column-major storage for data tables.

6.1 How can we implement data tables?

One way to store a table is **row-major** order, in which the values in each row are stored together in memory. This is sometimes also called **heterogeneous** storage because each "unit" of storage can contain values of different types. We can implement this design in JavaScript using an array of objects, each of which has the same keys (Figure 6.2).

Another option is **column-major** or **homogeneous** order, in which all the values in a column are stored together. In JavaScript, this could be implemented using an object whose members are all arrays of the same length.

To find out which is better we will construct one of each, try some operations, record their execution times and memory use, and then compare them. Crucially, the answer will depend on both the implementations themselves and on what mix of operations we measure. For example, if one strategy works better for filter and another for select, the ratio of filters to selects may determine which is "best".

> **Immutability**
>
> All of our implementations will treat each data table as **immutable**: once we have created it, we will not modify its contents. This doesn't actually have much impact on performance and makes the programming easier and safer, since shared data structures are a rich source of bugs.

For our first experiment, let's build a row-major table with some number of columns. To keep it simple, we will use the row indexes to fill the table:

```
export const buildRows = (nRows, labels) => {
  const result = []
  for (let iR = 0; iR < nRows; iR += 1) {
    const row = {}
    labels.forEach(label => {
      row[label] = iR
    })
    result.push(row)
  }
  return result
}
```

Next, we write `filter` and `select` for tables laid out this way. We need to provide a callback function to `filter` to determine which rows to keep like the callback for `Array.filter`; for selecting columns, we provide a list of the keys that identify the columns we want to

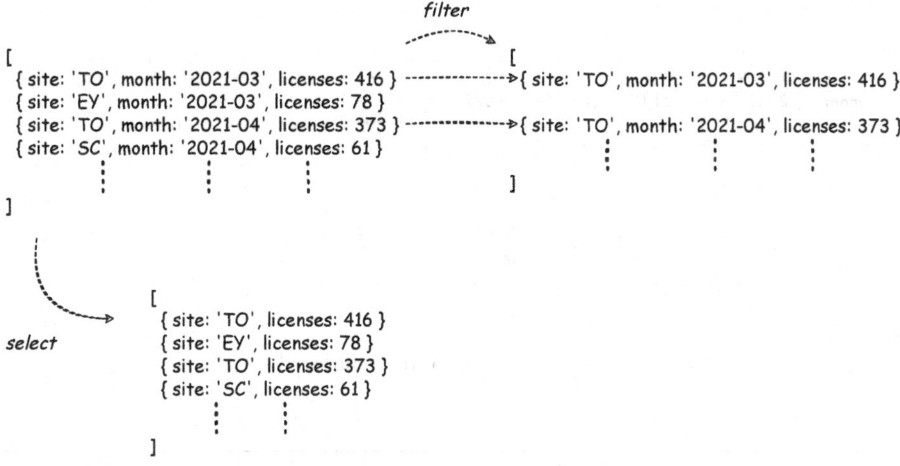

Figure 6.3: Operations on row-major data tables.

keep. We expect filtering to be relatively fast, since it is recycling rows, while selecting should be relatively slow because we have to construct a new set of arrays (Figure 6.3).

```
const rowFilter = (table, func) => {
  return table.filter(row => func(row))
}

const rowSelect = (table, toKeep) => {
  return table.map(row => {
    const newRow = {}
    toKeep.forEach(label => {
      newRow[label] = row[label]
    })
    return newRow
  })
}
```

Now let's do the same for column-major storage. Building the object that holds the columns is straightforward:

```
export const buildCols = (nRows, labels) => {
  const result = {}
  labels.forEach(label => {
    result[label] = []
    for (let iR = 0; iR < nRows; iR += 1) {
      result[label].push(iR)
    }
  })
  return result
}
```

Filtering is more complex because the values in each row are scattered across several arrays, but selecting is just a matter of recycling the arrays we want in the new table. We expect selecting to be relatively fast, since only the references to the columns need to be copied, but filtering will be relatively slow since we are constructing multiple new arrays (Figure 6.4). Note that this code assumes there is a column called `label_1` that it can look at to find out how many rows there are in the table. This would be a horrible thing to put into production, but is good enough for some simple performance testing.

Figure 6.4: Operations on column-major data tables.

```
const colFilter = (table, func) => {
  const result = {}
  const labels = Object.keys(table)
  labels.forEach(label => {
    result[label] = []
  })
  for (let iR = 0; iR < table.label_1.length; iR += 1) {
    if (func(table, iR)) {
      labels.forEach(label => {
        result[label].push(table[label][iR])
      })
    }
  }
  return result
}

const colSelect = (table, toKeep) => {
  const result = {}
  toKeep.forEach(label => {
    result[label] = table[label]
  })
  return result
}
```

Not quite polymorphic

Our tests would be simpler to write if the two versions of `filter` and `select` took exactly the same parameters, but the row-testing functions for `filter` are different because of the differences in the ways the tables are stored. We could force them to be the same by (for example) packing the values for each row in the column-major implementation into a temporary object and passing that to the same filtering function we used for the row-major implementation, but that extra work would bias the performance comparison in row-major's favor.

6.2 How can we test the performance of our implementations?

Now that we have our tables and operations, we can build a **test harness** to run those operations on data tables of varying sizes. We arbitrarily decide to keep half of the columns and one-third of the rows; these ratios will affect our decision about which is better, so if we were doing this for a real application we would test what happens as these fractions vary. And as we said earlier, the relative performance will also depend on how many filters we do for each select; our balance should be based on data from whatever application we intend to support.

Our performance measurement program looks like this:

```
const RANGE = 3

const main = () => {
  const nRows = parseInt(process.argv[2])
  const nCols = parseInt(process.argv[3])
  const filterPerSelect = parseFloat(process.argv[4])

  const labels = [...Array(nCols).keys()].map(i => `label_${i + 1}`)
  const someLabels = labels.slice(0, Math.floor(labels.length / 2))
  assert(someLabels.length > 0,
    'Must have some labels for select (array too short)')

  const [rowTable, rowSize, rowHeap] = memory(buildRows, nRows, labels)
  const [colTable, colSize, colHeap] = memory(buildCols, nRows, labels)

  const rowFilterTime =
    time(rowFilter, rowTable,
      row => ((row.label_1 % RANGE) === 0))
  const rowSelectTime =
    time(rowSelect, rowTable, someLabels)
  const colFilterTime =
    time(colFilter, colTable,
      (table, iR) => ((table.label_1[iR] % RANGE) === 0))
  const colSelectTime =
    time(colSelect, colTable, someLabels)

  const ratio = calculateRatio(filterPerSelect,
    rowFilterTime, rowSelectTime,
    colFilterTime, colSelectTime)

  const result = {
    nRows,
    nCols,
    filterPerSelect,
    rowSize,
    rowHeap,
    colSize,
    colHeap,
    rowFilterTime,
    rowSelectTime,
    colFilterTime,
    colSelectTime,
    ratio
  }
  console.log(yaml.safeDump(result))
}
```

The functions that actually do the measurements use the `microtime`[5] library to get microsecond level timing because JavaScript's `Date` only gives us millisecond-level resolution. We use `object-sizeof`[6] to estimate how much memory our structures require; we also call `process.memoryUsage()` and look at the `heapUsed` value to see how much memory Node[7] is using while the program runs, but that may be affected by **garbage collection** and a host of other factors outside our control.

```
const memory = (func, ...params) => {
  const before = process.memoryUsage()
  const result = func(...params)
  const after = process.memoryUsage()
  const heap = after.heapUsed - before.heapUsed
  const size = sizeof(result)
  return [result, size, heap]
}

const time = (func, ...params) => {
  const before = microtime.now()
  func(...params)
  const after = microtime.now()
  return after - before
}

const calculateRatio = (f2S, rFilterT, rSelectT, cFilterT, cSelectT) => {
  return ((f2S * rFilterT) + rSelectT) / ((f2S * cFilterT) + cSelectT)
}
```

Let's run our program for a table with 100 rows and 3 columns and a 3:1 ratio of filter to select:

```
node table-performance.js 100 3 3
```

```
nRows: 100
nCols: 3
filterPerSelect: 3
rowSize: 6600
rowHeap: 26512
colSize: 2442
colHeap: 8536
rowFilterTime: 75
rowSelectTime: 111
colFilterTime: 137
colSelectTime: 48
ratio: 0.7320261437908496
```

What if we increase the table size to 10,000 rows by 30 columns with the same 3:1 filter/select ratio?

```
nRows: 10000
nCols: 30
filterPerSelect: 3
rowSize: 7020000
rowHeap: 18392064
colSize: 2400462
colHeap: -3473800
rowFilterTime: 2929
```

[5]https://www.npmjs.com/package/microtime
[6]https://www.npmjs.com/package/object-sizeof
[7]https://nodejs.org/en/

value	100-03-03	10000-30-03	10000-30-10
nRows	100	10000	10000
nCols	3	30	30
filterPerSelect	3	3	10
rowFilterTime	75	2929	2376
rowSelectTime	111	15863	15566
colFilterTime	137	4529	4380
colSelectTime	48	104	90

Table 6.1: Relative performance of operations on row-major and column-major data tables.

```
rowSelectTime: 15863
colFilterTime: 4529
colSelectTime: 104
ratio: 1.8004528522386969
```

And what if we keep the table size the same but use a 10:1 filter/select ratio?

```
nRows: 10000
nCols: 30
filterPerSelect: 10
rowSize: 7020000
rowHeap: 18287160
colSize: 2400462
colHeap: -3645056
rowFilterTime: 2376
rowSelectTime: 15566
colFilterTime: 4380
colSelectTime: 90
ratio: 0.8960127591706539
```

The results in Table 6.1 show that column-major storage is better. It uses less memory (presumably because column labels aren't duplicated once per row) and the time required to construct new objects when doing select with row-major storage outweighs cost of appending to arrays when doing filter with column-major storage. Unfortunately, the code for column-major storage is a little more complicated to write, which is a cost that doesn't show up in experiments.

6.3 What is the most efficient way to save a table?

Data is valuable, so we are going to store data tables in files of some kind. If one storage scheme is much more efficient than another and we are reading or writing frequently, that could change our mind about which implementation to pick.

Two simple text-based schemes are row-oriented and column-oriented **JSON**—basically, just printing the data structures we have. Let's run the 10,000×30 test:

```
nRows: 10000
nCols: 30
rowStringTime: 57342
rowStringSize: 9393402
colStringTime: 13267
colStringSize: 2934164
```

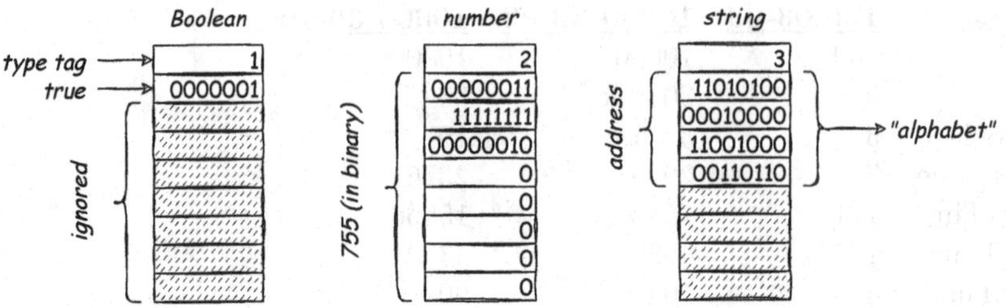

Figure 6.5: How JavaScript uses tagged data structures to store objects.

The time needed for the row-major version is almost ten times greater than that needed for the column-major version; we assume that the redundant printing of the labels is mostly to blame, just as redundant storage of the labels was to blame for row-major's greater memory requirements.

If that diagnosis is correct, then a packed version of row-major storage ought to be faster. We save the column headers once, then copy the data values into an array of arrays and save that:

```
const asPackedJson = (table) => {
  const temp = {}
  temp.keys = Object.keys(table[0])
  temp.values = table.map(row => temp.keys.map(k => row[k]))
  return JSON.stringify(temp)
}
```

```
nRows: 10000
nCols: 30
packedRowStringTime: 29659
packedRowStringSize: 2974084
```

These results show that changing layout for storage is faster than turning the data structure we have into a string. Again, we assume this is because copying data takes less time than turning labels into strings over and over, but column-major storage is still the best approach.

6.4 Does binary storage improve performance?

Let's try one more strategy for storing our tables. JavaScript stores values in **tagged** data structures: some bits define the value's type while other bits store the value itself in a type-dependent way (Figure 6.5).

We can save space by keeping track of the types ourselves and just storing the bits that represent the values. JavaScript has an `ArrayBuffer` class for exactly this purpose. It stores any value we want as a set of bits; we then access those bits through a view that presents the data as a particular type, such as Boolean (one byte per value) or number (64 bits per number). As Figure 6.6 shows, we can mix different types of data in a single `ArrayBuffer`, but it's up to us to keep track of which bytes belong to which values.

To store a column-major table we will fill an `ArrayBuffer` with:

1. Two integers that hold the table's size (number of rows and number of columns).

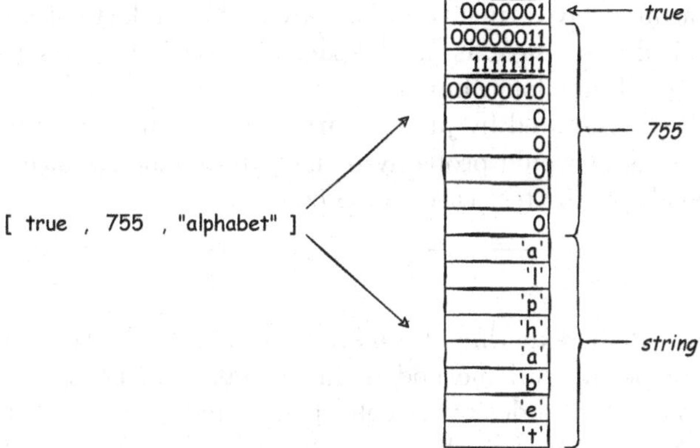

Figure 6.6: Storing object values as bits with lookup information.

2. A string with the column labels joined by newline characters. (We use newlines as a separator because we assume column labels can't contain them.)

3. The numbers themselves.

```
const asBinary = (table) => {
  const labels = Object.keys(table)

  const nCols = labels.length
  const nRows = table[labels[0]].length
  const dimensions = new Uint32Array([nCols, nRows])

  const allLabels = labels.join('\n')
  const encoder = new TextEncoder()
  const encodedLabels = encoder.encode(allLabels)

  const dataSize = sizeof(0) * nCols * nRows
  const totalSize =
    dimensions.byteLength + encodedLabels.byteLength + dataSize

  const buffer = new ArrayBuffer(totalSize)
  const result = new Uint8Array(buffer)
  result.set(dimensions, 0)
  result.set(encodedLabels, dimensions.byteLength)

  let current = dimensions.byteLength + encodedLabels.byteLength
  labels.forEach(label => {
    const temp = new Float64Array(table[label])
    result.set(temp, current)
    current += temp.byteLength
  })

  return result
}
```

```
nRows: 10000
nCols: 30
packedColBinaryTime: 6074
packedColBinarySize: 2400268
```

Packing the data table saves time because copying bits is faster than turning numbers into characters, but it doesn't save as much space as expected. The reason is that double-precision numbers are 8 bytes long, but because we have chosen simple integer values for our tests, they can be represented by just 5 characters (which is 10 bytes). If we had "real" numbers the storage benefit would probably be more pronounced; once again, the result of our experiment depends on the test cases we choose.

Engineering

If science is the use of the experimental method to investigate the world, engineering is the use of the experimental method to investigate and improve the things that people build. Good software designers collect and analyze data all the time to find out whether one website design works better than another [Kohavi2020] or to improve the performance of CPUs [Patterson2017]; a few simple experiments like these can sometimes save weeks or months of effort.

6.5 Exercises

Varying filter behavior

How does our decision about which storage format is better change if we keep 1% of rows when filtering instead of one-third? What if we keep 90% of rows?

Filtering by strings

Modify the comparison of filter and select to work with tables that contain columns of strings instead of columns of numbers and see how that changes performance. For testing, create random 4-letter strings using the characters A-Z and then filter by:

- an exact match,
- strings starting with a specific character, and
- strings that contain a specific character.

Join performance

A join combines data from two tables based on matching keys. For example, if the two tables are:

Key	Left
A	a1
B	b1
C	c1

and:

Key	Right
A	a2
A	a3
B	b2

then the join is:

Key	Left	Right
A	a1	a2
A	a1	a3
B	b1	b2

Write a test to compare the performance of row-wise vs. column-wise storage when joining two tables based on matching numeric keys. Does the answer depend on the fraction of keys that match?

Join optimization

The simplest way to **join** two tables is to look for matching keys using a double loop. An alternative is to build an **index** for each table and then use it to construct matches. For example, suppose the tables are:

Key	Left
A	a1
B	b1
C	c1

and:

Key	Right
A	a2
A	a3
B	b2

The first step is to create a `Map` showing where each key is found in the first table:

```
{A: [0], B: [1], C: [2]}
```

The second step is to create a similar `Map` for the second table:

```
{A: [0, 1], B: [2]}
```

We can then loop over the keys in one of the maps, look up values in the second map, and construct all of the matches.

Write a function that joins two tables this way. Is it faster or slower than using a double loop? How does the answer depend on the number of keys and the fraction that match?

Flipping storage

Our tests showed that storing row-oriented tables as JSON is much slower than storing column-oriented tables. Write a test to determine whether converting a row-oriented table to a column-oriented table and then saving the latter is faster than saving the row-oriented table directly.

Sparse storage

A **sparse matrix** is one in which most of the values are zero. Instead of storing them all, a program can use a map to store non-zero values and a lookup function to return zero for anything that isn't stored explicitly:

```
def spareMatrixGet(matrix, row, col) => {
  return matrix.contains(row, col)
    ? matrix.get(row, col)
    : 0
}
```

The same technique can be used if most of the entries in a data table are missing. Write a function that creates a sparse table in which a random 5% of the values are non-zero and the other 95% are zero, then compare the memory requirements and performance of filter and select for this implementation versus those of row-wise and column-wise storage.

Loading time

Modify the programs in this section to measure the time required to convert a data table from JSON or binary form back to a data structure.

Saving fixed-width strings

To improve performance, databases often store **fixed-width** strings, i.e., they limit the length of the strings in a column to some fixed size and **pad** strings that are shorter than that.

1. Write a function that takes an array of strings and an integer width and creates an `ArrayBuffer` containing the strings padded to that width. The function should throw an exception if any of the strings are longer than the specified width.

2. Write another function that takes an `ArrayBuffer` as input and returns an array of strings. This function should remove the padding so that strings shorter than the fixed width are restored to their original form.

Saving variable-width strings

Fixed-width storage is inefficient for large blocks of text such as contracts, novels, and resumés, since padding every document to the length of the longest will probably waste a lot of space. An alternative way to store these in binary is to save each entry as a (length, text) pair.

1. Write a function that takes a list of strings as input and returns an `ArrayBuffer` containing (length, text) pairs.

2. Write another function that takes such an `ArrayBuffer` and returns an array containing the original text.

3. Write tests with Mocha to confirm that your functions work correctly.

ASCII storage

The original ASCII standard specified a 7-bit **character encoding** for letters commonly used in English, and many data files still only use characters whose numeric codes are in the range 0–127.

1. Write a function that takes an array of single-letter strings and returns an `ArrayBuffer` that stores them using one byte per character if all of the characters will fit into 7 bits, and multiple bytes per character if any of the characters require more than 7 bits.

2. Write another function that takes an `ArrayBuffer` generated by the first function and re-creates the array of characters. The function must *only* take the `ArrayBuffer` as an argument, so the first element of the `ArrayBuffer` should indicate how to interpret the rest of its contents.

3. Write tests with Mocha to check that your functions work correctly.

7

Pattern Matching

Terms defined: **base class**, **Chain of Responsibility pattern**, **child (in a tree)**, **coupling**, **depth-first**, **derived class**, **Document Object Model**, **eager matching**, **greedy algorithm**, **lazy matching**, **node**, **Open-Closed Principle**, **polymorphism**, **query selector**, **regular expression**, **scope creep**, **test-driven development**

We have been globbing to match filenames against patterns since Chapter 2. This lesson will explore how that works by building a simple version of the **regular expressions** used to match text in everything from editor and shell commands to web scrapers. Our approach is inspired by Brian Kernighan's[1] entry in [Oram2007].

Regular expressions have inspired pattern matching for many other kinds of data, such as **query selectors** for HTML. They are easier to understand and implement than patterns for matching text, so we will start by looking at them.

7.1 How can we match query selectors?

Programs stores HTML pages in memory using a **document object model** or DOM. Each element in the page, such as a heading and or paragraph, is a **node**; the **children** of a node are the elements it contains (Figure 7.1).

The first step is to define the patterns we want to support (Table 7.1). According to this grammar, `blockquote#important p.highlight` is a highlighted paragraph inside the blockquote whose ID is `"important"`. To find elements in a page that match it, our `select` function breaks the query into pieces and uses `firstMatch` to search recursively down the

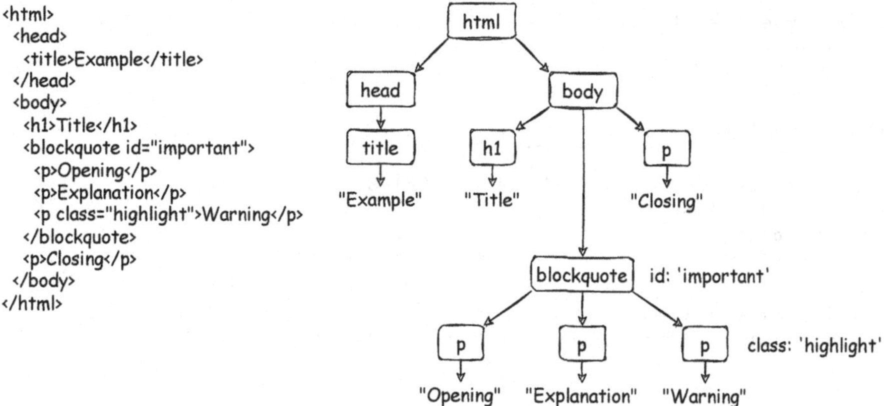

Figure 7.1: Representing an HTML document as a tree.

[1] https://en.wikipedia.org/wiki/Brian_Kernighan

Meaning	Selector
Element with tag "elt"	elt
Element with class="cls"	.cls
Element with id="ident"	#ident
child element inside a parent element	parent child

Table 7.1: Supported patterns.

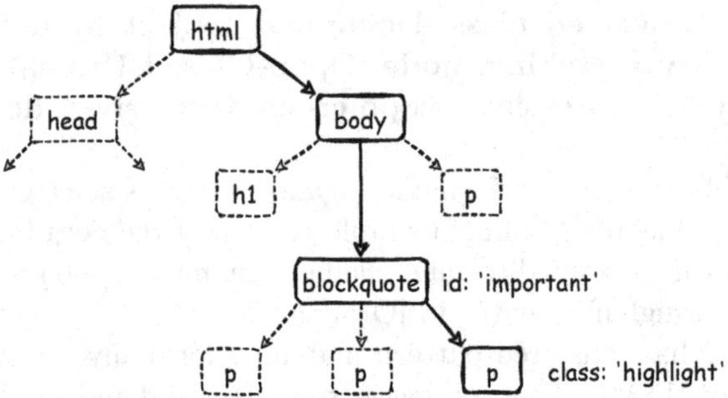

Figure 7.2: Matching a simple set of query selectors.

document tree until all the selectors in the query string have matched or no matches have been found (Figure 7.2).

```
import assert from 'assert'

const select = (root, selector) => {
  const selectors = selector.split(' ').filter(s => s.length > 0)
  return firstMatch(root, selectors)
}

const firstMatch = (node, selectors) => {
  assert(selectors.length > 0,
    'Require selector(s)')

  // Not a tag.
  if (node.type !== 'tag') {
    return null
  }

  // This node matches.
  if (matchHere(node, selectors[0])) {
    // This is the last selector, so matching worked.
    if (selectors.length === 1) {
      return node
    }

    // Try to match remaining selectors.
    return firstChildMatch(node, selectors.slice(1))
  }

  // This node doesn't match, so try further down.
  return firstChildMatch(node, selectors)
}

export default select
```

The `firstMatch` function handles three cases:

1. This node isn't an element, i.e., it is plain text or a comment. This can't match a selector, and these nodes don't have children, so the function returns `null` to indicate that matching has failed.

2. This node matches the current selector. If there aren't any selectors left then the whole pattern must have matched, so the function returns this node as the match. If there *are* more selectors, we try to match those that remain against this node's children and return whatever result that produces.

3. This node *doesn't* match the current selector, so we search the children one by one to see if there is a match further down.

This algorithm is called **depth-first search**: it explores one possible match to the end before considering any others. `firstMatch` relies on a helper function called `firstChildMatch`, which finds the first child of a node to match a set of selectors:

```
const firstChildMatch = (node, selectors) => {
  assert(node.type === 'tag',
    `Should only try to match first child of tags, not ${node.type}`)

  // First working match.
  for (const child of node.children) {
    const match = firstMatch(child, selectors)
    if (match) {
      return match
    }
  }

  // Nothing worked.
  return null
}
```

and on the function `matchHere` which compares a node against a selector:

```
const matchHere = (node, selector) => {
  let name = null
  let id = null
  let cls = null
  if (selector.includes('#')) {
    [name, id] = selector.split('#')
  } else if (selector.includes('.')) {
    [name, cls] = selector.split('.')
  } else {
    name = selector
  }
  return (node.name === name) &&
    ((id === null) || (node.attribs.id === id)) &&
    ((cls === null) || (node.attribs.class === cls))
}
```

This version of `matchHere` is simple but inefficient, since it breaks the selector into parts each time it is called rather than doing that once and re-using the results. We will build a more efficient version in the exercises, but let's try out the one we have. Our test cases are all in one piece of HTML:

```
const HTML = `<main>
  <p>text of first p</p>
```

```
  <p id="id-01">text of p#id-01</p>
  <p id="id-02">text of p#id-02</p>
  <p class="class-03">text of p.class-03</p>
  <div>
    <p>text of div / p</p>
    <p id="id-04">text of div / p#id-04</p>
    <p class="class-05">text of div / p.class-05</p>
    <p class="class-06">should not be found</p>
  </div>
  <div id="id-07">
    <p>text of div#id-07 / p</p>
    <p class="class-06">text of div#id-07 / p.class-06</p>
  </div>
</main>`
```

The program contains a table of queries and the expected matches. The function `main` loops over it to report whether each test passes or fails:

```
const main = () => {
  const doc = htmlparser2.parseDOM(HTML)[0]
  const tests = [
    ['p', 'text of first p'],
    ['p#id-01', 'text of p#id-01'],
    ['p#id-02', 'text of p#id-02'],
    ['p.class-03', 'text of p.class-03'],
    ['div p', 'text of div / p'],
    ['div p#id-04', 'text of div / p#id-04'],
    ['div p.class-05', 'text of div / p.class-05'],
    ['div#id-07 p', 'text of div#id-07 / p'],
    ['div#id-07 p.class-06', 'text of div#id-07 / p.class-06']
  ]
  tests.forEach(([selector, expected]) => {
    const node = select(doc, selector)
    const actual = getText(node)
    const result = (actual === expected) ? 'pass' : 'fail'
    console.log(`"${selector}": ${result}`)
  })
}

main()
```

`main` uses a helper function called `getText` to extract text from a node or return an error message if something has gone wrong:

```
const getText = (node) => {
  if (!node) {
    return 'MISSING NODE'
  }
  if (!('children' in node)) {
    return 'MISSING CHILDREN'
  }
  if (node.children.length !== 1) {
    return 'WRONG NUMBER OF CHILDREN'
  }
  if (node.children[0].type !== 'text') {
    return 'NOT TEXT'
  }
  return node.children[0].data
}
```

When we run our program it produces this result:

```
"p": pass
"p#id-01": pass
"p#id-02": pass
"p.class-03": pass
"div p": pass
"div p#id-04": pass
"div p.class-05": pass
"div#id-07 p": pass
"div#id-07 p.class-06": pass
```

We will rewrite these tests using Mocha[2] in the exercises.

Test then build

We actually wrote our test cases *before* implementing the code to match query selectors in order to give ourselves a goal to work toward. Doing this is called **test-driven development**, or TDD; while research doesn't support the claim that it makes programmers more productive [Fucci2016; Fucci2017], we find it helps prevent **scope creep** when writing lessons.

7.2 How can we implement a simple regular expression matcher?

Matching regular expressions against text relies on the same recursive strategy as matching query selectors against nodes in an HTML page. If the first element of the pattern matches where we are, we see if the rest of the pattern matches what's left; otherwise, we see if the the pattern will match further along. Our matcher will initially handle just the five cases shown in Table 7.2. These cases are a small subset of what JavaScript provides, but as Kernighan wrote, "This is quite a useful class; in my own experience of using regular expressions on a day-to-day basis, it easily accounts for 95 percent of all instances."

Meaning	Character
Any literal character *c*	*c*
Any single character	.
Beginning of input	^
End of input	$
Zero or more of the previous character	*

Table 7.2: Pattern matching cases.

The top-level function that users call handles the special case of ^ at the start of a pattern matching the start of the target string being searched. It then tries the pattern against each successive substring of the target string until it finds a match or runs out of characters:

```
const match = (pattern, text) => {
  // '^' at start of pattern matches start of text.
```

[2]https://mochajs.org/

```
  if (pattern[0] === '^') {
    return matchHere(pattern, 1, text, 0)
  }

  // Try all possible starting points for pattern.
  let iText = 0
  do {
    if (matchHere(pattern, 0, text, iText)) {
      return true
    }
    iText += 1
  } while (iText < text.length)

  // Nothing worked.
  return false
}
```

matchHere does the matching and recursing:

```
const matchHere = (pattern, iPattern, text, iText) => {
  // There is no more pattern to match.
  if (iPattern === pattern.length) {
    return true
  }

  // '$' at end of pattern matches end of text.
  if ((iPattern === (pattern.length - 1)) &&
      (pattern[iPattern] === '$') &&
      (iText === text.length)) {
    return true
  }

  // '*' following current character means match many.
  if (((pattern.length - iPattern) > 1) &&
      (pattern[iPattern + 1] === '*')) {
    while ((iText < text.length) && (text[iText] === pattern[iPattern])) {
      iText += 1
    }
    return matchHere(pattern, iPattern + 2, text, iText)
  }

  // Match a single character.
  if ((pattern[iPattern] === '.') ||
      (pattern[iPattern] === text[iText])) {
    return matchHere(pattern, iPattern + 1, text, iText + 1)
  }

  // Nothing worked.
  return false
}
```

Once again, we use a table of test cases and expected results to test it:

```
const main = () => {
  const tests = [
    ['a', 'a', true],
    ['b', 'a', false],
    ['a', 'ab', true],
    ['b', 'ab', true],
    ['ab', 'ba', false],
    ['^a', 'ab', true],
```

```
    ['^b', 'ab', false],
    ['a$', 'ab', false],
    ['a$', 'ba', true],
    ['a*', '', true],
    ['a*', 'baac', true],
    ['ab*c', 'ac', true],
    ['ab*c', 'abc', true],
    ['ab*c', 'abbbc', true],
    ['ab*c', 'abxc', false]
  ]
  tests.forEach(([regexp, text, expected]) => {
    const actual = match(regexp, text)
    const result = (actual === expected) ? 'pass' : 'fail'
    console.log(`"${regexp}" X "${text}": ${result}`)
  })
}

main()
```

```
"a" X "a": pass
"b" X "a": pass
"a" X "ab": pass
"b" X "ab": pass
"ab" X "ba": pass
"^a" X "ab": pass
"^b" X "ab": pass
"a$" X "ab": pass
"a$" X "ba": pass
"a*" X "": pass
"a*" X "baac": pass
"ab*c" X "ac": pass
"ab*c" X "abc": pass
"ab*c" X "abbbc": pass
"ab*c" X "abxc": pass
```

This program seems to work, but it actually contains an error that we will correct in the exercises. (Think about what happens if we match the pattern `/a*ab/` against the string `'aab'`.) Our design is also hard to extend: handling parentheses in patterns like `/a(bc)*d/` will require major changes. We need to explore a different approach.

7.3 How can we implement an extensible matcher?

Instead of packing all of our code into one long function, we can implement each kind of match as a separate function. Doing this makes it much easier to add more matchers: we just define a function that we can mix in with calls to the ones we already have.

Rather than having these functions do the matching immediately, though, we will have each one return an object that knows how to match itself against some text. Doing this allows us to build a complex match once and re-use it many times. This is a common pattern in text processing: we may want to apply a regular expression to each line in a large set of files, so recycling the matchers will make our programs more efficient.

Each matching object has a method that takes the target string and the index to start matching at as inputs. Its output is the index to continue matching at or `undefined`

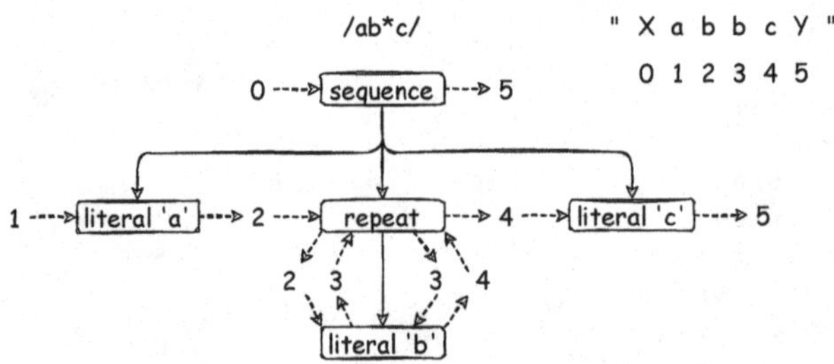

Figure 7.3: Using nested objects to match regular expressions.

indicating that matching failed. We can then combine these objects to match complex patterns (Figure 7.3).

The first step in implementing this is to write test cases, which forces us to define the syntax we are going to support:

```
import Alt from './regex-alt.js'
import Any from './regex-any.js'
import End from './regex-end.js'
import Lit from './regex-lit.js'
import Seq from './regex-seq.js'
import Start from './regex-start.js'

const main = () => {
  const tests = [
    ['a', 'a', true, Lit('a')],
    ['b', 'a', false, Lit('b')],
    ['a', 'ab', true, Lit('a')],
    ['b', 'ab', true, Lit('b')],
    ['ab', 'ab', true, Seq(Lit('a'), Lit('b'))],
    ['ba', 'ab', false, Seq(Lit('b'), Lit('a'))],
    ['ab', 'ba', false, Lit('ab')],
    ['^a', 'ab', true, Seq(Start(), Lit('a'))],
    ['^b', 'ab', false, Seq(Start(), Lit('b'))],
    ['a$', 'ab', false, Seq(Lit('a'), End())],
    ['a$', 'ba', true, Seq(Lit('a'), End())],
    ['a*', '', true, Any('a')],
    ['a*', 'baac', true, Any('a')],
    ['ab*c', 'ac', true, Seq(Lit('a'), Any('b'), Lit('c'))],
    ['ab*c', 'abc', true, Seq(Lit('a'), Any('b'), Lit('c'))],
    ['ab*c', 'abbbc', true, Seq(Lit('a'), Any('b'), Lit('c'))],
    ['ab*c', 'abxc', false, Seq(Lit('a'), Any('b'), Lit('c'))],
    ['ab|cd', 'xaby', true, Alt(Lit('ab'), Lit('cd'))],
    ['ab|cd', 'acdc', true, Alt(Lit('ab'), Lit('cd'))],
    ['a(b|c)d', 'xabdy', true,
      Seq(Lit('a'), Alt(Lit('b'), Lit('c')), Lit('d'))],
    ['a(b|c)d', 'xabady', false,
      Seq(Lit('a'), Alt(Lit('b'), Lit('c')), Lit('d'))]
  ]
  tests.forEach(([pattern, text, expected, matcher]) => {
    const actual = matcher.match(text)
    const result = (actual === expected) ? 'pass' : 'fail'
    console.log(`"${pattern}" X "${text}": ${result}`)
  })
}

main()
```

Next, we define a **base class** that all matchers will inherit from. This class contains the `match` method that users will call so that we can start matching right away no matter what kind of matcher we have at the top level of our pattern.

```
class RegexBase {
  match (text) {
    for (let i = 0; i < text.length; i += 1) {
      if (this._match(text, i)) {
        return true
      }
    }
    return false
  }

  _match (text, start) {
    throw new Error('derived classes must override "_match"')
  }
}

export default RegexBase
```

The base class also defines a `_match` method (with a leading underscore) that other classes will fill in with actual matching code. The base implementation of this method throws an exception so that if we forget to provide `_match` in a **derived class** our code will fail with a meaningful reminder.

One interface to call them all

Our design makes use of **polymorphism**, which literally means "having multiple forms". If a set of objects all have methods that can be called the same way, then those objects can be used interchangeably; putting it another way, a program can use them without knowing exactly what they are. Polymorphism reduces the **coupling** between different parts of our program, which in turn makes it easier for those programs to evolve.

We can now define empty versions of each matching class that all say "no match here" like this one for literal characters:

```
import RegexBase from './regex-base.js'

class RegexLit extends RegexBase {
  constructor (chars) {
    super()
    this.chars = chars
  }

  _match (text, start) {
    return undefined // FIXME
  }
}

export default (chars) => new RegexLit(chars)
```

Our tests now run, but most of them fail: "most" because we expect some tests not to match, so the test runner reports `true`.

```
"a" X "a": fail
"b" X "a": pass
```

```
"a" X "ab": fail
"b" X "ab": fail
"ab" X "ab": fail
"ba" X "ab": pass
"ab" X "ba": pass
"^a" X "ab": fail
"^b" X "ab": pass
"a$" X "ab": pass
"a$" X "ba": fail
"a*" X "": fail
"a*" X "baac": fail
"ab*c" X "ac": fail
"ab*c" X "abc": fail
"ab*c" X "abbbc": fail
"ab*c" X "abxc": pass
"ab|cd" X "xaby": fail
"ab|cd" X "acdc": fail
"a(b|c)d" X "xabdy": fail
"a(b|c)d" X "xabady": pass
```

This output tells us how much work we have left to do: when all of these tests pass, we're finished.

Let's implement a literal character string matcher first:

```
import RegexBase from './regex-base.js'

class RegexLit extends RegexBase {
  constructor (chars) {
    super()
    this.chars = chars
  }

  _match (text, start) {
    const nextIndex = start + this.chars.length
    if (nextIndex > text.length) {
      return undefined
    }
    if (text.slice(start, nextIndex) !== this.chars) {
      return undefined
    }
    return nextIndex
  }
}

export default (chars) => new RegexLit(chars)
```

Some tests now pass, others still fail as expected:

```
"a" X "a": pass
"b" X "a": pass
"a" X "ab": pass
"b" X "ab": pass
"ab" X "ab": fail
"ba" X "ab": pass
"ab" X "ba": pass
"^a" X "ab": fail
"^b" X "ab": pass
"a$" X "ab": pass
"a$" X "ba": fail
"a*" X "": fail
"a*" X "baac": fail
```

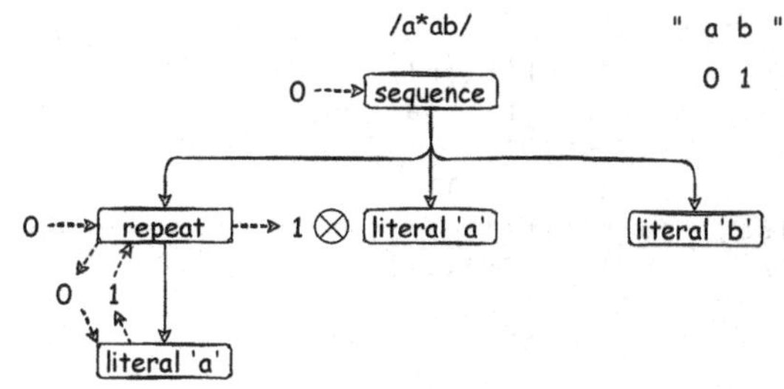

Figure 7.4: Why overly greedy matching doesn't work.

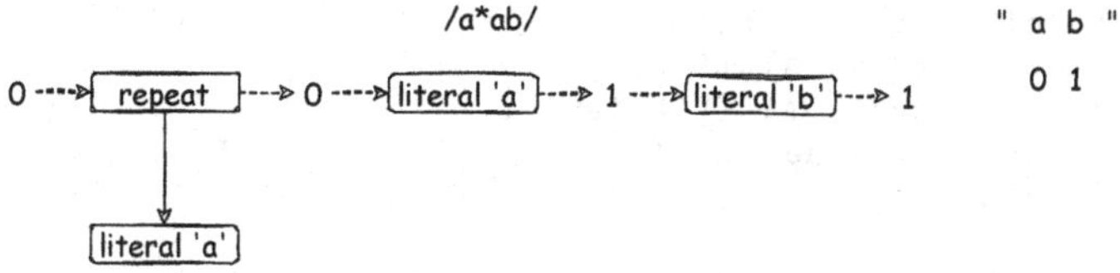

Figure 7.5: Using rest to match the remainder of a pattern.

```
"ab*c" X "ac": fail
"ab*c" X "abc": fail
"ab*c" X "abbbc": fail
"ab*c" X "abxc": pass
"ab|cd" X "xaby": fail
"ab|cd" X "acdc": fail
"a(b|c)d" X "xabdy": fail
"a(b|c)d" X "xabady": pass
```

We will tackle RegexSeq next so that we can combine other matchers. This is why we have tests for `Seq(Lit('a'), Lit('b'))` and `Lit('ab')`: all children have to match in order without gaps.

But wait: suppose we have the pattern `/a*ab/`. This ought to match the text `"ab"`, but will it? The `/*/` is **greedy**: it matches as much as it can (which is also called **eager matching**). As a result, `/a*/` will match the leading `"a"`, leaving nothing for the literal `/a/` to match (Figure 7.4). Our current implementation doesn't give us a way to try other possible matches when this happens.

Let's re-think our design and have each matcher take its own arguments and a `rest` parameter containing the rest of the matchers (Figure 7.5). (We will provide a default of `null` in the creation function so we don't have to type `null` over and over again.) Each matcher will try each of its possibilities and then see if the rest will also match.

This design means we can get rid of RegexSeq, but it does make our tests a little harder to read:

```
import Alt from './regex-alt.js'
import Any from './regex-any.js'
import End from './regex-end.js'
import Lit from './regex-lit.js'
import Start from './regex-start.js'

const main = () => {
  const tests = [
    ['a', 'a', true, Lit('a')],
    ['b', 'a', false, Lit('b')],
    ['a', 'ab', true, Lit('a')],
```

```
    ['b', 'ab', true, Lit('b')],
    ['ab', 'ab', true, Lit('a', Lit('b'))],
    ['ba', 'ab', false, Lit('b', Lit('a'))],
    ['ab', 'ba', false, Lit('ab')],
    ['^a', 'ab', true, Start(Lit('a'))],
    ['^b', 'ab', false, Start(Lit('b'))],
    ['a$', 'ab', false, Lit('a', End())],
    ['a$', 'ba', true, Lit('a', End())],
    ['a*', '', true, Any(Lit('a'))],
    ['a*', 'baac', true, Any(Lit('a'))],
    ['ab*c', 'ac', true, Lit('a', Any(Lit('b'), Lit('c')))],
    ['ab*c', 'abc', true, Lit('a', Any(Lit('b'), Lit('c')))],
    ['ab*c', 'abbbc', true, Lit('a', Any(Lit('b'), Lit('c')))],
    ['ab*c', 'abxc', false, Lit('a', Any(Lit('b'), Lit('c')))],
    ['ab|cd', 'xaby', true, Alt(Lit('ab'), Lit('cd'))],
    ['ab|cd', 'acdc', true, Alt(Lit('ab'), Lit('cd'))],
    ['a(b|c)d', 'xabdy', true, Lit('a', Alt(Lit('b'), Lit('c'), Lit('d')))],
    ['a(b|c)d', 'xabady', false, Lit('a', Alt(Lit('b'), Lit('c'), Lit('d')))]
  ]
  tests.forEach(([pattern, text, expected, matcher]) => {
    const actual = matcher.match(text)
    const result = (actual === expected) ? 'pass' : 'fail'
    console.log(`"${pattern}" X "${text}": ${result}`)
  })
}

main()
```

Here's how this works for matching a literal expression:

```
import RegexBase from './regex-base.js'

class RegexLit extends RegexBase {
  constructor (chars, rest) {
    super(rest)
    this.chars = chars
  }

  _match (text, start) {
    const nextIndex = start + this.chars.length
    if (nextIndex > text.length) {
      return undefined
    }
    if (text.slice(start, nextIndex) !== this.chars) {
      return undefined
    }
    if (this.rest === null) {
      return nextIndex
    }
    return this.rest._match(text, nextIndex)
  }
}

export default (chars, rest = null) => new RegexLit(chars, rest)
```

The `_match` method checks whether all of the pattern matches the target text starting at the current location. If so, it checks whether the rest of the overall pattern matches what's left. Matching the start `/^/` and end `/$/` anchors is just as straightforward:

```
import RegexBase from './regex-base.js'

class RegexStart extends RegexBase {
  _match (text, start) {
    if (start !== 0) {
      return undefined
    }
    if (this.rest === null) {
      return 0
    }
    return this.rest._match(text, start)
  }
}

export default (rest = null) => new RegexStart(rest)
```

```
import RegexBase from './regex-base.js'

class RegexEnd extends RegexBase {
  _match (text, start) {
    if (start !== text.length) {
      return undefined
    }
    if (this.rest === null) {
      return text.length
    }
    return this.rest._match(text, start)
  }
}

export default (rest = null) => new RegexEnd(rest)
```

Matching either/or is done by trying the first pattern and the rest, and if that fails, trying the second pattern and the rest:

```
import RegexBase from './regex-base.js'

class RegexAlt extends RegexBase {
  constructor (left, right, rest) {
    super(rest)
    this.left = left
    this.right = right
  }

  _match (text, start) {
    for (const pat of [this.left, this.right]) {
      const afterPat = pat._match(text, start)
      if (afterPat !== undefined) {
        if (this.rest === null) {
          return afterPat
        }
        const afterRest = this.rest._match(text, afterPat)
        if (afterRest !== undefined) {
          return afterRest
        }
      }
    }
    return undefined
  }
}
```

```
const create = (left, right, rest = null) => {
  return new RegexAlt(left, right, rest)
}

export default create
```

To match a repetition, we figure out the maximum number of matches that might be left, then count down until something succeeds. (We start with the maximum because matching is supposed to be greedy.) Each non-empty repetition matches at least one character, so the number of remaining characters is the maximum number of matches worth trying.

```
import RegexBase from './regex-base.js'

class RegexAny extends RegexBase {
  constructor (child, rest) {
    super(rest)
    this.child = child
  }

  _match (text, start) {
    const maxPossible = text.length - start
    for (let num = maxPossible; num >= 0; num -= 1) {
      const afterMany = this._matchMany(text, start, num)
      if (afterMany !== undefined) {
        return afterMany
      }
    }
    return undefined
  }

  _matchMany (text, start, num) {
    for (let i = 0; i < num; i += 1) {
      start = this.child._match(text, start)
      if (start === undefined) {
        return undefined
      }
    }
    if (this.rest !== null) {
      return this.rest._match(text, start)
    }
    return start
  }
}

const create = (child, rest = null) => {
  return new RegexAny(child, rest)
}

export default create
```

With these classes in place, our tests all pass:

```
"a" X "a": pass
"b" X "a": pass
"a" X "ab": pass
"b" X "ab": pass
"ab" X "ab": pass
"ba" X "ab": pass
"ab" X "ba": pass
"^a" X "ab": pass
```

```
"^b" X "ab": pass
"a$" X "ab": pass
"a$" X "ba": pass
"a*" X "": pass
"a*" X "baac": pass
"ab*c" X "ac": pass
"ab*c" X "abc": pass
"ab*c" X "abbbc": pass
"ab*c" X "abxc": pass
"ab|cd" X "xaby": pass
"ab|cd" X "acdc": pass
"a(b|c)d" X "xabdy": pass
"a(b|c)d" X "xabady": pass
```

The most important thing about this design is how extensible it is: if we want to add other kinds of matching, all we have to do is add more classes. That extensibility comes from the lack of centralized decision-making, which in turn comes from our use of polymorphism and the **Chain of Responsibility** design pattern. Each component does its part and asks something else to handle the remaining work; so long as each component takes the same inputs, we can put them together however we want.

The Open-Closed Principle

The **Open-Closed Principle** states that software should be open for extension but closed for modification, i.e., that it should be possible to extend functionality without having to rewrite existing code. As we said in Chapter 3, this allows old code to use new code, but only if our design permits the kinds of extensions people are going to want to make. Since we can't anticipate everything, it is normal to have to revise a design the first two or three times we try to extend it. Looking at it another way, the things we build learn how to do their jobs better as we use them and improve them [Brand1995].

7.4 Exercises

Split once

Modify the query selector code so that selectors like `div#id` and `div.class` are only split into pieces once rather than being re-split each time `matchHere` is called.

Find and fix the error

The first regular expression matcher contains an error: the pattern `'a*ab'` should match the string `'aab'` but doesn't. Figure out why it fails and fix it.

Unit tests

Rewrite the tests for selectors and regular expressions to use Mocha.

Find all with query selectors

Modify the query selector so that it returns *all* matches, not just the first one.

Select based on attributes

Modify the query selector to handle `[attribute="value"]` selectors, so that (for example) `div[align=center]` returns all `div` elements whose `align` attribute has the value `"center"`.

Child selectors

The expression `parent > child` selects all nodes of type `child` that are immediate children of nodes of type `parent`—for example, `div > p` selects all paragraphs that are immediate children of `div` elements. Modify `simple-selectors.js` to handle this kind of matching.

Find all with regular expressions

Modify the regular expression matcher to return *all* matches rather than just the first one.

Find one or more with regular expressions

Extend the regular expression matcher to support `+`, meaning "one or more".

Match sets of characters

Add a new regular expression matching class that matches any character from a set, so that `Charset('aeiou')` matches any lower-case vowel.

Make repetition more efficient

Rewrite `RegexAny` so that it does not repeatedly re-match text.

Lazy matching

The regular expressions we have seen so far are **eager**: they match as much as they can, as early as they can. An alternative is **lazy matching**, in which expressions match as little as they need to. For example, given the string `"ab"`, an eager match with the expression `/ab*/` will match both letters (because `/b*/` matches a 'b' if one is available) but a lazy match will only match the first letter (because `/b*/` can match no letters at all). Implement lazy matching for the `*` operator.

Optional matching

The `?` operator means "optional", so that `/a?/` matches either zero or one occurrences of the letter 'a'. Implement this operator.

8

Parsing Expressions

Terms defined: **finite state machine**, **literal**, **parser**, **precedence**, **token**, **Turing Machine**, **well formed**, **YAML**

In Chapter 7 we created regular expressions by constructing objects. It takes a lot less typing to write them as strings as we did for HTML selectors, but if we're going to do that we need something to convert those strings to the required objects. In other words, we need to write a **parser**.

Meaning	Character
Any literal character *c*	*c*
Beginning of input	^
End of input	$
Zero or more of the previous thing	*
Either/or	|
Grouping	(...)

Table 8.1: Regular expression grammar.

Table 8.1 shows the grammar we will handle. When we are done we should be able to parse `/^(a|b|$)*z$/` as "start of text", "any number of 'a', 'b', or '$'", "a single 'z', and "end of text". (We write regular expressions inside slashes to distinguish them from strings.) To keep things simple, we will create a tree of objects (Figure 8.1) rather than instances of the regular expression classes from Chapter 7; the exercises will tackle the latter.

> **Please don't write parsers**
>
> Languages that are comfortable for people to read are usually difficult for computers to understand and vice versa, so we need parsers to translate human-friendly notation into computer-friendly representations. However, the world doesn't need more file formats; if you need a configuration file or lookup table, please use CSV, JSON, **YAML**, or something else that already has an acronym rather than inventing a format of your own.

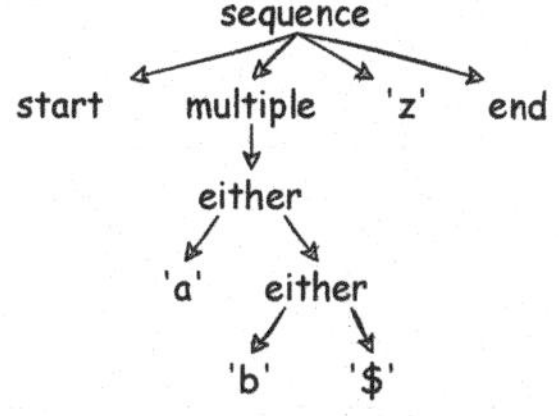

Figure 8.1: Representing the result of parsing a regular expression as an tree.

8.1 How can we break text into tokens?

A **token** is an atom of text, such as the digits making up a number or the letters making up a variable name. In our grammar the tokens are the special characters `*`, `|`, `(`, `)`, `^`, and `$`, plus any sequence of one or more other characters (which count as one multi-letter token). This classification guides the design of our parser:

1. If a character is special, create a token for it.
2. If it is a **literal** then combine it with the current literal if there is one or start a new literal.
3. Since `^` and `$` are either special or regular depending on position, we must treat them as separate tokens or as part of a literal based on where they appear.

We can translate these rules almost directly into code to create a list of objects whose keys are `kind` and `loc` (short for location), with the extra key `value` for literal values:

```
const SIMPLE = {
  '*': 'Any',
  '|': 'Alt',
  '(': 'GroupStart',
  ')': 'GroupEnd'
}

const tokenize = (text) => {
  const result = []
  for (let i = 0; i < text.length; i += 1) {
    const c = text[i]
    if (c in SIMPLE) {
      result.push({ kind: SIMPLE[c], loc: i })
    } else if (c === '^') {
      if (i === 0) {
        result.push({ kind: 'Start', loc: i })
      } else {
        combineOrPush(result, c, i)
      }
    } else if (c === '$') {
      if (i === (text.length - 1)) {
        result.push({ kind: 'End', loc: i })
      } else {
        combineOrPush(result, c, i)
      }
    } else {
      combineOrPush(result, c, i)
    }
  }

  return result
}

export default tokenize
```

The helper function `combineOrPush` does exactly what its name says. If the thing most recently added to the list of tokens isn't a literal, the new character becomes a new token; otherwise, we append the new character to the literal we're building:

```
const combineOrPush = (soFar, character, location) => {
  const topIndex = soFar.length - 1
  if ((soFar.length === 0) || (soFar[topIndex].token !== 'Lit')) {
    soFar.push({ kind: 'Lit', value: character, loc: location })
  } else {
    soFar[topIndex].value += character
  }
}
```

We can try this out with a three-line test program:

```
import tokenize from './tokenizer-collapse.js'

const test = '^a^b*'
const result = tokenize(test)
console.log(JSON.stringify(result, null, 2))
```

```
[
  {
    "kind": "Start",
    "loc": 0
  },
  {
    "kind": "Lit",
    "value": "a",
    "loc": 1
  },
  {
    "kind": "Lit",
    "value": "^",
    "loc": 2
  },
  {
    "kind": "Lit",
    "value": "b",
    "loc": 3
  },
  {
    "kind": "Any",
    "loc": 4
  }
]
```

This simple tokenizer is readable, efficient, and wrong. The problem is that the expression `/ab*/` means "a single `a` followed by zero or more `b`". If we combine the `a` and `b` as we read them, though, we wind up with "zero or more repetitions of `ab`". (Don't feel bad if you didn't spot this: we didn't notice the problem until we were implementing the next step.)

The solution is to treat each regular character as its own literal in this stage and then combine things later. Doing this lets us get rid of the nested `if` for handling `^` and `$` as well:

```
const SIMPLE = {
  '*': 'Any',
  '|': 'Alt',
  '(': 'GroupStart',
  ')': 'GroupEnd'
}

const tokenize = (text) => {
  const result = []
```

```
  for (let i = 0; i < text.length; i += 1) {
    const c = text[i]
    if (c in SIMPLE) {
      result.push({ kind: SIMPLE[c], loc: i })
    } else if ((c === '^') && (i === 0)) {
      result.push({ kind: 'Start', loc: i })
    } else if ((c === '$') && (i === (text.length - 1))) {
      result.push({ kind: 'End', loc: i })
    } else {
      result.push({ kind: 'Lit', loc: i, value: c })
    }
  }

  return result
}

export default tokenize
```

Software isn't done until it's tested, so let's build some Mocha[1] tests for our tokenizer. The listing below shows a few of these along with the output for the full set:

```
import assert from 'assert'

import tokenize from '../tokenizer.js'

describe('tokenizes correctly', async () => {
  it('tokenizes a single character', () => {
    assert.deepStrictEqual(tokenize('a'), [
      { kind: 'Lit', value: 'a', loc: 0 }
    ])
  })

  it('tokenizes a sequence of characters', () => {
    assert.deepStrictEqual(tokenize('ab'), [
      { kind: 'Lit', value: 'a', loc: 0 },
      { kind: 'Lit', value: 'b', loc: 1 }
    ])
  })

  it('tokenizes start anchor alone', () => {
    assert.deepStrictEqual(tokenize('^'), [
      { kind: 'Start', loc: 0 }
    ])
  })

  it('tokenizes start anchor followed by characters', () => {
    assert.deepStrictEqual(tokenize('^a'), [
      { kind: 'Start', loc: 0 },
      { kind: 'Lit', value: 'a', loc: 1 }
    ])
  })

  it('tokenizes a complex expression', () => {
    assert.deepStrictEqual(tokenize('^a*(bcd|e^)*f$gh$'), [
      { kind: 'Start', loc: 0 },
      { kind: 'Lit', loc: 1, value: 'a' },
      { kind: 'Any', loc: 2 },
      { kind: 'GroupStart', loc: 3 },
      { kind: 'Lit', loc: 4, value: 'b' },
```

[1] https://mochajs.org/

```
      { kind: 'Lit', loc: 5, value: 'c' },
      { kind: 'Lit', loc: 6, value: 'd' },
      { kind: 'Alt', loc: 7 },
      { kind: 'Lit', loc: 8, value: 'e' },
      { kind: 'Lit', loc: 9, value: '^' },
      { kind: 'GroupEnd', loc: 10 },
      { kind: 'Any', loc: 11 },
      { kind: 'Lit', loc: 12, value: 'f' },
      { kind: 'Lit', loc: 13, value: '$' },
      { kind: 'Lit', loc: 14, value: 'g' },
      { kind: 'Lit', loc: 15, value: 'h' },
      { kind: 'End', loc: 16 }
    ])
  })
})
```

```
> stjs@1.0.0 test /u/stjs
> mocha */test/test-*.js "-g" "tokenizes correctly"


  tokenizes correctly
    ✓ tokenizes a single character
    ✓ tokenizes a sequence of characters
    ✓ tokenizes start anchor alone
    ✓ tokenizes start anchor followed by characters
    ✓ tokenizes circumflex not at start
    ✓ tokenizes start anchor alone
    ✓ tokenizes end anchor preceded by characters
    ✓ tokenizes dollar sign not at end
    ✓ tokenizes repetition alone
    ✓ tokenizes repetition in string
    ✓ tokenizes repetition at end of string
    ✓ tokenizes alternation alone
    ✓ tokenizes alternation in string
    ✓ tokenizes alternation at start of string
    ✓ tokenizes the start of a group alone
    ✓ tokenizes the start of a group in a string
    ✓ tokenizes the end of a group alone
    ✓ tokenizes the end of a group at the end of a string
    ✓ tokenizes a complex expression


  19 passing (12ms)
```

8.2 How can we turn a list of tokens into a tree?

We now have a list of tokens, but we need a tree that captures the nesting introduced by parentheses and the way that * applies to whatever comes before it. Let's trace a few cases in order to see how to build this tree:

1. If the regular expression is /a/, we create a Lit token for the letter a (where "create" means "append to the output list").
2. What if the regular expression is /a*/? We first create a Lit token for the a and append

it to the output list. When we see the `*`, we take that `Lit` token off the tail of the output list and replace it with an `Any` token that has the `Lit` token as its child.

3. Our next thought experiment is `/(ab)/`. We don't know how long the group is going to be when we see the `(`, so we put the parenthesis onto the output as a marker. We then add the `Lit` tokens for the `a` and `b` until we see the `)`, at which point we pull tokens off the end of the output list until we get back to the `(` marker. When we find it, we put everything we have temporarily collected into a `Group` token and append it to the output list. This algorithm automatically handles `/(a*)/` and `/(a(b*)c)/`.

4. What about `/a|b/`? We append a `Lit` token for `a`, get the `|` and—and we're stuck, because we don't yet have the next token we need to finish building the `Alt`.

One way to solve this problem is to check if the thing on the top of the stack is waiting to combine each time we append a new token. However, this doesn't handle `/a|b*/` properly. The pattern is supposed to mean "one `a` or any number of `b`", but the check-and-combine strategy will turn it into the equivalent of `/(a|b)*/`.

A better (i.e., correct) solution is to leave some partially-completed tokens in the output and compress them later (Figure 8.2). If our input is the pattern `/a|b/`, we can:

1. Append a `Lit` token for `a`.

2. When we see `|`, make that `Lit` token the left child of the `Alt` and append that without filling in the right child.

3. Append the `Lit` token for `b`.

4. After all tokens have been handled, look for partially-completed `Alt` tokens and make whatever comes after them their right child.

Again, this automatically handles patterns like `/(ab)|c*|(de)/`.

It's time to turn these ideas into code. The main structure of our parser is:

```
import assert from 'assert'

import tokenize from './tokenizer.js'

const parse = (text) => {
  const result = []
  const allTokens = tokenize(text)
  for (let i = 0; i < allTokens.length; i += 1) {
    const token = allTokens[i]
    const last = i === allTokens.length - 1
    handle(result, token, last)
  }
  return compress(result)
}


export default parse
```

We handle tokens case-by-case (with a few assertions to check that patterns are **well formed**):

```
const handle = (result, token, last) => {
  if (token.kind === 'Lit') {
    result.push(token)
  } else if (token.kind === 'Start') {
```

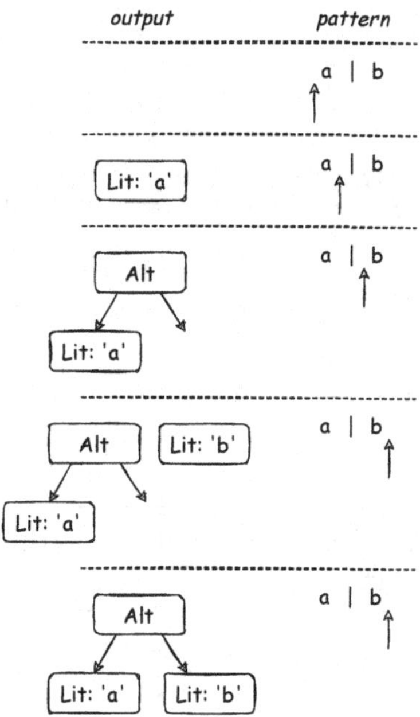

Figure 8.2: Mechanics of combining tokens while parsing regular expressions.

```
    assert(result.length === 0,
      'Should not have start token after other tokens')
    result.push(token)
  } else if (token.kind === 'End') {
    assert(last,
      'Should not have end token before other tokens')
    result.push(token)
  } else if (token.kind === 'GroupStart') {
    result.push(token)
  } else if (token.kind === 'GroupEnd') {
    result.push(groupEnd(result, token))
  } else if (token.kind === 'Any') {
    assert(result.length > 0,
      `No operand for '*' (location ${token.loc})`)
    token.child = result.pop()
    result.push(token)
  } else if (token.kind === 'Alt') {
    assert(result.length > 0,
      `No operand for '*' (location ${token.loc})`)
    token.left = result.pop()
    token.right = null
    result.push(token)
  } else {
    assert(false, 'UNIMPLEMENTED')
  }
}
```

When we find the `)` that marks the end of a group, we take items from the end of the output list until we find the matching start and use them to create a group:

```
const groupEnd = (result, token) => {
  const group = {
    kind: 'Group',
```

```
    loc: null,
    end: token.loc,
    children: []
  }
  while (true) {
    assert(result.length > 0,
           `Unmatched end parenthesis (location ${token.loc})`)
    const child = result.pop()
    if (child.kind === 'GroupStart') {
      group.loc = child.loc
      break
    }
    group.children.unshift(child)
  }
  return group
}
```

Finally, when we have finished with the input, we go through the output list one last time to fill in the right side of `Alts`:

```
const compress = (raw) => {
  const cooked = []
  while (raw.length > 0) {
    const token = raw.pop()
    if (token.kind === 'Alt') {
      assert(cooked.length > 0,
             `No right operand for alt (location ${token.loc})`)
      token.right = cooked.shift()
    }
    cooked.unshift(token)
  }
  return cooked
}
```

Once again, it's not done until we've tested it:

```
import assert from 'assert'

import parse from '../parser.js'

describe('parses correctly', async () => {
  it('parses the empty string', () => {
    assert.deepStrictEqual(parse(''), [])
  })

  it('parses a single literal', () => {
    assert.deepStrictEqual(parse('a'), [
      { kind: 'Lit', loc: 0, value: 'a' }
    ])
  })

  it('parses multiple literals', () => {
    assert.deepStrictEqual(parse('ab'), [
      { kind: 'Lit', loc: 0, value: 'a' },
      { kind: 'Lit', loc: 1, value: 'b' }
    ])
  })


  it('parses alt of groups', () => {
    assert.deepStrictEqual(parse('a|(bc)'), [
```

```
        {
          kind: 'Alt',
          loc: 1,
          left: { kind: 'Lit', loc: 0, value: 'a' },
          right: {
            kind: 'Group',
            loc: 2,
            end: 5,
            children: [
              { kind: 'Lit', loc: 3, value: 'b' },
              { kind: 'Lit', loc: 4, value: 'c' }
            ]
          }
        }
      ])
  })
})
```

```
> stjs@1.0.0 test /u/stjs
> mocha */test/test-*.js "-g" "parses correctly"


  parses correctly
    ✓ parses the empty string
    ✓ parses a single literal
    ✓ parses multiple literals
    ✓ parses start anchors
    ✓ handles circumflex not at start
    ✓ parses end anchors
    ✓ parses circumflex not at start
    ✓ parses empty groups
    ✓ parses groups containing characters
    ✓ parses two groups containing characters
    ✓ parses any
    ✓ parses any of group
    ✓ parses alt
    ✓ parses alt of any
    ✓ parses alt of groups

  15 passing (11ms)
```

While our final parser is less than 90 lines of code, it is doing a lot of complex things. Compared to parsers for things like JSON and YAML, though, it is still very simple. If we have more operators with different **precedences** we should switch to the shunting-yard algorithm[2], and if we need to handle a language like JavaScript we should explore tools like ANTLR[3], which can generate a parser automatically given a description of the language to be parsed. As we said at the start, though, if our design requires us to write a parser we should try to come up with a better design. CSV, JSON, YAML, and other formats have their quirks[4], but at least they're broken the same way everywhere.

[2]https://en.wikipedia.org/wiki/Shunting-yard_algorithm
[3]https://www.antlr.org/
[4]https://third-bit.com/2015/06/11/why-we-cant-have-nice-things/

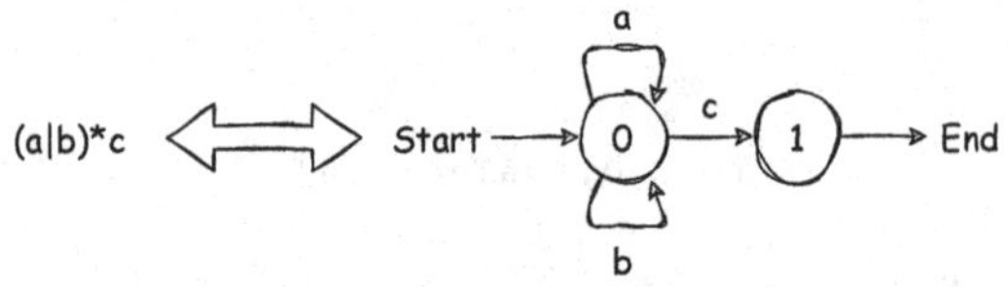

Figure 8.3: A finite state machine equivalent to a regular expression.

The limits of computing

One of the most important theoretical results in computer science is that every formal language corresponds to a type of abstract machine and vice versa, and that some languages (or machines) are more or less powerful than others. For example, every regular expression corresponds to a **finite state machine** (FSM) like the one in Figure 8.3. As powerful as FSMs are, they cannot match things like nested parentheses or HTML tags, and attempting to do so is a sin[5]. If you add a stack to the system you can process a much richer set of languages, and if you add two stacks you have something equivalent to a **Turing Machine** that can do any conceivable computation. [Conery2021] presents this idea and others for self-taught developers.

8.3 Exercises

Create objects

Modify the parser to return instances of classes derived from `RegexBase`.

Escape characters

Modify the parser to handle escape characters, so that (for example) `\*` is interpreted as "a literal asterisk" and `\\` is interpreted as "a literal backslash".

Lazy matching

Modify the parser so that `*?` is interpreted as a single token meaning "lazy match zero or more".

Character sets

Modify the parser so that expressions like `[xyz]` are interpreted to mean "match any one of the characters x, y, or z".

[5]https://stackoverflow.com/questions/1732348/regex-match-open-tags-except-xhtml-self-contained-tags/1732454#1732454

Back reference

Modify the tokenizer so that it recognizes `\1`, `\2`, and so on to mean "back reference". The number may contain any number of digits.

Named groups

1. Modify the tokenizer to recognize named groups. For example, the named group `/(?<triple>aaa)/` would create a named group called `triple` that matches exactly three consecutive occurrences of 'a'.

2. Write Mocha tests for your modified tokenizer. Does it handle nested named groups?

Object streams

Write a parser that turns files of key-value pairs separated by blank lines into objects. For example, if the input is:

```
left: "left value"
first: 1

middle: "middle value"
second: 2

right: "right value"
third: 3
```

then the output will be:

```
[
  {left: "left value", first: 1},
  {middle: "middle value", second: 2},
  {right: "right value", third: 3}
]
```

Keys are always upper- and lower-case characters; values may be strings in double quotes or unquoted numbers.

Tokenize HTML

1. Write a tokenizer for a subset of HTML that consists of:

   - Opening tags without attributes, such as `<div>` and `<p>`
   - Closing tags, such as `</p>` and `</div>`
   - Plain text between tags that does *not* contain '<' or '>' characters

2. Modify the tokenizer to handle `key="value"` attributes in opening tags.

3. Write Mocha tests for your tokenizer.

The Shunting-Yard Algorithm

1. Use the shunting-yard algorithm[6] to implement a tokenizer for a simple subset of arithmetic that includes:

[6] https://en.wikipedia.org/wiki/Shunting-yard_algorithm

- single-letter variable names
- single-digit numbers
- the `+`, `*`, and `^` operators, where `+` has the lowest precedence and `^` has the highest

2. Write Mocha tests for your tokenizer.

Handling errors

1. What does the regular expression tokenizer do with expressions that contain unmatched opening parentheses like `/a(b/`? What about expressions that contain unmatched closing parentheses like `/ab)/`?
2. Modify it so it produces a more useful error message.

9

Page Templates

Terms defined: **bare object**, **dynamic scoping**, **environment**, **lexical scoping**, **stack frame**, **static site generator**, **Visitor pattern**

Every program needs documentation in order to be usable, and the best place to put that documentation is on the web. Writing and updating pages by hand is time-consuming and error-prone, particularly when many parts are the same, so most documentation sites use some kind of **static site generator** to create web pages from templates.

At the heart of every static site generator is a page templating system. Thousands of these have been written in the last thirty years in every popular programming language (and one language, PHP[1], was created for this purpose). Most of these systems use one of three designs (Figure 9.1):

1. Mix commands in a language such as JavaScript with the HTML or Markdown using some kind of marker to indicate which parts are commands and which parts are to be taken as-is. This approach is taken by EJS[2], which we used to write these lessons.

2. Create a mini-language with its own commands like Jekyll[3] (which is used by GitHub Pages[4]). Mini-languages are appealing because they are smaller and safer than general-purpose languages, but experience shows that they eventually grow most of the features of a general-purpose language. Again, some kind of marker must be used to show which parts of the page are code and which are ordinary text.

3. Put directives in specially-named attributes in the HTML. This approach has been the least popular, but since pages are valid HTML, it eliminates the need for a special parser.

In this chapter we will build a simple page templating system using the third strategy. We will process each page independently by parsing the HTML and walking the DOM to find nodes with special attributes. Our program will execute the instructions in those nodes to do the equivalent of loops and if/else statements; other nodes will be copied as-is to create text.

EJS

```
<ul>
<% items.forEach(item => { %>
  <li><%- item.title %></li>
<% } %>
</ul>
```

Jekyll

```
<ul>
{% for item in items %}
  <li>{{ item.title }}</li>
{% endfor %}
</ul>
```

Argon

```
<ul z-loop="item:items">
  <li><span z-var="item"/></li>
</ul>
```

Figure 9.1: Three different ways to implement page templating.

[1]https://www.php.net/
[2]https://ejs.co/
[3]https://jekyllrb.com/
[4]https://pages.github.com/

9.1 What will our system look like?

Let's start by deciding what "done" looks like. Suppose we want to turn an array of strings into an HTML list. Our page will look like this:

```
<html>
  <body>
    <p>Expect three items</p>
    <ul z-loop="item:names">
      <li><span z-var="item"/></li>
    </ul>
  </body>
</html>
```

The attribute `z-loop` tells the tool to repeat the contents of that node; the loop variable and the collection being looped over are separated by a colon. The attribute `z-var` tells the tool to fill in the node with the value of the variable.

When our tool processes this page, the output will be standard HTML without any traces of how it was created:

```
<html>
  <body style="font-size: 200%; margin-left: 0.5em">
    <p>Expect three items</p>
    <ul>
      <li><span>Johnson</span></li>

      <li><span>Vaughan</span></li>

      <li><span>Jackson</span></li>
    </ul>
  </body>
</html>
```

Human-readable vs. machine-readable

The introduction said that mini-languages for page templating quickly start to accumulate extra features. We have already started down that road by putting the loop variable and loop target in a single attribute and splitting that attribute to get them out. Doing this makes loops easy for people to type, but hides important information from standard HTML processing tools. They can't know that this particular attribute of these particular elements contains multiple values or that those values should be extracted by splitting a string on a colon. We could instead require people to use two attributes, as in:

```
<ul z-loop="names" z-loop-var="item">
```

but we have decided to err on the side of minimal typing. And note that strictly speaking, we should call our attributes `data-something` instead of `z-something` to conform with the HTML5 specification[5], but by the time we're finished processing our templates, there shouldn't be any `z-*` attributes left to confuse a browser.

[5]https://developer.mozilla.org/en-US/docs/Learn/HTML/Howto/Use_data_attributes

The next step is to define the API for filling in templates. Our tool needs the template itself, somewhere to write its output, and some variables to use in the expansion. These variables might come from a configuration file, from a YAML header in the file itself, or from some mix of the two; for the moment, we will just pass them into the expansion function as an object:

```
const variables = {
  names: ['Johnson', 'Vaughan', 'Jackson']
}
const dom = readHtml('template.html')
const expander = new Expander(dom, variables)
expander.walk()
console.log(expander.result)
```

9.2 How can we keep track of values?

Speaking of variables, we need a way to keep track of their current values; we say "current" because the value of a loop variable changes each time we go around the loop. We also need to maintain multiple sets of variables so that variables used inside a loop don't conflict with ones used outside it. (We don't actually "need" to do this—we could just have one global set of variables—but experience teaches us that if all our variables are global, all of our programs will be buggy.)

The standard way to manage variables is to create a stack of lookup tables. Each **stack frame** is an object with names and values; when we need to find a variable, we look through the stack frames in order to find the uppermost definition of that variable..

Scoping rules

Searching the stack frame-by-frame while the program is running is called **dynamic scoping**, since we find variables while the program is running. In contrast, most programming languages used **lexical scoping**, which figures out what a variable name refers to based on the structure of the program text.

The values in a running program are sometimes called an **environment**, so we have named our stack-handling class `Env`. Its methods let us push and pop new stack frames and find a variable given its name; if the variable can't be found, `Env.find` returns `undefined` instead of throwing an exception (Figure 9.2).

```
class Env {
  constructor (initial) {
    this.stack = []
    this.push(Object.assign({}, initial))
  }

  push (frame) {
    this.stack.push(frame)
  }

  pop () {
    this.stack.pop()
  }
```

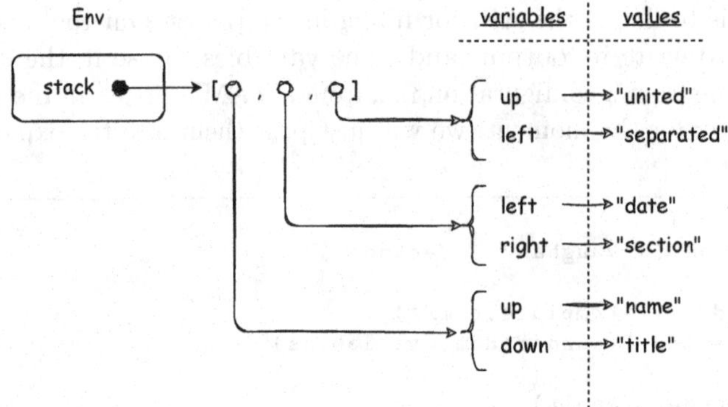

Figure 9.2: Using a stack to manage variables.

```
  find (name) {
    for (let i = this.stack.length - 1; i >= 0; i--) {
      if (name in this.stack[i]) {
        return this.stack[i][name]
      }
    }
    return undefined
  }

  toString () {
    return JSON.stringify(this.stack)
  }
}

export default Env
```

9.3 How do we handle nodes?

HTML pages have a nested structure, so we will process them using the **Visitor** design pattern. `Visitor`'s constructor takes the root node of the DOM tree as an argument and saves it. When we call `Visitor.walk` without a value, it starts recursing from that saved root; if `.walk` is given a value (as it is during recursive calls), it uses that instead.

```
import assert from 'assert'

class Visitor {
  constructor (root) {
    this.root = root
  }

  walk (node = null) {
    if (node === null) {
      node = this.root
    }
    if (this.open(node)) {
      node.children.forEach(child => {
        this.walk(child)
```

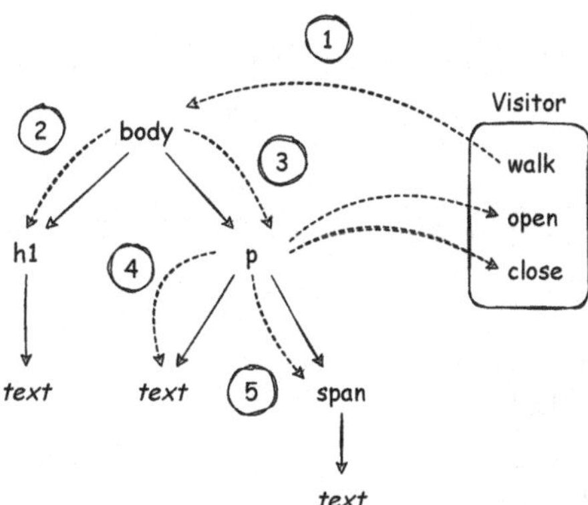

Figure 9.3: Using the Visitor pattern to evaluate a page template.

```
      })
    }
    this.close(node)
  }

  open (node) {
    assert(false,
      'Must implement "open"')
  }

  close (node) {
    assert(false,
      'Must implement "close"')
  }
}

export default Visitor
```

`Visitor` defines two methods called `open` and `close` that are called when we first arrive at a node and when we are finished with it (shown for the `p` node in Figure 9.3). The default implementations of these methods throw exceptions to remind the creators of derived classes to implement their own versions.

The `Expander` class is specialization of `Visitor` that uses an `Env` to keep track of variables. It imports a handler for each type of special node we support—we will write those in a moment—and uses them to process each type of node:

1. If the node is plain text, copy it to the output.

2. If there is a handler for the node, call the handler's `open` or `close` method.

3. Otherwise, open or close a regular tag.

```
import assert from 'assert'

import Visitor from './visitor.js'
import Env from './env.js'

import z_if from './z-if.js'
import z_loop from './z-loop.js'
import z_num from './z-num.js'
```

```
import z_var from './z-var.js'

const HANDLERS = {
  'z-if': z_if,
  'z-loop': z_loop,
  'z-num': z_num,
  'z-var': z_var
}

class Expander extends Visitor {
  constructor (root, vars) {
    super(root)
    this.env = new Env(vars)
    this.handlers = HANDLERS
    this.result = []
  }

  open (node) {
    if (node.type === 'text') {
      this.output(node.data)
      return false
    } else if (this.hasHandler(node)) {
      return this.getHandler(node).open(this, node)
    } else {
      this.showTag(node, false)
      return true
    }
  }

  close (node) {
    if (node.type === 'text') {
      return
    }
    if (this.hasHandler(node)) {
      this.getHandler(node).close(this, node)
    } else {
      this.showTag(node, true)
    }
  }
}

export default Expander
```

Checking to see if there is a handler for a particular node and getting that handler are straightforward—we just look at the node's attributes:

```
  hasHandler (node) {
    for (const name in node.attribs) {
      if (name in this.handlers) {
        return true
      }
    }
    return false
  }

  getHandler (node) {
    const possible = Object.keys(node.attribs)
      .filter(name => name in this.handlers)
    assert(possible.length === 1,
      'Should be exactly one handler')
```

```
    return this.handlers[possible[0]]
  }
```

Finally, we need a few helper methods to show tags and generate output:

```
  showTag (node, closing) {
    if (closing) {
      this.output(`</${node.name}>`)
      return
    }

    this.output(`<${node.name}`)
    if (node.name === 'body') {
      this.output(' style="font-size: 200%; margin-left: 0.5em"')
    }
    for (const name in node.attribs) {
      if (!name.startsWith('z-')) {
        this.output(` ${name}="${node.attribs[name]}"`)
      }
    }
    this.output('>')
  }

  output (text) {
    this.result.push((text === undefined) ? 'UNDEF' : text)
  }

  getResult () {
    return this.result.join('')
  }
```

Notice that this class adds strings to an array and joins them all right at the end rather than concatenating strings repeatedly. Doing this is more efficient and also helps with debugging, since each string in the array corresponds to a single method call.

9.4 How do we implement node handlers?

At this point we have built a lot of infrastructure but haven't actually processed any special nodes. To do that, let's write a handler that copies a constant number into the output:

```
export default {
  open: (expander, node) => {
    expander.showTag(node, false)
    expander.output(node.attribs['z-num'])
  },

  close: (expander, node) => {
    expander.showTag(node, true)
  }
}
```

When we enter a node like `<span z-num="123"/>` this handler asks the expander to show an opening tag followed by the value of the `z-num` attribute. When we exit the node, the handler asks the expander to close the tag. The handler doesn't know whether things are printed immediately, added to an output list, or something else; it just knows that whoever called it implements the low-level operations it needs.

Note that this expander is *not* a class, but instead an object with two functions stored under the keys `open` and `close`. We could use a class for each handler so that handlers can store any extra state they need, but **bare objects** are common and useful in JavaScript (though we will see below that we *should* have used classes).

So much for constants; what about variables?

```
export default {
  open: (expander, node) => {
    expander.showTag(node, false)
    expander.output(expander.env.find(node.attribs['z-var']))
  },

  close: (expander, node) => {
    expander.showTag(node, true)
  }
}
```

This code is almost the same as the previous example. The only difference is that instead of copying the attribute's value directly to the output, we use it as a key to look up a value in the environment.

These two pairs of handlers look plausible, but do they work? To find out, we can build a program that loads variable definitions from a JSON file, reads an HTML template, and does the expansion:

```
import fs from 'fs'
import htmlparser2 from 'htmlparser2'

import Expander from './expander.js'

const main = () => {
  const vars = readJSON(process.argv[2])
  const doc = readHtml(process.argv[3])
  const expander = new Expander(doc, vars)
  expander.walk()
  console.log(expander.getResult())
}

const readJSON = (filename) => {
  const text = fs.readFileSync(filename, 'utf-8')
  return JSON.parse(text)
}

const readHtml = (filename) => {
  const text = fs.readFileSync(filename, 'utf-8')
  return htmlparser2.parseDOM(text)[0]
}

main()
```

We added new variables for our test cases one-by-one as we were writing this chapter. To avoid repeating text repeatedly, we show the entire set once:

```
{
  "firstVariable": "firstValue",
  "secondVariable": "secondValue",
  "variableName": "variableValue",
  "showThis": true,
  "doNotShowThis": false,
  "names": ["Johnson", "Vaughan", "Jackson"]
}
```

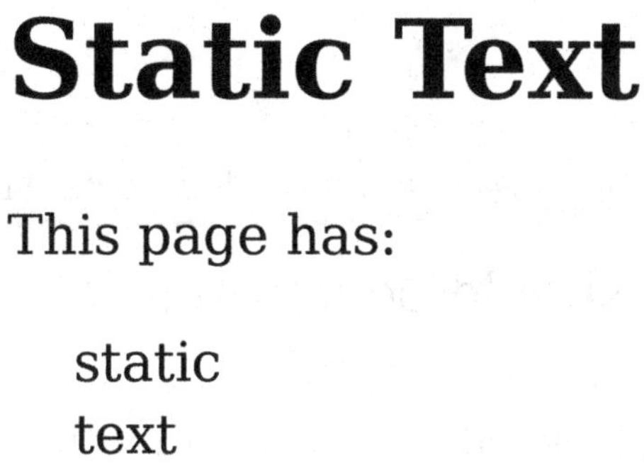

Static Text

This page has:

- static
- text

Figure 9.4: Static text generated by page templates.

Our first test: is static text copied over as-is (Figure 9.4)?

```
<html>
  <body>
    <h1>Static Text</h1>
    <p>This page has:</p>
    <ul>
      <li>static</li>
      <li>text</li>
    </ul>
  </body>
</html>
```

```
node template.js vars.json input-static-text.html
```

```
<html>
  <body style="font-size: 200%; margin-left: 0.5em">
    <h1>Static Text</h1>
    <p>This page has:</p>
    <ul>
      <li>static</li>
      <li>text</li>
    </ul>
  </body>
</html>
```

Good. Now, does the expander handle constants (Figure 9.5)?

```
<html>
  <body>
    <p><span z-num="123"/></p>
  </body>
</html>
```

```
<html>
  <body style="font-size: 200%; margin-left: 0.5em">
    <p><span>123</span></p>
  </body>
</html>
```

What about a single variable (Figure 9.6)?

123

Figure 9.5: A single constant generated by page templates.

This should be shown.

Figure 9.6: A single variable generated by page templates.

```
<html>
  <body>
    <p><span z-var="variableName"/></p>
  </body>
</html>
```

```
<html>
  <body style="font-size: 200%; margin-left: 0.5em">
    <p><span>variableValue</span></p>
  </body>
</html>
```

What about a page containing multiple variables? There's no reason it should fail if the single-variable case works, but we should still check—again, software isn't done until it has been tested (Figure 9.7).

```
<html>
  <body>
    <p><span z-var="firstVariable" /></p>
    <p><span z-var="secondVariable" /></p>
  </body>
</html>
```

```
<html>
  <body style="font-size: 200%; margin-left: 0.5em">
    <p><span>firstValue</span></p>
    <p><span>secondValue</span></p>
  </body>
</html>
```

firstValue

secondValue

Figure 9.7: Multiple variables generated by page templates.

This should be shown.

Figure 9.8: Conditional text generated by page templates.

9.5 How can we implement control flow?

Our tool supports two types of control flow: conditional expressions and loops. Since we don't support Boolean expressions like `and` and `or`, implementing a conditional is as simple as looking up a variable (which we know how to do) and then expanding the node if the value is true:

```
export default {
  open: (expander, node) => {
    const doRest = expander.env.find(node.attribs['z-if'])
    if (doRest) {
      expander.showTag(node, false)
    }
    return doRest
  },

  close: (expander, node) => {
    if (expander.env.find(node.attribs['z-if'])) {
      expander.showTag(node, true)
    }
  }
}
```

Let's test it (Figure 9.8):

```
<html>
  <body>
    <p z-if="showThis">This should be shown.</p>
    <p z-if="doNotShowThis">This should <em>not</em> be shown.</p>
  </body>
</html>
```

```
<html>
  <body style="font-size: 200%; margin-left: 0.5em">
    <p>This should be shown.</p>

  </body>
</html>
```

Spot the bug

The `open` and `close` functions for `if` both check the value of the control variable. If something inside the `if`'s body changes that value we could produce an opening tag without a matching closing tag. We haven't implemented assignment, so there's no way for that to happen now, but it could be a headache if we add it later.

Finally we come to loops. For these, we need to get the array we're looping over from the environment and do something for each of its elements. That "something" is:

1. Create a new stack frame holding the current value of the loop variable.
2. Expand all of the node's children with that stack frame in place.
3. Pop the stack frame to get rid of the temporary variable.

```
export default {
  open: (expander, node) => {
    const [indexName, targetName] = node.attribs['z-loop'].split(':')
    delete node.attribs['z-loop']
    expander.showTag(node, false)
    const target = expander.env.find(targetName)
    for (const index of target) {
      expander.env.push({ [indexName]: index })
      node.children.forEach(child => expander.walk(child))
      expander.env.pop()
    }
    return false
  },

  close: (expander, node) => {
    expander.showTag(node, true)
  }
}
```

Once again, it's not done until we test it (Figure 9.9):

```
<html>
  <body>
    <p>Expect three items</p>
    <ul z-loop="item:names">
      <li><span z-var="item"/></li>
    </ul>
  </body>
</html>
```

```
<html>
  <body style="font-size: 200%; margin-left: 0.5em">
    <p>Expect three items</p>
    <ul>
      <li><span>Johnson</span></li>

      <li><span>Vaughan</span></li>

      <li><span>Jackson</span></li>
    </ul>
  </body>
</html>
```

Notice how we create the new stack frame using:

```
{ [indexName]: index }
```

This is an ugly but useful trick. We can't write:

```
{ indexName: index }
```

because that would create an object with the string `indexName` as a key, rather than one with the value of the variable `indexName` as its key. We can't do this either:

Expect three items

Johnson
Vaughan
Jackson

Figure 9.9: Repeated text generated with a loop by page templates.

```
{ `${indexName}`: index }
```

though it seems like we should be able to. Instead, we create an array containing the string we want. Since JavaScript automatically converts arrays to strings by concatenating their elements when it needs to, our expression is a quick way to get the same effect as:

```
const temp = {}
temp[indexName] = index
expander.env.push(temp)
```

Those three lines *are* much easier to understand, though, so we should probably have been less clever.

9.6 How did we know how to do all of this?

We have just implemented a simple programming language. It can't do arithmetic, but if we wanted to add tags like:

```
<span z-math="+"><span z-var="width"/><span z-num="1"//>
```

we could. It's unlikely anyone would use the result—typing all of that is so much clumsier than typing `width+1` that people wouldn't use it unless they had no other choice—but the basic design is there.

We didn't invent any of this from scratch, any more than we invented the parsing algorithm of Chapter 8. Instead, we did what you are doing now: we read what other programmers had written and tried to make sense of the key ideas.

The problem is that "making sense" depends on who we are. When we use a low-level language, we incur the cognitive load of assembling micro-steps into something more meaningful. When we use a high-level language, on the other hand, we incur a similar load translating functions of functions (of functions...) (or meta-classes templated on object factories) into actual operations on actual data.

More experienced programmers are more capable at both ends of the curve, but that's not the only thing that changes. If a novice's comprehension curve looks like the lower curve in Figure 9.10, then an expert's looks like the upper one. Experts don't just understand more at all levels of abstraction; their *preferred* level has also shifted so that $\sqrt{x^2 + y^2}$ is actually more readable than the medieval expression "the side of the square whose area is the sum of the areas of the two squares whose sides are given by the first part and the second part".

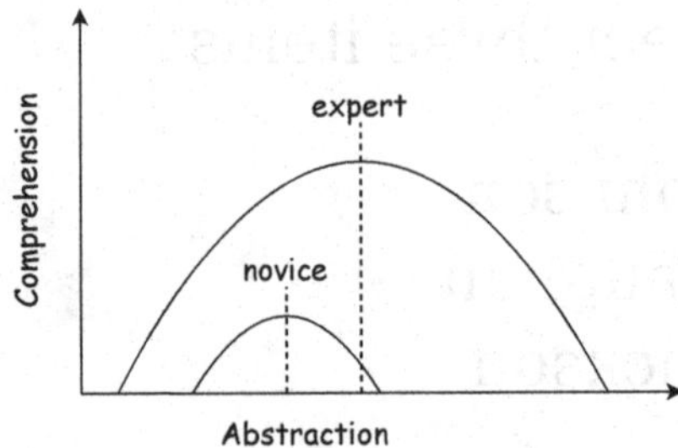

Figure 9.10: Novice and expert comprehension curves.

One implication of this is that for any given task, the software that is quickest for a novice to comprehend will almost certainly be different from the software that an expert can understand most quickly. In an ideal world our tools would automatically re-represent programs at different levels, so that with a click of a button we could view our code as either:

```
const hosts = links.map(a => a.href.split(':')[1].split('/')[2]).unique()
```

or:

```
hosts = []
for (each a in links) do
  temp <- attr(a, 'href').split(':')[1].split('/')[2]
  if (not (temp in hosts)) do
    hosts.append(temp)
  end
end
```

just as we could change the colors used for syntax highlighting or the depth to which loop bodies are indented. But today's tools don't do that, and I suspect that any tool smart enough to translate between comprehension levels automatically would also be smart enough to write the code without our help.

9.7 Exercises

Tracing execution

Add a directive `<span z-trace="variable"/>` that prints the current value of a variable using `console.error` for debugging.

Unit tests

Write unit tests for template expansion using Mocha.

Trimming text

Modify all of the directives to take an extra optional attribute `z-trim="true"`. If this attribute is set, leading and trailing whitespace is trimmed from the directive's expansion.

Literal text

Add a directive `<div z-literal="true">...</div>` that copies the enclosed text as-is without interpreting or expanding any contained directives. (A directive like this would be needed when writing documentation for the template expander.)

Including other files

1. Add a directive `<div z-include="filename.html"/>` that includes another file in the file being processed.
2. Should included files be processed and the result copied into the including file, or should the text be copied in and then processed? What difference does it make to the way variables are evaluated?

HTML snippets

Add a directive `<div z-snippet="variable">...</div>` that saves some text in a variable so that it can be displayed later. For example:

```
<html>
  <body>
    <div z-snippet="prefix"><strong>Important:</strong></div>
    <p>Expect three items</p>
    <ul>
      <li z-loop="item:names">
        <span z-var="prefix"><span z-var="item"/>
      </li>
    </ul>
  </body>
</html>
```

would printed the word "Important:" in bold before each item in the list.

YAML headers

Modify the template expander to handle variables defined in a YAML header in the page being processed. For example, if the page is:

```
---
name: "Dorothy Johnson Vaughan"
---
<html>
  <body>
    <p><span z-var="name"/></p>
  </body>
</html>
```

will create a paragraph containing the given name.

Expanding all files

Write a program `expand-all.js` that takes two directory names as command-line arguments and builds a website in the second directory by expanding all of the HTML files found in the first or in sub-directories of the first.

Counting loops

Add a directive `<div z-index="indexName" z-limit="limitName">...</div>` that loops from zero to the value in the variable `limitName`, putting the current iteration index in `indexName`.

Auxiliary functions

1. Modify `Expander` so that it takes an extra argument `auxiliaries` containing zero or more named functions:

```
const expander = new Expander(root, vars, {
  max: Math.max,
  trim: (x) => x.trim()
})
```

2. Add a directive `<span z-call="functionName" z-args="var,var"/>` that looks up a function in `auxiliaries` and calls it with the given variables as arguments.

10

Build Manager

Terms defined: **automatic variable**, **build manager**, **build recipe**, **build rule**, **build target**, **compiled language**, **cycle (in a graph)**, **dependency**, **directed acyclic graph**, **driver**, **interpreted language**, **link (a program)**, **pattern rule**, **runnable documentation**, **stale (in build)**, **Template Method pattern**, **topological order**

Suppose we are using a page templating system to create a website (Chapter 9). If we change a single page our tool should translate it, but it shouldn't waste time translating others. If we change a template, on the other hand, the tool should realize that every page in the site is potentially affected and automatically re-translate all of them.

Choosing what actions to take based on how files depend on one another is a common pattern. For example, programs in **compiled languages** like C and Java have to be translated into lower-level forms before they can run. In fact, there are usually two stages to the translation: compiling each source file into some intermediate form, and then **linking** the compiled modules to each other and to libraries to create a runnable program (Figure 10.1). If a source file hasn't changed, there's no need to recompile it before linking.

A **build manager** takes a description of what depends on what, figures out which files are out of date, determines an order in which to rebuild things, and then executes any necessary steps. Originally created to manage compilation, they are also useful for programs written in **interpreted languages** like JavaScript when we want to bundle multiple modules into a single loadable file (Chapter 17) or re-create documentation from source code (Chapter 16). In this chapter we will create a simple build manager based on Make[1], Bajel[2], Jake[3], and other systems discussed in [Smith2011].

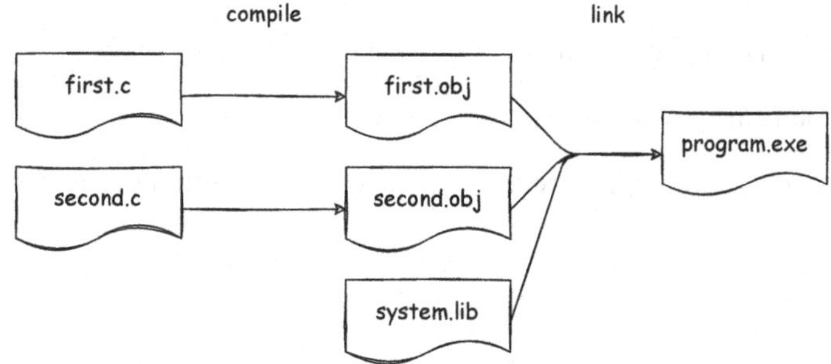

Figure 10.1: Compiling source files and linking the resulting modules.

[1]https://www.gnu.org/software/make/
[2]https://www.npmjs.com/package/bajel
[3]https://jakejs.com/

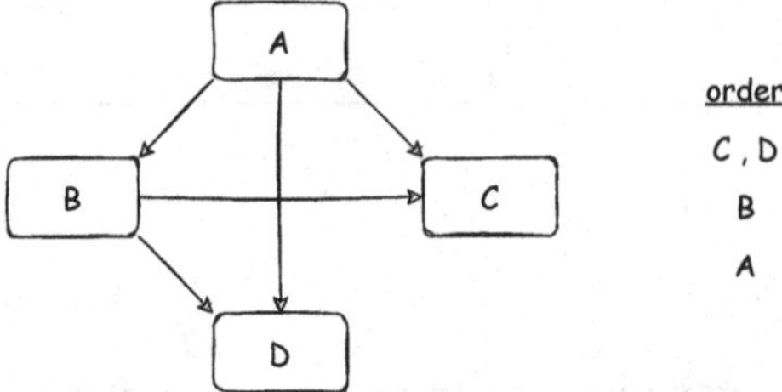

Figure 10.2: How a build manager finds and respects dependencies.

10.1 What's in a build manager?

The input to a build manager is a set of rules, each of which has:

- a **target**, which is the file to be updated;
- some **dependencies**, which are the things that file depends on; and
- a **recipe** that specifies how to update the target if it is out of date compared to its dependencies.

The target of one rule can be a dependency of another rule, so the relationships between the files form a **directed acyclic graph** or DAG (Figure 10.2). The graph is directed because "A depends on B" is a one-way relationship; it cannot contain cycles (or loops) because if something depends on itself we can never finish updating it. We say that a target is **stale** if it is older than any of its dependencies. When this happens, we use the recipes to bring it up to date.

Our build manager must:

1. Read a file containing rules.
2. Construct the dependency graph.
3. Figure out which targets are stale.
4. Build those targets, making sure to build things *before* anything that depends on them is built.

> **Topological order**
>
> A **topological ordering** of a graph arranges the nodes so that every node comes after everything it depends on. For example, if A depends on both B and C, then (B, C, A) and (C, B, A) are both valid topological orders of the graph.

10.2 Where should we start?

We will store our rules in YAML files like this:

```
- target: A
  depends:
  - B
  - C
  recipes:
  - "update A from B and C"
- target: B
  depends:
  - C
  recipes:
  - "update B from C"
- target: C
  depends: []
  recipes: []
```

We could equally well have used JSON, but it wouldn't have made sense to use CSV: rules have a nested structure, and CSV doesn't represent nesting particularly gracefully.

We are going to create our build manager in stages, so we start by writing a simple **driver** that loads a JavaScript source file, creates an object of whatever class that file exports, and runs the `.build` method of that object with the rest of the command-line parameters:

```
const main = async () => {
  const BuilderClass = (await import(process.argv[2])).default
  const builder = new BuilderClass(...process.argv.slice(3))
  try {
    builder.build()
  } catch (err) {
    console.error('Build failed:', err)
  }
}

main()
```

We use the `import` function to dynamically load files in Chapter 4 as well. It only saves us a few lines of code in this case, but we will use this idea of a general-purpose driver for larger programs in future chapters.

To work with our driver, each version of our build manager must be a class that satisfies two requirements:

1. Its constructor must take a configuration file as an argument.

2. It must provide a `build` method that needs no arguments.

The `build` method must create a graph from the configuration file, check that it does not contain any **cycles**, and then run whatever commands are needed to update stale targets. Just as we built a generic `Visitor` class in Chapter 9, we can build a generic base class for our build manager that does these steps in this order without actually implementing any of them:

```
import assert from 'assert'

class SkeletonBuilder {
  constructor (configFile) {
    this.configFile = configFile
  }

  build () {
```

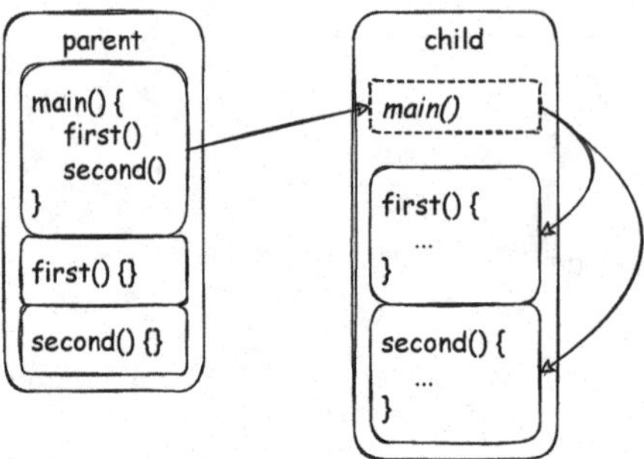

Figure 10.3: The Template Method pattern in action.

```
    this.loadConfig()
    this.buildGraph()
    this.checkCycles()
    this.run()
  }

  loadConfig () {
    assert(false, 'not implemented')
  }

  buildGraph () {
    assert(false, 'not implemented')
  }

  checkCycles () {
    assert(false, 'not implemented')
  }

  run () {
    assert.fail('run method not implemented')
  }
}

export default SkeletonBuilder
```

This is an example of the **Template Method** design pattern: the parent class defines the order of the steps and child classes fill them in (Figure 10.3). This design pattern ensures that every child does the same things in the same order, even if the details of *how* vary from case to case.

We would normally implement all of the methods required by the `build` method at the same time; here, we will write them one-by-one to make the evolving code easier to follow. The `loadConfig` method loads the configuration file as the builder object is being constructed:

```
import assert from 'assert'
import fs from 'fs'
import yaml from 'js-yaml'

import SkeletonBuilder from './skeleton-builder.js'

class ConfigLoader extends SkeletonBuilder {
  loadConfig () {
    this.config = yaml.safeLoad(fs.readFileSync(this.configFile, 'utf-8'))
```

```
    assert(Array.isArray(this.config),
      'Configuration must be array')

    this.config.forEach(rule => {
      assert(('target' in rule) && (typeof rule.target === 'string'),
        `Rule ${JSON.stringify(rule)} does not string as 'target'`)

      assert(('depends' in rule) &&
        Array.isArray(rule.depends) &&
        rule.depends.every(dep => (typeof dep === 'string')),
        `Bad 'depends' for rule ${JSON.stringify(rule)}`)

      assert(('recipes' in rule) &&
        Array.isArray(rule.recipes) &&
        rule.recipes.every(recipe => (typeof recipe === 'string')),
        `Bad 'recipes' for rule ${JSON.stringify(rule)}`)
    })
  }
}

export default ConfigLoader
```

The first line does the loading; the rest of the method checks that the rules are at least superficially plausible. We need these checks because YAML is a generic file format that doesn't know anything about the extra requirements of our rules. And as we first saw in Chapter 3, we have to specify that the character encoding of our file is UTF-8 so that JavaScript knows how to convert bytes into text.

The next step is to turn the configuration into a graph in memory. We use the `graphlib`[4] module to manage nodes and links rather than writing our own classes for graphs, and store the recipe to rebuild a node in that node. Two features of `graphlib` that took us a while to figure out are that:

1. links go *from* the dependency *to* the target, and

2. `setEdge` automatically adds nodes if they aren't already present.

`graphlib` provides implementations of some common graph algorithms, including one to check for cycles, so we might as well write that method at this point too:

```
import assert from 'assert'
import graphlib from '@dagrejs/graphlib'

import ConfigLoader from './config-loader.js'

class GraphCreator extends ConfigLoader {
  buildGraph () {
    this.graph = new graphlib.Graph()
    this.config.forEach(rule => {
      this.graph.setNode(rule.target, {
        recipes: rule.recipes
      })
      rule.depends.forEach(dep => this.graph.setEdge(dep, rule.target))
    })
  }

  checkCycles () {
    const cycles = graphlib.alg.findCycles(this.graph)
```

[4]https://www.npmjs.com/package/graphlib

```
    assert.strictEqual(cycles.length, 0,
      `Dependency graph contains cycles ${cycles}`)
  }
}

export default GraphCreator
```

We can now create something that displays our configuration when it runs but does nothing else:

```
import graphlib from '@dagrejs/graphlib'

import GraphCreator from './graph-creator.js'

class DisplayOnly extends GraphCreator {
  run () {
    console.log('Graph')
    console.log(graphlib.json.write(this.graph))
    console.log('Sorted')
    console.log(graphlib.alg.topsort(this.graph))
  }
}

export default DisplayOnly
```

If we run this with our three simple rules as input, it shows the graph with v and w keys to represent the ends of the links:

```
node driver.js ./display-only.js three-simple-rules.yml
```

```
Graph
{
  options: { directed: true, multigraph: false, compound: false },
  nodes: [
    { v: 'A', value: [Object] },
    { v: 'B', value: [Object] },
    { v: 'C', value: [Object] }
  ],
  edges: [ { v: 'B', w: 'A' }, { v: 'C', w: 'A' }, { v: 'C', w: 'B' } ]
}
Sorted
[ 'C', 'B', 'A' ]
```

Let's write a quick test to make sure the cycle detector works as intended:

```
- target: A
  depends:
  - B
  recipes:
  - "update A from B"
- target: B
  depends:
  - A
  recipes:
  - "update B from A"
```

```
node driver.js ./display-only.js circular-rules.yml
```

```
Build failed: AssertionError [ERR_ASSERTION]: Dependency graph contains \
 cycles B,A
    at DisplayOnly.checkCycles \
     (/u/stjs/build-manager/graph-creator.js:19:12)
    at DisplayOnly.build \
     (/u/stjs/build-manager/skeleton-builder.js:11:10)
    at main (/u/stjs/build-manager/driver.js:5:13) {
  generatedMessage: false,
  code: 'ERR_ASSERTION',
  actual: 1,
  expected: 0,
  operator: 'strictEqual'
}
```

10.3 How can we specify that a file is out-of-date?

The next step is to figure out which files are out-of-date. Make does this by comparing the timestamps of the files in question, but this isn't always reliable because computers' clocks may be slightly out of sync, which can produce a wrong answer on a networked filesystem, and the operating system may only report file update times to the nearest millisecond (which seemed very short in 1970 but seems very long today).

More modern build systems store a hash of each file's contents and compare the current hash to the stored one to see if the file has changed. Since we already looked at hashing in Chapter 5, we will use the timestamp approach here. And instead of using a mock filesystem as we did in Chapter 5, we will simply load another configuration file that specifies fake timestamps for files:

```
A: 2
B: 5
C: 8
```

Since we want to associate those timestamps with files, we add a step to `buildGraph` to read the timestamp file and add information to the graph's nodes:

```
import assert from 'assert'
import fs from 'fs'
import yaml from 'js-yaml'

import GraphCreator from './graph-creator.js'

class AddTimestamps extends GraphCreator {
  constructor (configFile, timesFile) {
    super(configFile)
    this.timesFile = timesFile
  }

  buildGraph () {
    super.buildGraph()
    this.addTimestamps()
  }

  addTimestamps () {
    const times = yaml.safeLoad(fs.readFileSync(this.timesFile, 'utf-8'))
    for (const node of Object.keys(times)) {
```

```
      assert(this.graph.hasNode(node),
             `Graph does not have node ${node}`)
      this.graph.node(node).timestamp = times[node]
    }
    const missing = this.graph.nodes().filter(
      n => !('timestamp' in this.graph.node(n))
    )
    assert.strictEqual(missing.length, 0,
      `Timestamp missing for node(s) ${missing}`)
  }

  run () {
    console.log(this.graph.nodes().map(
      n => `${n}: ${JSON.stringify(this.graph.node(n))}`
    ))
  }
}

export default AddTimestamps
```

Not quite what we were expecting

The steps defined in `SkeletonBuilder.build` don't change when we do this, so people reading the code don't have to change their mental model of what it does overall. However, if we had realized in advance that we were going to want to add timestamps from a file, we would probably have added a step for that in the template method. And if someone ever wants to inject a new step between building the graph and adding timestamps, they will have to override `addTimestamps` and put their step at the top before calling `super.addTimestamps`, which will make the code a lot harder to understand.

Before we move on, let's make sure that adding timestamps works as we want:

```
node driver.js ./add-stamps.js three-simple-rules.yml add-stamps.yml
```

```
[
  'A: {"recipes":["update A from B and C"],"timestamp":2}',
  'B: {"recipes":["update B from C"],"timestamp":5}',
  'C: {"recipes":[],"timestamp":8}'
]
```

10.4 How can we update out-of-date files?

To figure out which recipes to execute and in which order, we set the pretended current time to the latest time of any file, then look at each file in topological order. If a file is older than any of its dependencies, we update the file *and* its pretended timestamp to trigger an update of anything that depends on it.

We can pretend that updating a file always takes one unit of time, so we advance our fictional clock by one for each build. Using `graphlib.alg.topsort` to create the topological order, we get this:

```
import graphlib from '@dagrejs/graphlib'

import AddTimestamps from './add-stamps.js'

class UpdateOnTimestamps extends AddTimestamps {
  run () {
    const sorted = graphlib.alg.topsort(this.graph)
    const startTime = 1 + Math.max(...sorted.map(
      n => this.graph.node(n).timestamp))
    console.log(`${startTime}: START`)
    const endTime = sorted.reduce((currTime, node) => {
      if (this.isStale(node)) {
        console.log(`${currTime}: ${node}`)
        this.graph.node(node).recipes.forEach(
          a => console.log(`    ${a}`))
        this.graph.node(node).timestamp = currTime
        currTime += 1
      }
      return currTime
    }, startTime)
    console.log(`${endTime}: END`)
  }

  isStale (node) {
    return this.graph.predecessors(node).some(
      other => this.graph.node(other).timestamp >=
        this.graph.node(node).timestamp
    )
  }
}

export default UpdateOnTimestamps
```

The `run` method:

1. gets a sorted list of nodes;
2. sets the starting time to be one unit past the largest file time; and then
3. uses `Array.reduce` to operate on each node (i.e., each file) in order. If that file is stale, we print the steps we would run and then update the file's timestamp. We only advance the notional current time when we do an update.

To check if a file is stale, we see if any of its dependencies currently have timestamps greater than or equal to its own. When we run this, it seems to do the right thing:

```
node driver.js ./update-stamps.js three-simple-rules.yml add-stamps.yml
```

```
9: START
9: B
    update B from C
10: A
    update A from B and C
11: END
```

10.5 How can we add generic build rules?

If our website has a hundred blog posts or a hundred pages of documentation about particular JavaScript files, we don't want to have to write a hundred nearly-identical recipes. Instead, we want to be able to write generic **build rules** that say, "Build all things of this kind the same way." These generic rules need:

- a way to define a set of files;
- a way to specify a generic rule; and
- a way to fill in parts of that rule.

We will achieve this by overriding `buildGraph` to replace variables in recipes with values. Once again, object-oriented programming helps us change only what we need to change, provided we divided our problem into sensible chunks in the first place.

Make provides **automatic variables** with names like `$<` and `$@` to represent the parts of a rule. Ours will be more readable: we will use `@TARGET` for the target, `@DEPENDENCIES` for the dependencies (in order), and `@DEP[1]`, `@DEP[2]`, and so on for specific dependencies (Figure 10.4). Our variable expander looks like this:

```
import UpdateOnTimestamps from './update-stamps.js'

class VariableExpander extends UpdateOnTimestamps {
  buildGraph () {
    super.buildGraph()
    this.expandVariables()
  }

  expandVariables () {
    this.graph.nodes().forEach(target => {
      try {
        const dependencies = this.graph.predecessors(target)
        const recipes = this.graph.node(target).recipes
        this.graph.node(target).recipes = recipes.map(act => {
          act = act
            .replace('@TARGET', target)
            .replace('@DEPENDENCIES', dependencies.join(' '))
          dependencies.forEach((dep, i) => {
            act = act.replace(`@DEP[${i}]`, dependencies[i])
          })
          return act
        })
      } catch (error) {
        console.error(`Cannot find ${target} in graph`)
        process.exit(1)
      }
    })
  }
}

export default VariableExpander
```

The first thing we do is test that it works when there *aren't* any variables to expand by running it on the same example we used previously:

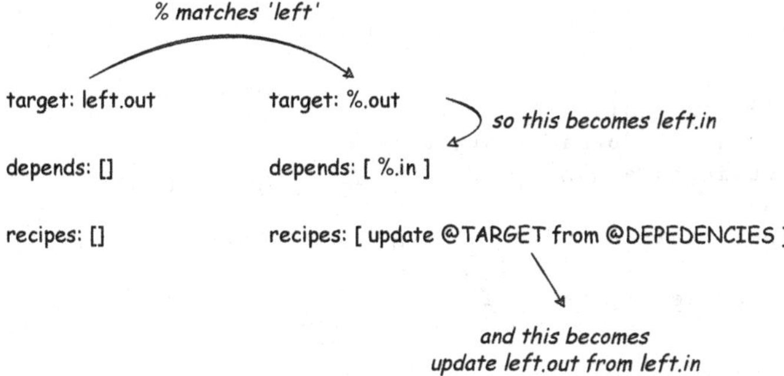

Figure 10.4: Turning patterns rules into runnable commands.

```
9: START
9: B
   update B from C
10: A
   update A from B C
11: END
```

This is perhaps the most important reason to create tests: they tell us right away if something we have added or changed has broken something that used to work. That gives us a firm base to build on as we debug the new code.

Now we need to add **pattern rules**. Our first attempt at a rules file looks like this:

```
- target: left.out
  depends: []
  recipes: []
  timestamp: 1
- target: left.in
  depends: []
  recipes: []
  timestamp: 2
- target: right.out
  depends: []
  recipes: []
  timestamp: 1
- target: right.in
  depends: []
  recipes: []
  timestamp: 3
- target: "%.out"
  depends:
  - "%.in"
  recipes:
  - "update @TARGET from @DEPENDENCIES"
```

and our first attempt at reading it extracts rules before expanding variables:

```
import VariableExpander from './variable-expander.js'

class PatternUserAttempt extends VariableExpander {
  buildGraph () {
    super.buildGraph()
    this.extractRules()
    this.expandVariables()
```

```
  }

  extractRules () {
    this.rules = new Map()
    this.graph.nodes().forEach(target => {
      if (target.includes('%')) {
        const data = {
          recipes: this.graph.node(target).recipes
        }
        this.rules.set(target, data)
      }
    })
    this.rules.forEach((value, key) => {
      this.graph.removeNode(key)
    })
  }
}

export default PatternUserAttempt
```

However, that doesn't work:

```
Build failed: AssertionError [ERR_ASSERTION]: Graph does not have node A
    at PatternUserAttempt.addTimestamps \
    (/u/stjs/build-manager/add-stamps.js:21:7)
    at PatternUserAttempt.buildGraph \
    (/u/stjs/build-manager/add-stamps.js:15:10)
    at PatternUserAttempt.buildGraph \
    (/u/stjs/build-manager/variable-expander.js:5:11)
    at PatternUserAttempt.buildGraph \
    (/u/stjs/build-manager/pattern-user-attempt.js:5:11)
    at PatternUserAttempt.build \
    (/u/stjs/build-manager/skeleton-builder.js:10:10)
    at main (/u/stjs/build-manager/driver.js:5:13) {
  generatedMessage: false,
  code: 'ERR_ASSERTION',
  actual: false,
  expected: true,
  operator: '=='
}
```

The problem is that our simple graph loader creates nodes for dependencies even if they aren't targets. As a result, we wind up tripping over the lack of a node for `%.in` before we get to extracting rules.

Errors become assertions

When we first wrote `add-stamps.js`, it didn't contain the assertion that printed the error message shown above. Once we tracked down our bug, though, we added the assertion to ensure we didn't make the same mistake again, and as **runnable documentation** to tell the next programmer more about the code. Regular code tells the computer what to do; assertions with meaningful error messages tell the reader why.

We can fix our problem by rewriting the rule loader to separate pattern rules from simple rules; we can tell the two apart by checking if the rule's dependencies include `%`. While we're here, we will enable timestamps as an optional field in the rules for testing purposes rather than having them in a separate file:

```
import assert from 'assert'
import graphlib from '@dagrejs/graphlib'

import VariableExpander from './variable-expander.js'

class PatternUserRead extends VariableExpander {
  buildGraph () {
    this.buildGraphAndRules()
    this.expandVariables()
  }

  buildGraphAndRules () {
    this.graph = new graphlib.Graph()
    this.rules = new Map()
    this.config.forEach(rule => {
      if (rule.target.includes('%')) {
        const data = {
          recipes: rule.recipes,
          depends: rule.depends
        }
        this.rules.set(rule.target, data)
      } else {
        const timestamp = ('timestamp' in rule) ? rule.timestamp : null
        this.graph.setNode(rule.target, {
          recipes: rule.recipes,
          timestamp: timestamp
        })
        rule.depends.forEach(dep => {
          assert(!dep.includes('%'),
            'Cannot have "%" in a non-pattern rule')
          this.graph.setEdge(dep, rule.target)
        })
      }
    })
  }
}

export default PatternUserRead
```

Before we run this, let's add methods to show the state of our data structures:

```
import graphlib from '@dagrejs/graphlib'

import PatternUserRead from './pattern-user-read.js'

class PatternUserShow extends PatternUserRead {
  run () {
    console.log(JSON.stringify(this.toJSON(), null, 2))
  }

  toJSON () {
    return {
      graph: graphlib.json.write(this.graph),
      rules: Array.from(this.rules.keys()).map(key => {
        return { k: key, v: this.rules.get(key) }
      })
    }
  }
```

```
}

export default PatternUserShow
```

```
node driver.js ./pattern-user-show.js pattern-rules.yml
```


```
{
  "graph": {
    "options": {
      "directed": true,
      "multigraph": false,
      "compound": false
    },
    "nodes": [
      {
        "v": "left.out",
        "value": {
          "recipes": [],
          "timestamp": 1
        }
      },
      {
        "v": "left.in",
        "value": {
          "recipes": [],
          "timestamp": 2
        }
      },
      {
        "v": "right.out",
        "value": {
          "recipes": [],
          "timestamp": 1
        }
      },
      {
        "v": "right.in",
        "value": {
          "recipes": [],
          "timestamp": 3
        }
      }
    ],
    "edges": []
  },
  "rules": [
    {
      "k": "%.out",
      "v": {
        "recipes": [
          "update @TARGET from @DEPENDENCIES"
        ],
        "depends": [
          "%.in"
        ]
      }
    }
  ]
}
```

The output seems to be right, so let's try expanding rules *after* building the graph and rules but *before* expanding variables:

```
import PatternUserRead from './pattern-user-read.js'

class PatternUserRun extends PatternUserRead {
  buildGraph () {
    this.buildGraphAndRules()
    this.expandAllRules()
    this.expandVariables()
  }

  expandAllRules () {
    this.graph.nodes().forEach(target => {
      if (this.graph.predecessors(target).length > 0) {
        return
      }
      const data = this.graph.node(target)
      if (data.recipes.length > 0) {
        return
      }
      const rule = this.findRule(target)
      if (!rule) {
        return
      }
      this.expandRule(target, rule)
    })
  }

  findRule (target) {
    const pattern = `%.${target.split('.')[1]}`
    return this.rules.has(pattern)
      ? this.rules.get(pattern)
      : null
  }

  expandRule (target, rule) {
    const stem = target.split('.')[0]
    rule.depends
      .map(dep => dep.replace('%', stem))
      .forEach(dep => this.graph.setEdge(dep, target))
    const recipes = rule.recipes.map(act => act.replace('%', stem))
    const timestamp = this.graph.node(target).timestamp
    this.graph.setNode(target, {
      recipes: recipes,
      timestamp: timestamp
    })
  }
}

export default PatternUserRun
```

```
4: START
4: left.out
   update left.out from left.in
5: right.out
   update right.out from right.in
6: END
```

10.6 What should we do next?

We have added a lot of steps to our original template method, which makes it a bit of a stretch to claim that the overall operation hasn't changed. Knowing what we know now, we could go back and modify the original `SkeletonBuilder.build` method to include those extra steps and provide do-nothing implementations.

The root of the problem is that we didn't anticipate all the steps that would be involved when we wrote our template method. It typically takes a few child classes for this to settle down; if it never does, then Template Method is probably the wrong pattern for our situation. This isn't a failure in initial design: we always learn about our problem as we try to capture it in code, and if we know enough to anticipate 100% of the issues that are going to come up, it's time to put what we've learned in a library for future use.

10.7 Exercises

Handle failure

1. Modify the build manager to accommodate build steps that fail.
2. Write Mocha tests to check that this change works correctly.

Dry run

Add an option to the build manager to show what commands would be executed and why if a build were actually run. For example, the output should display things like, "'update A' because A older than B".

Change directories

Modify the build manager so that:

```
node build.js -C some/sub/directory rules.yml timestamps.yml
```

runs the build in the specified directory rather than the current directory.

Merge files

Modify the build manager so that it can read multiple configuration files and execute their combined rules.

Show recipes

Add a method to build manager to display all unique recipes, i.e., all of the commands it might execute if asked to rebuild everything.

Conditional execution

Modify the build manager so that:

1. The user can pass `variable=true` and `variable=false` arguments on the command-line to define variables.
2. Rules can contain an `if: variable` field.
3. Those rules are only executed if the variable is defined and true.
4. Write Mocha tests to check that this works correctly.

Define filesets

Modify the build manager so that users can define sets of files:

```
fileset:
  name: everything
  contains:
    - X
    - Y
    - Z
```

and then refer to them later:

```
- target: P
  depends:
  - @everything
```

Globbing

Modify the build manager so that it can dynamically construct a set of files:

```
glob:
  name: allAvailableInputs
  pattern: "./*.in"
```

and then refer to them later:

```
- target: P
  depends:
  - @allAvailableInputs
```

Use hashes

1. Write a program called `build-init.js` that calculates a hash for every file mentioned in the build configuration and stores the hash along with the file's name in `build-hash.json`.
2. Modify the build manager to compare the current hashes of files with those stored in `build-hash.json` in order to determine what is out of date, and to update `build-hash.json` each time it runs.

Auxiliary functions

1. Modify the builder manager so that it takes an extra argument `auxiliaries` containing zero or more named functions:

```
const builder = new ExtensibleBuilder(configFile, timesFile, {
  slice: (node, graph) => simplify(node, graph, 1)
})
```

2. Modify the `run` method to call these functions before executing the rules for a node, and to only execute the rules if all of them return `true`.

3. Write Mocha tests to check that this works correctly.

11

Layout Engine

Terms defined: **attribute**, **cache**, **confirmation bias**, **design by contract**, **easy mode**, **layout engine**, **Liskov Substitution Principle**, **query selector**, **signature**, **z-buffering**

You might be reading this as an HTML page, an e-book (which is basically the same thing), or on the printed page. In all three cases, a **layout engine** took some text and some layout instructions and decided where to put each character and image. We will build a small layout engine in this chapter based on Matt Brubeck's[1] tutorial[2] to explore how browsers decide what to put where.

Our inputs will be a very small subset of HTML and an equally small subset of CSS. We will create our own classes to represent these instead of using those provided by various Node[3] libraries; to translate the combination of HTML and CSS into text on the screen, we will label each node in the DOM tree with the appropriate styles, walk that tree to figure out where each visible element belongs, and then draw the result as text on the screen.

> **Upside down**
>
> The coordinate systems for screens puts (0, 0) in the upper left corner instead of the lower left. X increases to the right as usual, but Y increases as we go down, rather than up (Figure 11.1). This convention is a holdover from the days of teletype terminals that printed lines on rolls of paper; as Mike Hoye[4] has repeatedly observed[5], the past is all around us.

```
  0 1 2 3 4 5
 ┌──────────────→ X
0│F i r s t
1│S e c o n d
2│T h i r d
 ↓
 Y
```

Figure 11.1: Coordinate system with (0, 0) in the upper left corner.

[1]https://limpet.net/mbrubeck/
[2]https://limpet.net/mbrubeck/2014/08/08/toy-layout-engine-1.html
[3]https://nodejs.org/en/
[4]http://exple.tive.org/blarg/
[5]http://exple.tive.org/blarg/2020/11/26/punching-holes/

11.1 How can we size rows and columns?

Let's start on **easy mode** without margins, padding, line-wrapping, or other complications. Everything we can put on the screen is represented as a rectangular cell, and every cell is either a row, a column, or a block. A block has a fixed width and height:

```
export class Block {
  constructor (width, height) {
    this.width = width
    this.height = height
  }

  getWidth () {
    return this.width
  }

  getHeight () {
    return this.height
  }
}
```

A row arranges one or more cells horizontally; its width is the sum of the widths of its children, while its height is the height of its tallest child (Figure 11.2):

```
export class Row {
  constructor (...children) {
    this.children = children
  }

  getWidth () {
    let result = 0
    for (const child of this.children) {
      result += child.getWidth()
    }
    return result
  }

  getHeight () {
    let result = 0
    for (const child of this.children) {
      result = Math.max(result, child.getHeight())
    }
    return result
  }
}
```

Finally, a column arranges one or more cells vertically; its width is the width of its widest child and its height is the sum of the heights of its children. (Here and elsewhere we use the abbreviation `col` when referring to columns.)

```
export class Col {
  constructor (...children) {
    this.children = children
  }

  getWidth () {
    let result = 0
    for (const child of this.children) {
      result = Math.max(result, child.getWidth())
```

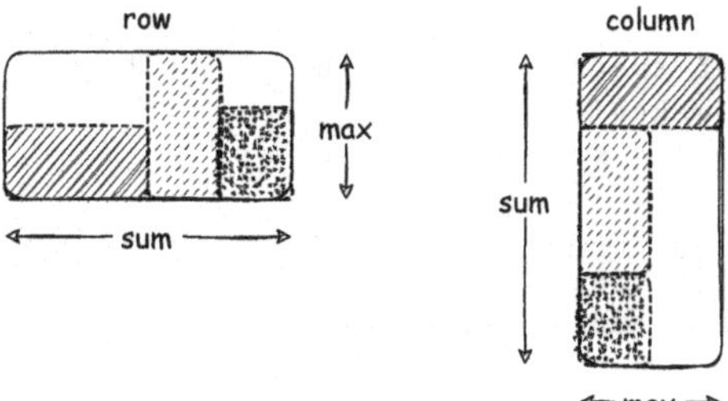

Figure 11.2: Calculating sizes of blocks with fixed width and height.

```
    }
    return result
  }

  getHeight () {
    let result = 0
    for (const child of this.children) {
      result += child.getHeight()
    }
    return result
  }
}
```

Rows and columns nest inside one another: a row cannot span two or more columns, and a column cannot cross the boundary between two rows. Any time we have a structure with that property we can represent it as a tree of nested objects. Given such a tree, we can calculate the width and height of each cell every time we need to. This is simple but inefficient: we could calculate both width and height at the same time and **cache** those values to avoid recalculation, but we called this "easy mode" for a reason.

As simple as it is, this code could still contain errors (and did during development), so we write some Mocha[6] tests to check that it works as desired before trying to build anything more complicated:

```
import assert from 'assert'

import {
  Block,
  Row,
  Col
} from '../easy-mode.js'

describe('lays out in easy mode', () => {
  it('lays out a single unit block', async () => {
    const fixture = new Block(1, 1)
    assert.strictEqual(fixture.getWidth(), 1)
    assert.strictEqual(fixture.getHeight(), 1)
  })

  it('lays out a large block', async () => {
    const fixture = new Block(3, 4)
    assert.strictEqual(fixture.getWidth(), 3)
    assert.strictEqual(fixture.getHeight(), 4)
  })
```

[6] https://mochajs.org/

```
  it('lays out a row of two blocks', async () => {
    const fixture = new Row(
      new Block(1, 1),
      new Block(2, 4)
    )
    assert.strictEqual(fixture.getWidth(), 3)
    assert.strictEqual(fixture.getHeight(), 4)
  })

  it('lays out a column of two blocks', async () => {
    const fixture = new Col(
      new Block(1, 1),
      new Block(2, 4)
    )
    assert.strictEqual(fixture.getWidth(), 2)
    assert.strictEqual(fixture.getHeight(), 5)
  })

  it('lays out a grid of rows of columns', async () => {
    const fixture = new Col(
      new Row(
        new Block(1, 2),
        new Block(3, 4)
      ),
      new Row(
        new Block(5, 6),
        new Col(
          new Block(7, 8),
          new Block(9, 10)
        )
      )
    )
    assert.strictEqual(fixture.getWidth(), 14)
    assert.strictEqual(fixture.getHeight(), 22)
  })
})
```

```
> stjs@1.0.0 test /u/stjs
> mocha */test/test-*.js "-g" "easy mode"



  lays out in easy mode
    ✓ lays out a single unit block
    ✓ lays out a large block
    ✓ lays out a row of two blocks
    ✓ lays out a column of two blocks
    ✓ lays out a grid of rows of columns


  5 passing (7ms)
```

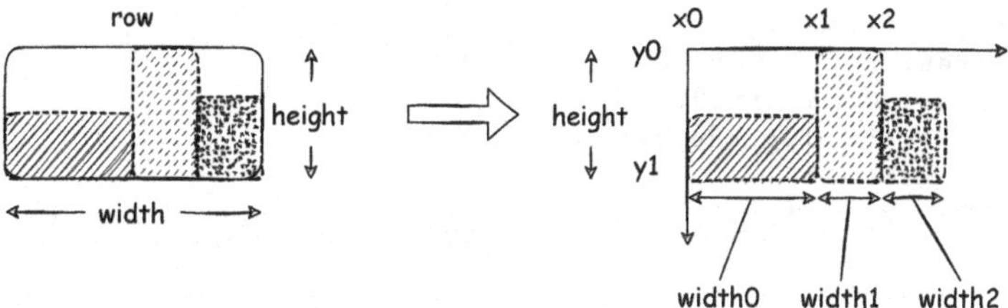

Figure 11.3: Laying out rows and columns of fixed-size blocks.

11.2 How can we position rows and columns?

Now that we know how big each cell is we can figure out where to put it. Suppose we start with the upper left corner of the browser: upper because we lay out the page top-to-bottom and left because we are doing left-to-right layout. If the cell is a block, we place it there. If the cell is a row, on the other hand, we get its height and then calculate its lower edge as y1 = y0 + height. We then place the first child's lower-left corner at (x0, y1), the second child's at (x0 + width0, y1), and so on (Figure 11.3). Similarly, if the cell is a column we place the first child at (x0, y0), the next at (x0, y0 + height0), and so on.

To save ourselves some testing we will derive the classes that know how to do layout from the classes we wrote before. Our blocks are:

```
export class PlacedBlock extends Block {
  constructor (width, height) {
    super(width, height)
    this.x0 = null
    this.y0 = null
  }

  place (x0, y0) {
    this.x0 = x0
    this.y0 = y0
  }

  report () {
    return [
      'block', this.x0, this.y0,
      this.x0 + this.width,
      this.y0 + this.height
    ]
  }
}
```

while our columns are:

```
export class PlacedCol extends Col {
  constructor (...children) {
    super(...children)
    this.x0 = null
    this.y1 = null
  }

  place (x0, y0) {
    this.x0 = x0
    this.y0 = y0
```

```
    let yCurrent = this.y0
    this.children.forEach(child => {
      child.place(x0, yCurrent)
      yCurrent += child.getHeight()
    })
  }

  report () {
    return [
      'col', this.x0, this.y0,
      this.x0 + this.getWidth(),
      this.y0 + this.getHeight(),
      ...this.children.map(child => child.report())
    ]
  }
}
```

and our rows are:

```
export class PlacedRow extends Row {
  constructor (...children) {
    super(...children)
    this.x0 = null
    this.y0 = null
  }

  place (x0, y0) {
    this.x0 = x0
    this.y0 = y0
    const y1 = this.y0 + this.getHeight()
    let xCurrent = x0
    this.children.forEach(child => {
      const childY = y1 - child.getHeight()
      child.place(xCurrent, childY)
      xCurrent += child.getWidth()
    })
  }

  report () {
    return [
      'row', this.x0, this.y0,
      this.x0 + this.getWidth(),
      this.y0 + this.getHeight(),
      ...this.children.map(child => child.report())
    ]
  }
}
```

Once again, we write and run some tests to check that everything is doing what it's supposed to:

```
import assert from 'assert'

import {
  PlacedBlock as Block,
  PlacedCol as Col,
  PlacedRow as Row
} from '../placed.js'

describe('places blocks', () => {
  it('places a single unit block', async () => {
```

```
    const fixture = new Block(1, 1)
    fixture.place(0, 0)
    assert.deepStrictEqual(
      fixture.report(),
      ['block', 0, 0, 1, 1]
    )
  })

  it('places a large block', async () => {
    const fixture = new Block(3, 4)
    fixture.place(0, 0)
    assert.deepStrictEqual(
      fixture.report(),
      ['block', 0, 0, 3, 4]
    )
  })

  it('places a row of two blocks', async () => {
    const fixture = new Row(
      new Block(1, 1),
      new Block(2, 4)
    )
    fixture.place(0, 0)
    assert.deepStrictEqual(
      fixture.report(),
      ['row', 0, 0, 3, 4,
        ['block', 0, 3, 1, 4],
        ['block', 1, 0, 3, 4]
      ]
    )
  })
})
```

```
> stjs@1.0.0 test /u/stjs
> mocha */test/test-*.js "-g" "places blocks"

  places blocks
    ✓ places a single unit block
    ✓ places a large block
    ✓ places a row of two blocks
    ✓ places a column of two blocks
    ✓ places a grid of rows of columns


  5 passing (8ms)
```

11.3 How can we render elements?

We drew the blocks on a piece of graph paper in order to figure out the expected answers for the tests shown above. We can do something similar in software by creating a "screen" of space characters and then having each block draw itself in the right place. If we do this starting at the root of the tree, child blocks will overwrite the markings made by their parents, which will automatically produce the right appearance (Figure 11.4). (A more

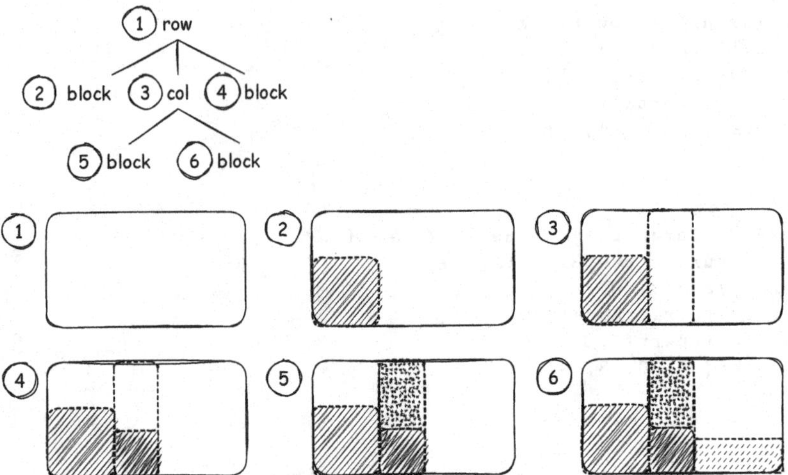

Figure 11.4: Render blocks by drawing child nodes on top of parent nodes.

sophisticated version of this called **z-buffering** keeps track of the visual depth of each pixel in order to draw things in three dimensions.)

Our pretended screen is just an array of arrays of characters:

```
const makeScreen = (width, height) => {
  const screen = []
  for (let i = 0; i < height; i += 1) {
    screen.push(new Array(width).fill(' '))
  }
  return screen
}
```

We will use successive lower-case characters to show each block, i.e., the root block will draw itself using the letter a, while its children will use b, c, and so on.

```
const draw = (screen, node, fill = null) => {
  fill = nextFill(fill)
  node.render(screen, fill)
  if ('children' in node) {
    node.children.forEach(child => {
      fill = draw(screen, child, fill)
    })
  }
  return fill
}

const nextFill = (fill) => {
  return (fill === null)
    ? 'a'
    : String.fromCharCode(fill.charCodeAt() + 1)
}
```

To teach each kind of cell how to render itself, we have to derive a new class from each of the ones we have and give the new class a `render` method with the same **signature**:

```
export class RenderedBlock extends PlacedBlock {
  render (screen, fill) {
    drawBlock(screen, this, fill)
  }
```

```
}

export class RenderedCol extends PlacedCol {
  render (screen, fill) {
    drawBlock(screen, this, fill)
  }
}

export class RenderedRow extends PlacedRow {
  render (screen, fill) {
    drawBlock(screen, this, fill)
  }
}

const drawBlock = (screen, node, fill) => {
  for (let ix = 0; ix < node.getWidth(); ix += 1) {
    for (let iy = 0; iy < node.getHeight(); iy += 1) {
      screen[node.y0 + iy][node.x0 + ix] = fill
    }
  }
}
```

These **render** methods do exactly the same thing, so we have each one call a shared function that does the actual work. If we were building a real layout engine, a cleaner solution would be to go back and create a class called `Cell` with this **render** method, then derive our `Block`, `Row`, and `Col` classes from that. In general, if two or more classes need to be able to do something, we should add a method to do that to their lowest common ancestor.

Our simpler tests are a little easier to read once we have rendering in place, though we still had to draw things on paper to figure out our complex ones:

```
  it('renders a grid of rows of columns', async () => {
    const fixture = new Col(
      new Row(
        new Block(1, 2),
        new Block(3, 4)
      ),
      new Row(
        new Block(1, 2),
        new Col(
          new Block(3, 4),
          new Block(2, 3)
        )
      )
    )
    fixture.place(0, 0)
    assert.deepStrictEqual(
      render(fixture),
      [
        'bddd',
        'bddd',
        'cddd',
        'cddd',
        'ehhh',
        'ehhh',
        'ehhh',
        'ehhh',
        'eiig',
        'fiig',
        'fiig'
      ].join('\n')
```

```
    )
  })
```

The fact that we find our own tests difficult to understand is a sign that we should do more testing. It would be very easy for us to get a wrong result and convince ourselves that it was actually correct; **confirmation bias** of this kind is very common in software development.

11.4 How can we wrap elements to fit?

One of the biggest differences between a browser and a printed page is that the text in the browser wraps itself automatically as the window is resized. (The other, these days, is that the printed page doesn't spy on us, though someone is undoubtedly working on that.)

To add wrapping to our layout engine, suppose we fix the width of a row. If the total width of the children is greater than the row's width, the layout engine needs to wrap the children around. This assumes that columns can be made as big as they need to be, i.e., that we can grow vertically to make up for limited space horizontally. It also assumes that all of the row's children are no wider than the width of the row; we will look at what happens when they're not in the exercises.

Our layout engine manages wrapping by transforming the tree. The height and width of blocks are fixed, so they become themselves. Columns become themselves as well, but since they have children that might need to wrap, the class representing columns needs a new method:

```
export class WrappedBlock extends PlacedBlock {
  wrap () {
    return this
  }
}

export class WrappedCol extends PlacedCol {
  wrap () {
    const children = this.children.map(child => child.wrap())
    return new PlacedCol(...children)
  }
}
```

Rows do all the hard work. Each original row is replaced with a new row that contains a single column with one or more rows, each of which is one "line" of wrapped cells (Figure 11.5). This replacement is unnecessary when everything will fit on a single row, but it's easiest to write the code that does it every time; we will look at making this more efficient in the exercises.

Our new wrappable row's constructor takes a fixed width followed by the children and returns that fixed width when asked for its size:

```
export class WrappedRow extends PlacedRow {
  constructor (width, ...children) {
    super(...children)
    assert(width >= 0,
      'Need non-negative width')
    this.width = width
  }

  getWidth () {
```

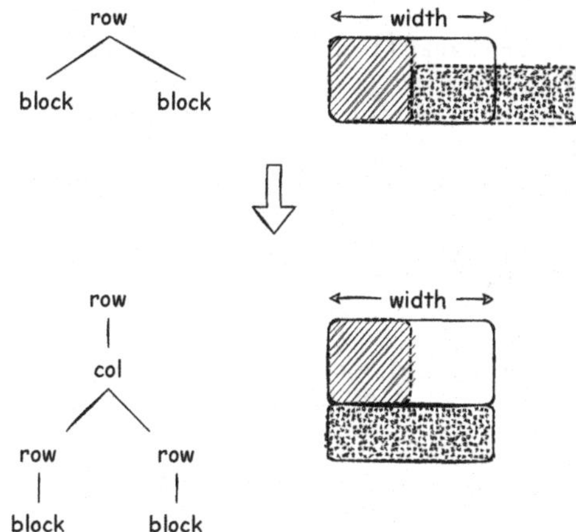

Figure 11.5: Wrapping rows by introducing a new row and column.

```
    return this.width
  }
}
```

Wrapping puts the row's children into buckets, then converts the buckets to a row of a column of rows:

```
  wrap () {
    const children = this.children.map(child => child.wrap())
    const rows = []
    let currentRow = []
    let currentX = 0

    children.forEach(child => {
      const childWidth = child.getWidth()
      if ((currentX + childWidth) <= this.width) {
        currentRow.push(child)
        currentX += childWidth
      } else {
        rows.push(currentRow)
        currentRow = [child]
        currentX = childWidth
      }
    })
    rows.push(currentRow)

    const newRows = rows.map(row => new PlacedRow(...row))
    const newCol = new PlacedCol(...newRows)
    return new PlacedRow(newCol)
  }
```

Once again we bring forward all the previous tests and write some new ones to test the functionality we've added:

```
  it('wrap a row of two blocks that do not fit on one row', async () => {
    const fixture = new Row(
      3,
      new Block(2, 1),
      new Block(2, 1)
```

```
  )
  const wrapped = fixture.wrap()
  wrapped.place(0, 0)
  assert.deepStrictEqual(
    wrapped.report(),
    ['row', 0, 0, 2, 2,
      ['col', 0, 0, 2, 2,
        ['row', 0, 0, 2, 1,
          ['block', 0, 0, 2, 1]
        ],
        ['row', 0, 1, 2, 2,
          ['block', 0, 1, 2, 2]
        ]
      ]
    ]
  )
})
```

```
> stjs@1.0.0 test /u/stjs
> mocha */test/test-*.js "-g" "wraps blocks"



  wraps blocks
    ✓ wraps a single unit block
    ✓ wraps a large block
    ✓ wrap a row of two blocks that fit on one row
    ✓ wraps a column of two blocks
    ✓ wraps a grid of rows of columns that all fit on their row
    ✓ wrap a row of two blocks that do not fit on one row
    ✓ wrap multiple blocks that do not fit on one row


  7 passing (10ms)
```

The Liskov Substitution Principle

We are able to re-use tests like this because of the **Liskov Substitution Principle**, which states that it should be possible to replace objects in a program with objects of derived classes without breaking anything. In order to satisfy this principle, new code must handle the same set of inputs as the old code, though it may be able to process more inputs as well. Conversely, its output must be a subset of what the old code produced so that whatever is downstream from it won't be surprised. Thinking in these terms leads to a methodology called **design by contract**.

11.5 What subset of CSS will we support?

It's finally time to style pages that contain text. Our final subset of HTML has rows, columns, and text blocks as before. Each text block has one or more lines of text; the number of lines determines the block's height and the length of the longest line determines its width.

Rows and columns can have **attributes** just as they can in real HTML, and each attribute must have a single value in quotes. Rows no longer take a fixed width: instead, we will specify that with our little subset of CSS. Together, these three classes are just over 40 lines of code:

```
export class DomBlock extends WrappedBlock {
  constructor (lines) {
    super(
      Math.max(...lines.split('\n').map(line => line.length)),
      lines.length
    )
    this.lines = lines
    this.tag = 'text'
    this.rules = null
  }

  findRules (css) {
    this.rules = css.findRules(this)
  }
}

export class DomCol extends WrappedCol {
  constructor (attributes, ...children) {
    super(...children)
    this.attributes = attributes
    this.tag = 'col'
    this.rules = null
  }

  findRules (css) {
    this.rules = css.findRules(this)
    this.children.forEach(child => child.findRules(css))
  }
}

export class DomRow extends WrappedRow {
  constructor (attributes, ...children) {
    super(0, ...children)
    this.attributes = attributes
    this.tag = 'row'
    this.rules = null
  }

  findRules (css) {
    this.rules = css.findRules(this)
    this.children.forEach(child => child.findRules(css))
  }
}
```

We will use regular expressions to parse HTML (though as we explained in Chapter 8, this is a sin[7]). The main body of our parser is:

```
import assert from 'assert'

import {
  DomBlock,
  DomCol,
  DomRow
```

[7]https://stackoverflow.com/questions/1732348/regex-match-open-tags-except-xhtml-self-contained-tags/1732454#1732454

```
} from './micro-dom.js'

const TEXT_AND_TAG = /^([^<]*)(<[^]+?>)(.*)$/ms
const TAG_AND_ATTR = /<(\w+)([^>]*)>/
const KEY_AND_VALUE = /\s*(\w+)="([^"]*)"\s*/g

const parseHTML = (text) => {
  const chunks = chunkify(text.trim())
  assert(isElement(chunks[0]),
    'Must have enclosing outer node')
  const [node, remainder] = makeNode(chunks)
  assert(remainder.length === 0,
    'Cannot have dangling content')
  return node
}

const chunkify = (text) => {
  const raw = []
  while (text) {
    const matches = text.match(TEXT_AND_TAG)
    if (!matches) {
      break
    }
    raw.push(matches[1])
    raw.push(matches[2])
    text = matches[3]
  }
  if (text) {
    raw.push(text)
  }
  const nonEmpty = raw.filter(chunk => (chunk.length > 0))
  return nonEmpty
}

const isElement = (chunk) => {
  return chunk && (chunk[0] === '<')
}


export default parseHTML
```

while the two functions that do most of the work are:

```
const makeNode = (chunks) => {
  assert(chunks.length > 0,
    'Cannot make nodes without chunks')

  if (!isElement(chunks[0])) {
    return [new DomBlock(chunks[0]), chunks.slice(1)]
  }

  const node = makeOpening(chunks[0])
  const closing = `</${node.tag}>`

  let remainder = chunks.slice(1)
  let child = null
  while (remainder && (remainder[0] !== closing)) {
    [child, remainder] = makeNode(remainder)
    node.children.push(child)
  }
```

```
  assert(remainder && (remainder[0] === closing),
    `Node with tag ${node.tag} not closed`)
  return [node, remainder.slice(1)]
}
```

and:

```
const makeOpening = (chunk) => {
  const outer = chunk.match(TAG_AND_ATTR)
  const tag = outer[1]
  const attributes = [...outer[2].trim().matchAll(KEY_AND_VALUE)]
    .reduce((obj, [all, key, value]) => {
      obj[key] = value
      return obj
    }, {})
  let Cls = null
  if (tag === 'col') {
    Cls = DomCol
  } else if (tag === 'row') {
    Cls = DomRow
  }
  assert(Cls !== null,
    `Unrecognized tag name ${tag}`)
  return new Cls(attributes)
}
```

The next step is to define a generic class for CSS rules with a subclass for each type of rule. From highest precedence to lowest, the three types of rules we support identify specific nodes via their ID, classes of nodes via their `class` attribute, and types of nodes via their element name. We keep track of which rules take precedence over which through the simple expedient of numbering the classes:

```
export class CssRule {
  constructor (order, selector, styles) {
    this.order = order
    this.selector = selector
    this.styles = styles
  }
}
```

An ID rule's **query selector** is written as `#name` and matches HTML like `<tag id="name">...</tag>` (where `tag` is `row` or `col`):

```
export class IdRule extends CssRule {
  constructor (selector, styles) {
    assert(selector.startsWith('#') && (selector.length > 1),
      `ID rule ${selector} must start with # and have a selector`)
    super(IdRule.ORDER, selector.slice(1), styles)
  }

  match (node) {
    return ('attributes' in node) &&
      ('id' in node.attributes) &&
      (node.attributes.id === this.selector)
  }
}
IdRule.ORDER = 0
```

A class rule's query selector is written as `.kind` and matches HTML like `<tag class="kind">...</tag>`. Unlike real CSS, we only allow one class per node:

```
export class ClassRule extends CssRule {
  constructor (selector, styles) {
    assert(selector.startsWith('.') && (selector.length > 1),
      `Class rule ${selector} must start with . and have a selector`)
    super(ClassRule.ORDER, selector.slice(1), styles)
  }

  match (node) {
    return ('attributes' in node) &&
      ('class' in node.attributes) &&
      (node.attributes.class === this.selector)
  }
}
ClassRule.ORDER = 1
```

Finally, tag rules just have the name of the type of node they apply to without any punctuation:

```
export class TagRule extends CssRule {
  constructor (selector, styles) {
    super(TagRule.ORDER, selector, styles)
  }

  match (node) {
    return this.selector === node.tag
  }
}
TagRule.ORDER = 2
```

We could build yet another parser to read a subset of CSS and convert it to objects, but this chapter is long enough, so we will write our rules as JSON:

```
{
  'row': { width: 20 },
  '.kind': { width: 5 },
  '#name': { height: 10 }
}
```

and build a class that converts this representation to a set of objects:

```
export class CssRuleSet {
  constructor (json, mergeDefaults = true) {
    this.rules = this.jsonToRules(json)
  }

  jsonToRules (json) {
    return Object.keys(json).map(selector => {
      assert((typeof selector === 'string') && (selector.length > 0),
        'Require non-empty string as selector')
      if (selector.startsWith('#')) {
        return new IdRule(selector, json[selector])
      }
      if (selector.startsWith('.')) {
        return new ClassRule(selector, json[selector])
      }
      return new TagRule(selector, json[selector])
    })
  }

  findRules (node) {
    const matches = this.rules.filter(rule => rule.match(node))
```

```
    const sorted = matches.sort((left, right) => left.order - right.order)
    return sorted
  }
}
```

Our CSS ruleset class also has a method for finding the rules for a given DOM node. This method relies on the precedence values we defined for our classes in order to sort them so that we can find the most specific.

Here's our final set of tests:

```
it('styles a tree of nodes with multiple rules', async () => {
  const html = [
    '<col id="name">',
    '<row class="kind">first\nsecond</row>',
    '<row>third\nfourth</row>',
    '</col>'
  ]
  const dom = parseHTML(html.join(''))
  const rules = new CssRuleSet({
    '.kind': { height: 3 },
    '#name': { height: 5 },
    row: { width: 10 }
  })
  dom.findRules(rules)
  assert.deepStrictEqual(dom.rules, [
    new IdRule('#name', { height: 5 })
  ])
  assert.deepStrictEqual(dom.children[0].rules, [
    new ClassRule('.kind', { height: 3 }),
    new TagRule('row', { width: 10 })
  ])
  assert.deepStrictEqual(dom.children[1].rules, [
    new TagRule('row', { width: 10 })
  ])
})
```

If we were going on, we would override the cells' **getWidth** and **getHeight** methods to pay attention to styles. We would also decide what to do with cells that don't have any styles defined: use a default, flag it as an error, or make a choice based on the contents of the child nodes. We will explore these possibilities in the exercises.

Where it all started

This chapter's topic was one of the seeds from which this entire book grew (the other being debuggers discussed in Chapter 20). After struggling with CSS for several years, I began wondering whether it really had to be so complicated. That question led to others, which eventually led to all of this. The moral is, be careful what you ask.

11.6 Exercises

Refactoring the node classes

Refactor the classes used to represent blocks, rows, and columns so that:

1. They all derive from a common parent.
2. All common behavior is defined in that parent (if only with placeholder methods).

Handling rule conflicts

Modify the rule lookup mechanism so that if two conflicting rules are defined, the one that is defined second takes precedence. For example, if there are two definitions for `row.bold`, whichever comes last in the JSON representation of the CSS wins.

Handling arbitrary tags

Modify the existing code to handle arbitrary HTML elements.

1. The parser should recognize `<anyTag>...</anyTag>`.
2. Instead of separate classes for rows and columns, there should be one class `Node` whose `tag` attribute identifies its type.

Recycling nodes

Modify the wrapping code so that new rows and columns are only created if needed. For example, if a row of width 10 contains a text node with the string "fits", a new row and column are *not* inserted.

Rendering a clear background

Modify the rendering code so that only the text in block nodes is shown, i.e., so that the empty space in rows and columns is rendered as spaces.

Clipping text

1. Modify the wrapping and rendering so that if a block of text is too wide for the available space the extra characters are clipped. For example, if a column of width 5 contains a line "unfittable", only "unfit" appears.
2. Extend your solution to break lines on spaces as needed in order to avoid clipping.

Bidirectional rendering

Modify the existing software to do either left-to-right or right-to-left rendering upon request.

Equal sizing

Modify the existing code to support elastic columns, i.e., so that all of the columns in a row are automatically sized to have the same width. If the number of columns does not divide evenly into the width of the row, allocate the extra space as equally as possible from left to right.

Padding elements

Modify the existing code so that:

1. Authors can define a padding attribute for row and column elements.
2. When the node is rendered, that many blank spaces are added on all four sides of the contents.

For example, the HTML <row>text</row> would render as:

```
+------+
|      |
| text |
|      |
+------+
```

where the lines show the outer border of the rendering.

Drawing borders

1. Modify the existing code so that elements may specify `border: true` or `border: false` (with the latter being the default). If an element's `border` property is `true`, it is drawn with a dashed border. For example, if the `border` property of `row` is `true`, then `<row>text</row>` is rendered as:

   ```
   +----+
   |text|
   +----+
   ```

2. Extend your solution so that if two adjacent cells both have borders, only a single border is drawn. For example, if the `border` property of `col` is `true`, then:

   ```
   <row><col>left</col><col>right</col></row>
   ```

   is rendered as:

   ```
   +----+-----+
   |left|right|
   +----+-----+
   ```

12

File Interpolator

Terms defined: **header file**, **literate programming**, **loader**, **sandbox**, **search path**, **shell variable**

Many of the examples in these lessons are too long to show comfortably in one block of code on a printed page, so we needed a way to break them up. As an experiment, we wrote a custom **module loader** that reads a source file containing specially-formatted comments and then reads and inserts the files specified in those comments before running the code (Figure 12.1). Modern programming languages don't work this way, but C and C++ do this with **header files**, and static site generators (Chapter 9) do this to share fragments of HTML.

The special comments in our source files contain the text to put in the displayed version and file to include when loading:

```
class Something {
  /*+ constructor + constructor.js +*/

  /*+ a long method + long_method.js +*/

  /*+ another method + another_method.js +*/
}
```

We got this to work, but decided to use a different approach in this book. The stumbling block was that the style-checking tool ESLint[1] didn't know what to make of our inclusions, so we would either have to modify it or build a style checker of our own. (We will actually do that in Chapter 14, but we won't go nearly as far as ESLint.)

Despite being a dead end, the inclusion tool is a good way to show how JavaScript turns source code into something it can execute. We need to be able to do this in the next couple of chapters, so we might as well tackle it now.

12.1 How can we evaluate JavaScript dynamically?

We want to display files as they are on the web and in print, but interpolate the files referenced in special comments when we load things with `import`. To do this, we need to understand the lifecycle of a JavaScript program. When we ask for a file, Node[2] reads the text, translates it into runnable instructions, and runs those instructions. We can do the second and third steps whenever we want using a function called `eval`, which takes a string as input and executes it as if it were part of the program (Figure 12.2).

[1] https://eslint.org/
[2] https://nodejs.org/en/

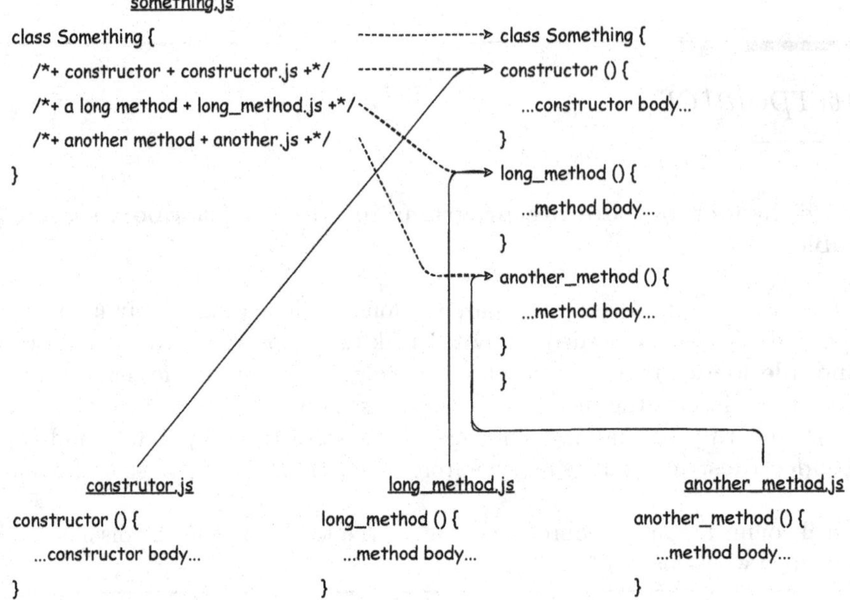

Figure 12.1: Including fragments of code to create runnable programs.

> **This is not a good idea**
>
> `eval` is a security risk: arbitrary code can do arbitrary things, so if we take a string typed in by a user and execute it without any checks it could email our bookmark list to villains all over the world, erase our hard drive, or do anything else that code can do (which is pretty much anything). Browsers do their best to run code in a **sandbox** for safety, but Node doesn't, so it's up to us to be (very) careful.

To see `eval` in action, let's evaluate an expression:

```
console.log(eval('2 + 2'))
```

```
4
```

Notice that the input to `eval` is *not* `2 + 2`, but rather a string containing the digit 2, a space, a plus sign, another space, and another 2. When we call `eval`, it translates this string using exactly the same parser that Node uses for our program and immediately runs the result.

We can make the example a little more interesting by constructing the string dynamically:

```
const x = 1
const y = 3
const z = 5
for (const name of ['x', 'y', 'z', 'oops']) {
  const expr = `${name} + 1`
  console.log(name, '+ 1 =', eval(expr))
}
```

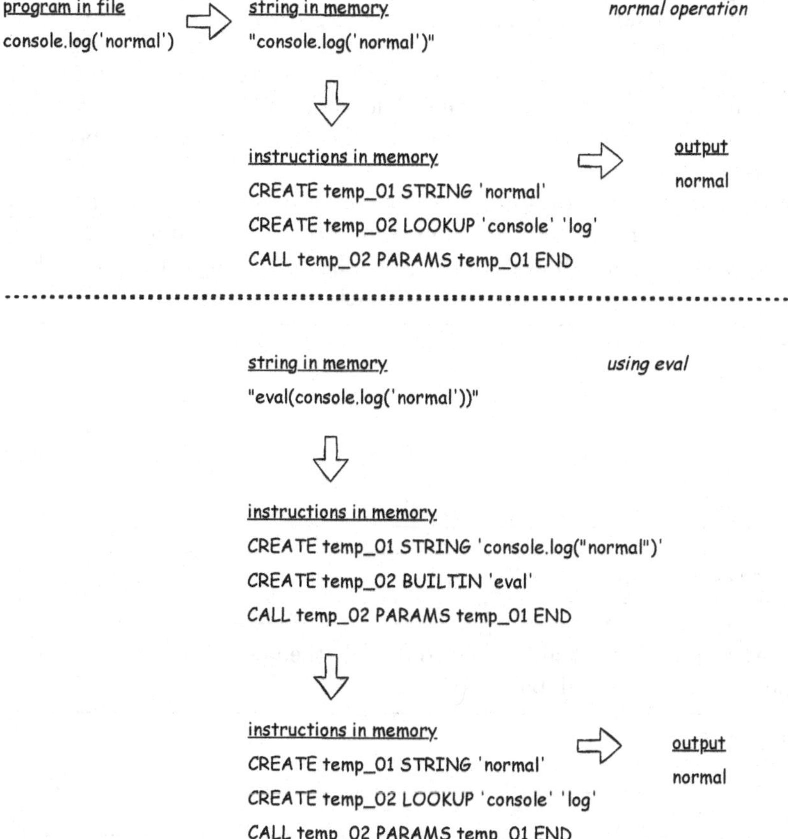

Figure 12.2: `eval` vs. normal translation and execution.

```
x + 1 = 2
y + 1 = 4
z + 1 = 6
undefined:1
oops + 1
^

ReferenceError: oops is not defined
    at eval (eval at <anonymous> \
    (/u/stjs/file-interpolator/eval-loop.js:7:30), <anonymous>:1:1)
    at /u/stjs/file-interpolator/eval-loop.js:7:30
    at ModuleJob.run (internal/modules/esm/module_job.js:152:23)
    at async Loader.import (internal/modules/esm/loader.js:166:24)
    at async Object.loadESM (internal/process/esm_loader.js:68:5)
```

The first time the loop runs the string is `'x + 1'`; since there's a variable called `x` in scope, `eval` does the addition and we print the result. The same thing happens for the variables `y` and `z`, but we get an error when we try to evaluate the string `'oops + 1'` because there is no variable in scope called `oops`.

`eval` can use whatever variables are in scope when it's called, but what happens to any variables it defines? This example creates a variable called `x` and runs `console.log` to display it, but as the output shows, `x` is local to the `eval` call just as variables created inside a function only exist during a call to that function:

```
const code = `
  const x = 'hello'
  console.log('x in eval is', x)
`

eval(code)
console.log('typeof x after eval', typeof x)
```

```
x in eval is hello
typeof x after eval undefined
```

However, `eval` can modify variables defined outside the text being evaluated in the same way that a function can modify global variables:

```
let x = 'original'
eval('x = "modified"')
console.log('x after eval is', x)
```

```
x after eval is modified
```

This means that if the text we give to `eval` modifies a structure that is defined outside the text, that change outlives the call to `eval`:

```
const seen = {}

for (const name of ['x', 'y', 'z']) {
  const expr = `seen["${name}"] = "${name.toUpperCase()}"`
  eval(expr)
}

console.log(seen)
```

```
{ x: 'X', y: 'Y', z: 'Z' }
```

The examples so far have all evaluated strings embedded in the program itself, but `eval` doesn't care where its input comes from. Let's move the code that does the modifying into `to-be-loaded.js`:

```
// Modify a global structure defined by whoever loads us.
Seen.from_loaded_file = 'from loaded file'
```

This doesn't work on its own because `Seen` isn't defined:

```
/u/stjs/file-interpolator/to-be-loaded.js:3
Seen.from_loaded_file = 'from loaded file'
^

ReferenceError: Seen is not defined
    at /u/stjs/file-interpolator/to-be-loaded.js:3:1
    at ModuleJob.run (internal/modules/esm/module_job.js:152:23)
    at async Loader.import (internal/modules/esm/loader.js:166:24)
    at async Object.loadESM (internal/process/esm_loader.js:68:5)
```

But if we read the file and `eval` the text *after* defining `Seen`, it does what we want:

```
import fs from 'fs'

const Seen = {}

const filename = process.argv[2]
const content = fs.readFileSync(filename, 'utf-8')
console.log('before eval, Seen is', Seen)
eval(content)
console.log('after eval, Seen is', Seen)
```

```
node does-the-loading.js to-be-loaded.js
```

```
before eval, Seen is {}
after eval, Seen is { from_loaded_file: 'from loaded file' }
```

12.2 How can we manage files?

The source files in this book are small enough that we don't have to worry about reading them repeatedly, but we would like to avoid re-reading things unnecessarily in large systems or when there might be network delays. The usual approach is to create a cache using the Singleton pattern that we first met in Chapter 4. Whenever we want to read a file, we check to see if it's already in the cache (Figure 12.3). If it is, we use that copy; if not, we read it and add it to the cache using the file path as a lookup key.

We can write a simple cache in just a few lines of code:

```
import fs from 'fs'

class Cache {
  constructor () {
    this.loaded = new Map()
  }

  need (name) {
```

```
    if (this.loaded.has(name)) {
      console.log(`returning cached value for ${name}`)
      return this.loaded.get(name)
    }
    console.log(`loading ${name}`)
    const content = fs.readFileSync(name, 'utf-8')
    const result = eval(content)
    this.loaded.set(name, result)
    return result
  }
}

const cache = new Cache()

export default (name) => {
  return cache.need(name)
}
```

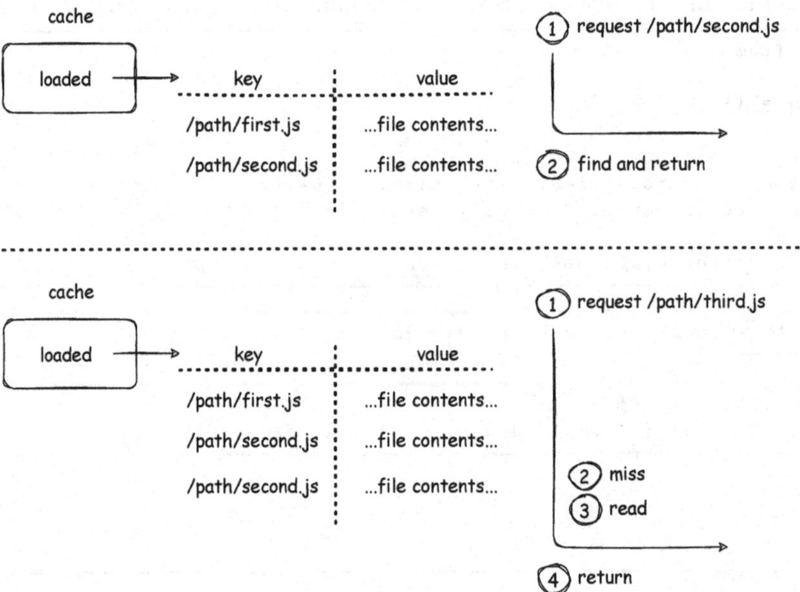

Figure 12.3: Using the Singleton pattern to implement a cache of loaded files.

Since we are using `eval`, though, we can't rely on `export` to make things available to the rest of the program. Instead, we rely on the fact that the result of an `eval` call is the value of the last expression evaluated. Since a variable name on its own evaluates to the variable's value, we can create a function and then use its name to "export" it from the evaluated file:

```
// Define.
const report = (message) => {
  console.log(`report in import-01.js with message "${message}"`)
}

// Export.
report
```

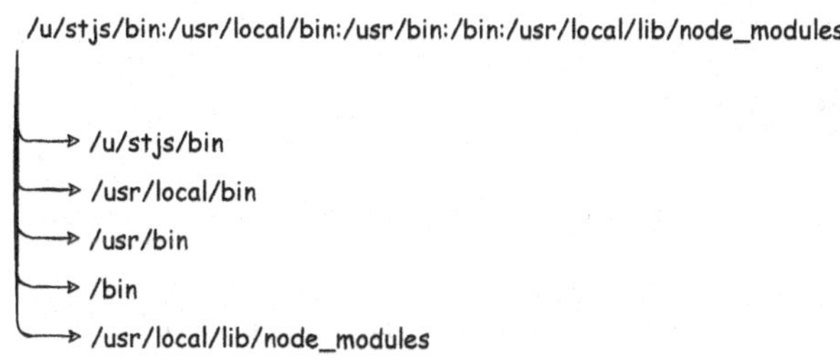

Figure 12.4: Using a colon-separated list of directories as a search path.

To test our program, we load the implementation of the cache using `import`, then use it to load and evaluate another file. This example expects that "other file" to define a function, which we call in order to show that everything is working:

```
import need from './need-simple.js'

const imported = need('./import-simple.js')
imported('called from test-simple.js')
```

```
node test-simple.js
```

12.3 How can we find files?

Each of the files included in our examples is in the same directory as the file including it, but in C/C++ or a page templating system we might include a particular file in several different places. We don't want to have to put all of our files in a single directory, so we need a way to specify where to look for files that are being included.

One option is to use relative paths, but another option is to give our program a list of directories to look in. This is called a **search path**, and many programs use them, including Node itself. By convention, a search path is written as a colon-separated list of directories on Unix or using semi-colons on Windows. If the path to an included file starts with `./`, we look for it locally; if not, we go through the directories in the search path in order until we find a file with a matching name (Figure 12.4).

> **That's just how it is**
>
> The rules about search paths in the paragraph above are a convention: somebody did it this way years ago and (almost) everyone has imitated it since. We could implement search paths some other way, but as with configuration file formats, variable naming conventions, and many other things, the last thing the world needs is more innovation.

Since the cache is responsible for finding files, it should also handle the search path. The outline of the class stays the same:

```
import fs from 'fs'
import path from 'path'
```

```
class Cache {
  constructor () {
    this.loaded = new Map()
    this.constructSearchPath()
  }

  need (fileSpec) {
    if (this.loaded.has(fileSpec)) {
      console.log(`returning cached value for ${fileSpec}`)
      return this.loaded.get(fileSpec)
    }
    console.log(`loading value for ${fileSpec}`)
    const filePath = this.find(fileSpec)
    const content = fs.readFileSync(filePath, 'utf-8')
    const result = eval(content)
    this.loaded.set(fileSpec, result)
    return result
  }

}

const cache = new Cache()

export default (fileSpec) => {
  return cache.need(fileSpec)
}
```

To get the search path, we look for the **shell variable** `NEED_PATH`. (Writing shell variables' names in upper case is another convention.) If `NEED_PATH` exists, we split it on colons to create a list of directories:

```
  constructSearchPath () {
    this.searchPath = []
    if ('NEED_PATH' in process.env) {
      this.searchPath = process.env.NEED_PATH
        .split(':')
        .filter(x => x.length > 0)
    }
  }
```

When we need to find a file we first check to see if the path is local. If it's not, we try the directories in the search path in order:

```
  constructSearchPath () {
    this.searchPath = []
    if ('NEED_PATH' in process.env) {
      this.searchPath = process.env.NEED_PATH
        .split(':')
        .filter(x => x.length > 0)
    }
  }
```

To test this, we put the file to import in a subdirectory called `modules`:

```
// Define.
const report = (message) => {
  console.log(`in LEFT with message "${message}"`)
}

// Export.
report
```

and then put the file doing the importing in the current directory:

```
import need from './need-path.js'
const imported = need('imported-left.js')
imported('called from test-import-left.js')
```

We now need to set the variable NEED_PATH. There are many ways to do this in shell; if we only need the variable to exist for a single command, the simplest is to write it as:

```
NAME=value command
```

right before the command (on the same line). Here's the shell command that runs our test case using $PWD to get the current working directory:

```
NEED_PATH=$PWD/modules/ node test-import-left.js
```

```
loading value for imported-left.js
trying /u/stjs/file-interpolator/modules/imported-left.js for \
imported-left.js
in LEFT with message "called from test-import-left.js"
```

Now let's create a second importable file in the modules directory:

```
// Define.
const report = (message) => {
  console.log(`in RIGHT with message "${message}"`)
}

// Export.
report
```

and load that twice to check that caching works:

```
import need from './need-path.js'

const imported = need('imported-right.js')
imported('called from test-import-right.js')

const alsoImported = need('imported-right.js')
alsoImported('called from test-import-right.js')
```

```
loading value for imported-right.js
trying /u/stjs/file-interpolator/modules/imported-right.js for \
imported-right.js
in RIGHT with message "called from test-import-right.js"
returning cached value for imported-right.js
in RIGHT with message "called from test-import-right.js"
```

12.4 How can we interpolate pieces of code?

Interpolating files is straightforward once we have this machinery in place. We modify Cache.find to return a directory and a file path, then add an interpolate method to replace special comments:

```
class Cache {
  // ...
  interpolate (fileDir, outer) {
    return outer.replace(Cache.INTERPOLATE_PAT,
                         (match, comment, filename) => {
      filename = filename.trim()
      const filePath = path.join(fileDir, filename)
      if (!fs.existsSync(filePath)) {
        throw new Error(`Cannot find ${filePath}`)
      }
      const inner = fs.readFileSync(filePath, 'utf-8')
      return inner
    })
  }
  // ...
}
Cache.INTERPOLATE_PAT = /\/\*\+(.+?)\+(.+?)\+\*\//g
```

We can now have a file like this:

```
class Example {
  constructor (msg) {
    this.constructorMessage = msg
  }
  /*+ top method + import-interpolate-topmethod.js +*/
  /*+ bottom method + import-interpolate-bottommethod.js +*/
}

Example
```

and subfiles like this:

```
topMethod (msg) {
  this.bottomMethod(`(topMethod ${msg})`)
}
```

and this:

```
bottomMethod (msg) {
  console.log(`(bottomMethod ${msg})`)
}
```

Let's test it:

```
node test-import-interpolate.js
```

```
(bottomMethod (topMethod called from test-import-interpolate.js))
```

When this program runs, its lifecycle is:

1. Node starts to run `test-import-interpolate.js`.
2. It sees the `import` of `need-interpolate` so it reads and evaluates that code.
3. Doing this creates a singleton cache object.
4. The program then calls `need('./import-interpolate.js')`.
5. This checks the cache: nope, nothing there.
6. So it loads `import-interpolate.js`.

7. It finds two specially-formatted comments in the text...
8. ...so it loads the file described by each one and inserts the text in place of the comment.
9. Now that it has the complete text, it calls `eval`...
10. ...and stores the result of `eval` (which is a class) in the cache.
11. It also returns that class.
12. We then create an instance of that class and call its method.

This works, but as we said in the introduction we decided not to use it because it didn't play well with other tools. No piece of software exists in isolation; when we evaluate a design, we always have to ask how it fits into everything else we have.

12.5 What did we do instead?

Rather than interpolating file fragments, we extract or erase parts of regular JavaScript files based on specially formatted comments like the `<fragment>...</fragment>` pair shown below.

```
class Example {
  constructor (name) {
    this.name = name
  }

  // <fragment>
  fragment (message) {
    console.log(`${name}: ${message}`)
  }
  // </fragment>
}
```

The code that selects the part of the file we want to display is part of our page templating system. It re-extracts code for display every time the web version of this site is built, which ensures that we always shows what's in the current version of our examples. However, this system doesn't automatically update the description of the code: if we write, "It does X," then modify the code to do Y, our lesson can be inconsistent. **Literate programming** was invented to try to prevent this from happening, but it never really caught on—unfortunately, most programming systems that describe themselves as "literate" these days only implement part of Donald Knuth's[3] original vision.

12.6 Exercises

Security concerns

1. Write a function `loadAndRun` that reads a file, evaluates it, and returns the result.

[3] https://www-cs-faculty.stanford.edu/ knuth/

2. Create a file `trust-me.js` that prints "nothing happening here" when it is evaluated, but also deletes everything in the directory called `target`.
3. Write tests for this using `mock-fs`[4].

Please be careful doing this exercise.

Loading functions

Write a function that reads a file containing single-argument functions like this:

```
addOne: (x) => x + 1
halve: (x) => x / 2
array: (x) => Array(x).fill(0)
```

and returns an object containing callable functions.

Registering functions

Write a function that loads one or more files containing function definitions like this:

```
const double = (x) => {
  return 2 * x
}

EXPORTS.append(double)
```

and returns a list containing all the loaded functions.

Indenting inclusions

Modify the file inclusion system so that inclusions are indented by the same amount as the including comment. For example, if the including file is:

```
const withLogging = (args) => {
  /*+ logging call + logging.js +*/
}

withLogging
```

and the included file is:

```
console.log('first message')
console.log('second message')
```

then the result will be:

```
const withLogging = (args) => {
  console.log('first message')
  console.log('second message')
}

withLogging
```

i.e., all lines of the inclusion will be indented to match the first.

[4]https://www.npmjs.com/package/mock-fs

Interpolating from subdirectories

Modify the file interpolator so that snippets can be included from sub-directories using relative paths.

Recursive search for inclusions

1. Modify the file interpolator so that it searches recursively through all subdirectories of the directories on the search path to find inclusions.
2. Explain why this is a bad idea.

Defining variables

Modify the file inclusion system so that users can pass in a `Map` containing name-value pairs and have these interpolated into the text of the files being loaded. To interpolate a value, the included file must use `@@name@@`.

Specifying markers

Modify the file inclusion system so that the user can override the inclusion comment markers. For example, the user should be able to specify that `/*!` and `!*/` be used to mark inclusions. (This is often used in tutorials that need to show the inclusion markers without them being interpreted.)

Recursive inclusions

Modify the file interpolator to support recursive includes, i.e., to handle inclusion markers in files that are being included. Be sure to check for the case of infinite includes.

Slicing files

Write a function that reads a JavaScript source file containing specially-formatted comments like the ones shown below and extracts the indicated section.

```
const toBeLeftOut = (args) => {
  console.log('this should not appear')
}

// <keepThis>
const toBeKept = (args) => {
  console.log('only this function should appear')
}
// </keepThis>
```

Users should be able to specify any tag they want, and if that tag occurs multiple times, all of the sections marked with that tag should be kept. (This is the approach we took for this book instead of file interpolation.)

13

Module Loader

Terms defined: **absolute path**, **alias**, **circular dependency**, **closure**, **directed graph**, **encapsulate**, **immediately-invoked function expression**, **inner function**, **Least Recently Used cache**, **namespace**, **plugin architecture**

Chapter 12 showed how to use `eval` to load code dynamically. We can use this to build our own version of JavaScript's `require` function. Our function will take the name of a source file as an argument and return whatever that file exports. The key requirement for such a function is to avoid accidentally overwriting things: if we just `eval` some code and it happens to assign to a variable called `x`, anything called `x` already in our program might be overwritten. We therefore need a way to **encapsulate** the contents of what we're loading. Our approach is based on [Casciaro2020], which contains a lot of other useful information as well.

13.1 How can we implement namespaces?

A **namespace** is a collection of names in a program that are isolated from other namespaces. Most modern languages provide namespaces as a built-in feature so that programmers don't accidentally step on each other's toes. JavaScript doesn't, so we have to implement them ourselves.

We can do this using **closures**. Every function is a namespace: variables defined inside the function are distinct from variables defined outside it (Figure 13.1). If we create the variables we want to manage inside a function, then define another function inside the first and return that **inner function**, that inner function will be the only thing with references to those variables.

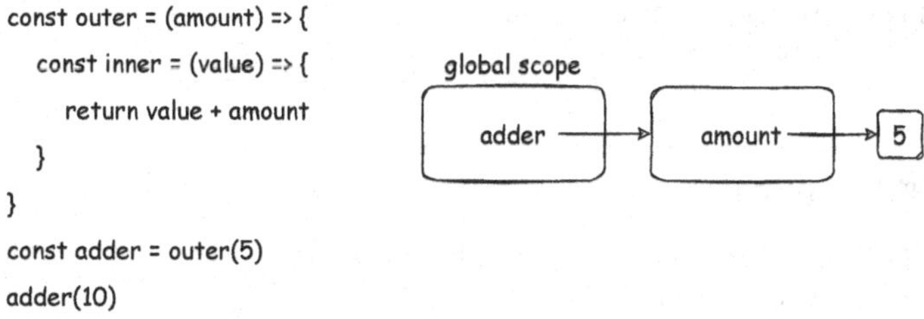

Figure 13.1: Using closures to create private variables.

For example, let's create a function that always appends the same string to its argument:

```
const createAppender = (suffix) => {
  const appender = (text) => {
    return text + suffix
  }
  return appender
```

```
}

const exampleFunction = createAppender(' and that')
console.log(exampleFunction('this'))
console.log('suffix is', suffix)
```

When we run it, the value that was assigned to the parameter `suffix` still exists but can only be reached by the inner function:

```
this and that
/u/stjs/module-loader/manual-namespacing.js:10
console.log('suffix is', suffix)
                         ^

ReferenceError: suffix is not defined
    at /u/stjs/module-loader/manual-namespacing.js:10:26
    at ModuleJob.run (internal/modules/esm/module_job.js:152:23)
    at async Loader.import (internal/modules/esm/loader.js:166:24)
    at async Object.loadESM (internal/process/esm_loader.js:68:5)
```

We could require every module to define a setup function like this for users to call, but thanks to `eval` we can wrap the file's contents in a function and call it automatically. To do this we will create something called an **immediately-invoked function expression** (IIFE). The syntax `() => {...}` defines a function. If we put the definition in parentheses and then put another pair of parentheses right after it:

```
(() => {...})()
```

we have code that defines a function of no arguments and immediately calls it. We can use this trick to achieve the same effect as the previous example in one step:

```
const contents = (() => {
  const privateValue = 'private value'
  const publicValue = 'public value'
  return { publicValue }
})()

console.log(`contents.publicValue is ${contents.publicValue}`)
console.log(`contents.privateValue is ${contents.privateValue}`)
```

```
contents.publicValue is public value
contents.privateValue is undefined
```

Unconfusing the parser

The extra parentheses around the original definition force the parser to evaluate things in the right order; if we write:

```
() => {...}()
```

then JavaScript interprets it as a function definition followed by an empty expression rather than an immediate call to the function just defined.

loader.js

```
1 const loadModule = (filename) => {
2   const source = ...read file...
3   const result = {}
4   const fullText = `...`
5   eval(fullText)
    return result.exports
  }
```

source.js

```
module.exports = 'hello'
```

Figure 13.2: Using IIFEs to encapsulate modules and get their exports (part 1).

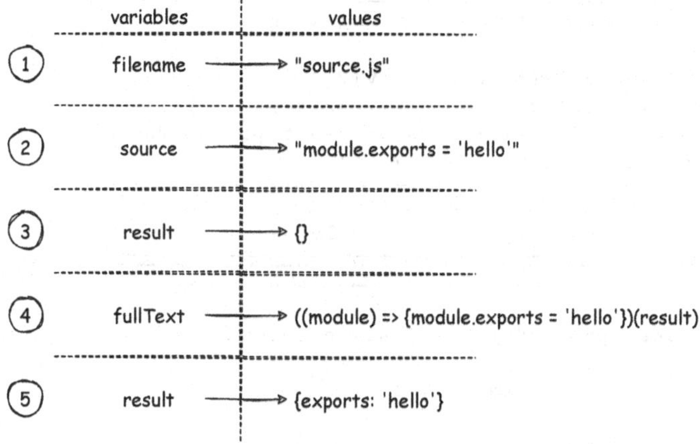

Figure 13.3: Using IIFEs to encapsulate modules and get their exports (part 2).

13.2 How can we load a module?

We want the module we are loading to export names by assigning to `module.exports` just as `require` does, so we need to provide an object called `module` and create a IIFE. (We will handle the problem of the module loading other modules later.) Our `loadModule` function takes a filename and returns a newly created module object; the parameter to the function we build and `eval` must be called `module` so that we can assign to `module.exports`. For clarity, we call the object we pass in `result` in `loadModule`.

```
import fs from 'fs'

const loadModule = (filename) => {
  const source = fs.readFileSync(filename, 'utf-8')
  const result = {}
  const fullText = `((module) => {${source}})(result)`
  console.log(`full text for eval:\n${fullText}\n`)
  eval(fullText)
  return result.exports
}

export default loadModule
```

Figure 13.2 and Figure 13.3 show the structure of our loader so far. We can use this code as a test:

```
const publicValue = 'public value'

const privateValue = 'private value'

const publicFunction = (caller) => {
  return `publicFunction called from ${caller}`
}

module.exports = { publicValue, publicFunction }
```

and this short program to load the test and check its exports:

```
import loadModule from './load-module-only.js'

const result = loadModule(process.argv[2])
console.log(`result.publicValue is ${result.publicValue}`)
console.log(`result.privateValue is ${result.privateValue}`)
console.log(result.publicFunction('main'))
```

```
node test-load-module-only.js small-module.js
```

```
full text for eval:
((module) => {const publicValue = 'public value'

const privateValue = 'private value'

const publicFunction = (caller) => {
  return `publicFunction called from ${caller}`
}

module.exports = { publicValue, publicFunction }
})(result)

result.publicValue is public value
result.privateValue is undefined
publicFunction called from main
```

13.3 Do we need to handle circular dependencies?

What if the code we are loading loads other code? We can visualize the network of who requires whom as a **directed graph**: if X requires Y, we draw an arrow from X to Y. Unlike the directed *acyclic* graphs we met in Chapter 10, though, these graphs can contain cycles: we say a **circular dependency** exists if X depends on Y and Y depends on X either directly or indirectly. This may seem nonsensical, but can easily arise with **plugin architectures**: the file containing the main program loads an extension, and that extension calls utility functions defined in the file containing the main program.

Most compiled languages can handle circular dependencies easily: they compile each module into low-level instructions, then link those to resolve dependencies before running anything (Figure 13.4). But interpreted languages usually run code as they're loading it, so if X is in the process of loading Y and Y tries to call X, X may not (fully) exist yet.

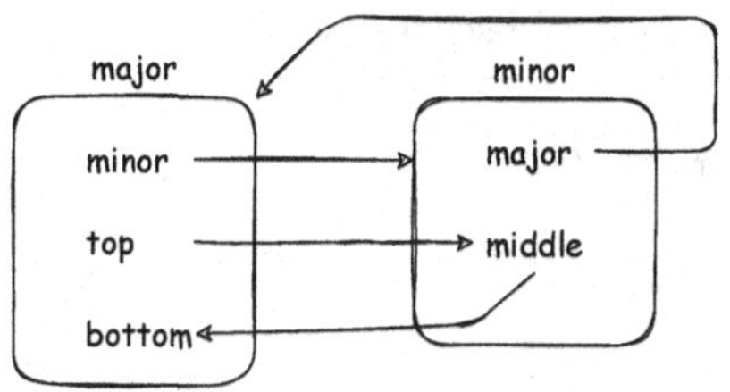

Figure 13.4: Testing circular imports.

Circular dependencies work in Python[1], but only sort of. Let's create two files called `major.py` and `minor.py`:

```
# major.py

import minor

def top():
    print("top")
    minor.middle()

def bottom():
    print("bottom")

top()
```

```
# minor.py

import major

def middle():
    print("middle")
    major.bottom()
```

Loading fails when we run `major.py` from the command line:

```
top
Traceback (most recent call last):
  File "major.py", line 3, in <module>
    import minor
  File "/u/stjs/module-loader/checking/minor.py", line 3, in <module>
    import major
  File "/u/stjs/module-loader/checking/major.py", line 12, in <module>
    top()
  File "/u/stjs/module-loader/checking/major.py", line 7, in top
    minor.middle()
AttributeError: module 'minor' has no attribute 'middle'
```

but works in the interactive interpreter:

```
$ python
>>> import major
top
middle
bottom
```

[1] https://www.python.org/

The equivalent test in JavaScript also has two files:

```
// major.js
const { middle } = require('./minor')

const top = () => {
  console.log('top')
  middle()
}

const bottom = () => {
  console.log('bottom')
}

top()

module.exports = { top, bottom }
```

```
// minor.js
const { bottom } = require('./major')

const middle = () => {
  console.log('middle')
  bottom()
}

module.exports = { middle }
```

It fails on the command line:

```
top
middle
/u/stjs/module-loader/checking/minor.js:6
  bottom()
  ^

TypeError: bottom is not a function
    at middle (/u/stjs/module-loader/checking/minor.js:6:3)
    at top (/u/stjs/module-loader/checking/major.js:6:3)
    at Object.<anonymous> (/u/stjs/module-loader/checking/major.js:13:1)
    at Module._compile (internal/modules/cjs/loader.js:1063:30)
    at Object.Module._extensions..js \
 (internal/modules/cjs/loader.js:1092:10)
    at Module.load (internal/modules/cjs/loader.js:928:32)
    at Function.Module._load (internal/modules/cjs/loader.js:769:14)
    at Function.executeUserEntryPoint [as runMain] \
 (internal/modules/run_main.js:72:12)
    at internal/main/run_main_module.js:17:47
```

and also fails in the interactive interpreter (which is more consistent):

```
$ node
> require('./major')
top
middle
/u/stjs/module-loader/checking/minor.js:6
  bottom()
  ^

TypeError: bottom is not a function
    at middle (/u/stjs/module-loader/checking/minor.js:6:3)
```

```
    at top (/u/stjs/module-loader/checking/major.js:6:3)
    at Object.<anonymous> (/u/stjs/module-loader/checking/major.js:13:1)
    at Module._compile (internal/modules/cjs/loader.js:1063:30)
    at Object.Module._extensions..js \
(internal/modules/cjs/loader.js:1092:10)
    at Module.load (internal/modules/cjs/loader.js:928:32)
    at Function.Module._load (internal/modules/cjs/loader.js:769:14)
    at Module.require (internal/modules/cjs/loader.js:952:19)
    at require (internal/modules/cjs/helpers.js:88:18)
    at [stdin]:1:1
```

We therefore won't try to handle circular dependencies. However, we will detect them and generate a sensible error message.

import vs. require

Circular dependencies work JavaScript's `import` syntax because we can analyze files to determine what needs what, get everything into memory, and then resolve dependencies. We can't do this with `require`-based code because someone might create an **alias** and call `require` through that or `eval` a string that contains a `require` call. (Of course, they can also do these things with the function version of `import`.)

13.4 How can a module load another module?

While we're not going to handle circular dependencies, modules do need to be able to load other modules. To enable this, we need to provide the module with a function called `require` that it can call as it loads. As in Chapter 12, this function checks a cache to see if the file being asked for has already been loaded. If not, it loads it and saves it; either way, it returns the result.

Our cache needs to be careful about how it identifies files so that it can detect duplicates loading attempts that use different names. For example, suppose that `major.js` loads `subdir/first.js` and `subdir/second.js`. When `subdir/second.js` loads `./first.js`, our system needs to realize that it already has that file even though the path looks different. We will use **absolute paths** as cache keys so that every file has a unique, predictable key.

To reduce confusion, we will call our function `need` instead of `require`. In order to make the cache available to modules while they're loading, we will make it a property of `need`. (Remember, a function is just another kind of object in JavaScript; every function gets several properties automatically, and we can always add more.) Since we're using the built-in `Map` class as a cache, the entire implementation of `need` is just 15 lines long:

```
import path from 'path'

import loadModule from './load-module.js'

const need = (name) => {
  const absPath = path.resolve(name)
  if (!need.cache.has(absPath)) {
    const contents = loadModule(absPath, need)
    need.cache.set(absPath, contents)
  }
  return need.cache.get(absPath)
```

```
}
need.cache = new Map()

export default need
```

We now need to modify `loadModule` to take our function `need` as a parameter. (Again, we'll have our modules call `need('something.js')` instead of `require('something')` for clarity.) Let's test it with the same small module that doesn't need anything else to make sure we haven't broken anything:

```
import need from './need.js'

const small = need('small-module.js')
console.log(`small.publicValue is ${small.publicValue}`)
console.log(`small.privateValue is ${small.privateValue}`)
console.log(small.publicFunction('main'))
```

```
full text for eval:
((module, need) => {
const publicValue = 'public value'

const privateValue = 'private value'

const publicFunction = (caller) => {
  return `publicFunction called from ${caller}`
}

module.exports = { publicValue, publicFunction }

})(result, need)

small.publicValue is public value
small.privateValue is undefined
publicFunction called from main
```

What if we test it with a module that *does* load something else?

```
import need from './need'

const small = need('small-module.js')

const large = (caller) => {
  console.log(`large from ${caller}`)
  small.publicFunction(`${caller} to large`)
}

export default large
```

```
import need from './need.js'

const large = need('large-module.js')
console.log(large.large('main'))
```

```
full text for eval:
((module, need) => {
import need from './need'

const small = need('small-module.js')
```

```
const large = (caller) => {
  console.log(`large from ${caller}`)
  small.publicFunction(`${caller} to large`)
}

export default large

})(result, need)

undefined:2
import need from './need'
^^^^^^

SyntaxError: Cannot use import statement outside a module
    at loadModule (/u/stjs/module-loader/load-module.js:8:8)
    at need (/u/stjs/module-loader/need.js:8:22)
    at /u/stjs/module-loader/test-need-large-module.js:3:15
    at ModuleJob.run (internal/modules/esm/module_job.js:152:23)
    at async Loader.import (internal/modules/esm/loader.js:166:24)
    at async Object.loadESM (internal/process/esm_loader.js:68:5)
```

This doesn't work because `import` only works at the top level of a program, not inside a function. Our system can therefore only run loaded modules by `need`ing them:

```
const small = need('small-module.js')

const large = (caller) => {
  return small.publicFunction(`large called from ${caller}`)
}

module.exports = large
```

```
import need from './need.js'

const large = need('large-needless.js')
console.log(large('main'))
```

```
full text for eval:
((module, need) => {
const small = need('small-module.js')

const large = (caller) => {
  return small.publicFunction(`large called from ${caller}`)
}

module.exports = large

})(result, need)

full text for eval:
((module, need) => {
const publicValue = 'public value'

const privateValue = 'private value'

const publicFunction = (caller) => {
  return `publicFunction called from ${caller}`
}

module.exports = { publicValue, publicFunction }
```

```
})(result, need)

publicFunction called from large called from main
```

"It's so deep it's meaningless"

The programs we have written in this chapter are harder to understand than most of the programs in earlier chapters because they are so abstract. Reading through them, it's easy to get the feeling that everything is happening somewhere else. Programmers' tools are often like this: there's always a risk of confusing the thing in the program with the thing the program is working on. Drawing pictures of data structures can help, and so can practicing with closures (which are one of the most powerful ideas in programming), but a lot of the difficulty is irreducible, so don't feel bad if it takes you a while to wrap your head around it.

13.5 Exercises

Counting with closures

Write a function `makeCounter` that returns a function that produces the next integer in sequence starting from zero each time it is called. Each function returned by `makeCounter` must count independently, so:

```
left = makeCounter()
right = makeCounter()
console.log(`left ${left()}`)
console.log(`right ${right()}`)
console.log(`left ${left()}`)
console.log(`right ${right()}`)
```

must produce:

```
left 0
right 0
left 1
right `
```

Objects and namespaces

A JavaScript object stores key-value pairs, and the keys in one object are separate from the keys in another. Why doesn't this provide the same level of safety as a closure?

Testing module loading

Write tests for `need.js` using Mocha and `mock-fs`.

Using module as a name

What happens if we define the variable `module` in `loadModule` so that it is in scope when `eval` is called rather than creating a variable called `result` and passing that in:

```
const loadModule = (filename) => {
  const source = fs.readFileSync(filename, 'utf-8')
  const module = {}
  const fullText = `(() => {${source}})()`
  eval(fullText)
  return module.exports
}
```

Implementing a search path

Add a search path to `need.js` so that if a module isn't found locally, it will be looked for in each directory in the search path in order.

Using a setup function

Rewrite the module loader so that every module has a function called `setup` that must be called after loading it to create its exports rather than using `module.exports`.

Handling errors while loading

1. Modify `need.js` so that it does something graceful if an exception is thrown while a module is being loaded.
2. Write unit tests for this using Mocha.

Refactoring circularity

Suppose that `main.js` contains this:

```
const PLUGINS = []

const plugin = require('./plugin')

const main = () => {
  PLUGINS.forEach(p => p())
}

const loadPlugin = (plugin) => {
  PLUGINS.push(plugin)
}

module.exports = {
  main,
  loadPlugin
}
```

and `plugin.js` contains this:

```
const { loadPlugin } = require('./main')

const printMessage = () => {
  console.log('running plugin')
```

```
}

loadPlugin(printMessage)
```

Refactor this code so that it works correctly while still using `require` rather than `import`.

An LRU cache

A **Least Recently Used (LRU) cache** reduces access time while limiting the amount of memory used by keeping track of the N items that have been used most recently. For example, if the cache size is 3 and objects are accessed in the order shown in the first column, the cache's contents will be as shown in the second column:

Item	Action	Cache After Access
A	read A	[A]
A	get A from cache	[A]
B	read B	[B, A]
A	get A from cache	[A, B]
C	read C	[C, A, B]
D	read D	[D, C, A]
B	read B	[B, D, C]

1. Implement a function `cachedRead` that takes the number of entries in the cache as an argument and returns a function that uses an LRU cache to either read files or return cached copies.
2. Modify `cachedRead` so that the number of items in the cache is determined by their combined size rather than by the number of files.

Make functions safe for renaming

Our implementation of `need` implemented the cache as a property of the function itself.

1. How can this go wrong? (Hint: thing about aliases.)
2. Modify the implementation to solve this problem using a closure.

14

Style Checker

Terms defined: **abstract syntax tree**, **Adapter pattern**, **column-major storage**, **dynamic lookup**, **generator function**, **intrinsic complexity**, **Iterator pattern**, **linter**, **Markdown**, **row-major storage**, **walk (a tree)**

Programmers argue endlessly about the best way to format their programs, but everyone agrees that the most important thing is to be consistent [Binkley2012; Johnson2019]. Since checking rules by hand is tedious, most programmers use tools to compare code against various rules and report any violations. Programs that do this are often called **linters** in honor of an early one for C named `lint` (because it looked for fluff in source code).

In this chapter we will build a simple linter of our own inspired by ESLint[1], which we use to check the code in this book. Our tool will parse source code to create a data structure, then go through that data structure and apply rules for each part of the program. It will also introduce us to one of the key ideas of this book, which is that source code is just another kind of data.

> **Don't define your own style**
>
> Just as the world doesn't need more file format (Chapter 8) it also doesn't need more programming styles, or more arguments among programmers about whether there should be spaces before curly braces or not. Standard JS[2] may not do everything exactly the way you want, but adopting it increases the odds that other programmers will be able to read your code at first glance.

14.1 How can we parse JavaScript to create an AST?

A parser for a simple language like arithmetic or JSON is relatively easy to write. A parser for a language as complex as JavaScript is much more work, so we will use one called Acorn[3] instead. Acorn takes a string containing source code as input and produces an **abstract syntax tree** (AST) whose nodes store information about what's in the program (Figure 14.1). An AST is for a program what the DOM is for HTML: an in-memory representation that is easy for software to inspect and manipulate.

ASTs can be quite complex—for example, the JSON representation of the AST for a single constant declaration is 84 lines long:

```
import acorn from 'acorn'
const ast = acorn.parse('const x = 0', { locations: true })
console.log(JSON.stringify(ast, null, 2))
```

[1]https://eslint.org/
[2]https://standardjs.com/
[3]https://github.com/acornjs/acorn

```
{
  "type": "Program",
  "start": 0,
  "end": 11,
  "loc": {
    "start": {
      "line": 1,
      "column": 0
    },
    "end": {
...
              "value": 0,
              "raw": "0"
            }
          }
        ],
        "kind": "const"
      }
  ],
  "sourceType": "script"
}
```

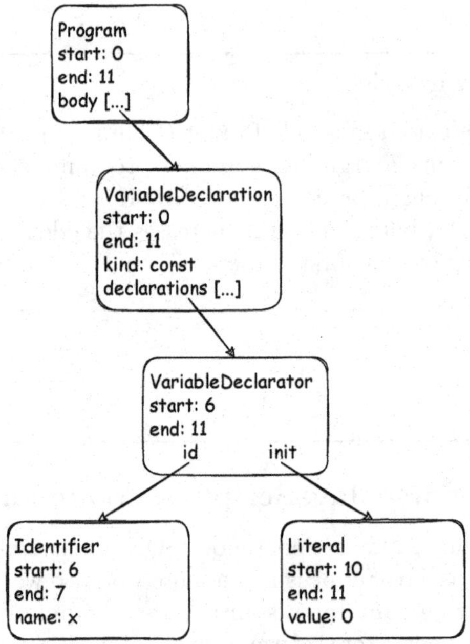

Figure 14.1: The parse tree of a simple program.

Acorn's output is in Esprima[4] format (so-called because it was originally defined by a tool with that name). The format's specification is very detailed, but we can usually figure out most of what we need by inspection. For example, here is the output for a 15-line program:

```
import acorn from 'acorn'

const program = `const value = 2
```

[4]https://esprima.org/

```
const double = (x) => {
  const y = 2 * x
  return y
}

const result = double(value)
console.log(result)
`

const ast = acorn.parse(program, { locations: true })
console.log(JSON.stringify(ast, null, 2))
```


```
{
  "type": "Program",
  "start": 0,
  "end": 122,
  "loc": {
    "start": {
      "line": 1,
      "column": 0
    },
    "end": {
...
        "line": 1,
        "column": 0
      },
      "end": {
        "line": 1,
        "column": 15
      }
    },
    "declarations": [
...480 more lines...
```


Yes, it really is almost 500 lines long...

14.2 How can we find things in an AST?

If we want to find functions, variables, or anything else in an AST we need to **walk the tree**, i.e., to visit each node in turn. The `acorn-walk`[5] library will do this for us using the Visitor design pattern we first saw in Chapter 9. If we provide a function to act on nodes of type `Identifier`, `acorn-walk` will call that function each time it finds an identifier. We can use other options to say that we want to record the locations of nodes (i.e., their line numbers) and to collect comments in an array called `onComment`. Our function can do whatever we want; for demonstration purposes we will add nodes to an array called `state` and report them all at the end (Figure 14.2).

```
import acorn from 'acorn'
import walk from 'acorn-walk'

const program = `// Constant
const value = 2
```

[5]https://www.npmjs.com/package/acorn-walk

```
// Function
const double = (x) => {
  const y = 2 * x
  return y
}

// Main body
const result = double(value)
console.log(result)
`

const options = {
  locations: true,
  onComment: []
}
const ast = acorn.parse(program, options)

const state = []
walk.simple(ast, {
  Identifier: (node, state) => {
    state.push(node)
  }
}, null, state)

state.forEach(node => console.log(
  `identifier ${node.name} on line ${node.loc.start.line}`
))
const comments = options.onComment.map(
  node => node.loc.start.line
).join(', ')
console.log(`comments on lines ${comments}`)
```

```
identifier x on line 6
identifier y on line 7
identifier double on line 11
identifier value on line 11
identifier console on line 12
identifier result on line 12
comments on lines 1, 4, 10
```

There's more than one way to do it

`walk.simple` takes four arguments:

1. The root node of the AST, which is used as the starting point.
2. An object containing callback functions for handling various kinds of nodes.
3. Another object that specifies what algorithm to use—we have set this to `null` to use the default because we don't particularly care about the order in which the nodes are processed.
4. Something we want passed in to each of the node handlers, which in our case is the `state` array. If our node handling functions don't require any extra data from one call to the next we can leave this out; if we want to accumulate information across calls, this argument acts as the Visitor's memory.

Any general-purpose implementation of the Visitor pattern is going to need these four things, but as we will see below, we can implement them in different ways.

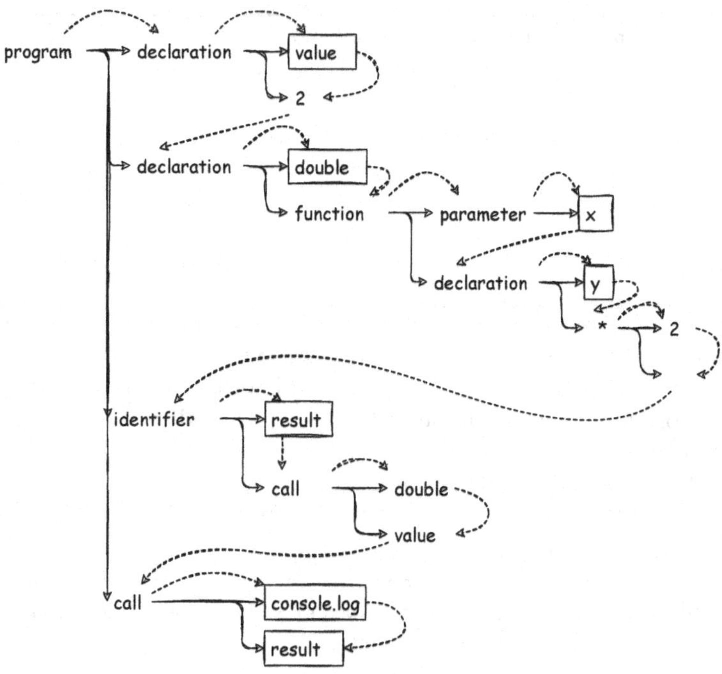

Figure 14.2: Walking a tree to perform an operation at each node.

14.3 How can we apply checks?

We don't just want to collect nodes: we want to check their properties against a set of rules. One way to do this would be to call `walk.simple` once for each rule, passing it a function that checks just that rule. Another way—the one we'll use—is to write a generic function that checks a rule and records any nodes that don't satisfy it, and then call that function once for each rule inside our `Identifier` handler. This may seem like extra work, but it ensures that all of our rule-checkers store their results in the same way, which in turn means that we can write one reporting function and be sure it will handle everything.

The function `applyCheck` takes the current state (where we are accumulating rule violations), a label that identifies this rule (so that violations of it can be stored together), the node, and a logical value telling it whether the node passed the test or not. If the node failed the test we make sure that `state` contains a list with the appropriate label and then append this node to it. This "create storage space on demand" pattern is widely used but doesn't have a well-known name.

```
const applyCheck = (state, label, node, passes) => {
  if (!passes) {
    if (!(label in state)) {
      state[label] = []
    }
```

```
    state[label].push(node)
  }
}
```

We can now put a call to **applyCheck** inside the handler for **Identifier**:

```
const ast = acorn.parse(program, { locations: true })

const state = {}
walk.simple(ast, {
  Identifier: (node, state) => {
    applyCheck(state, 'name_length', node, node.name.length >= 4)
  }
}, null, state)

state.name_length.forEach(
  node => console.log(`${node.name} at line ${node.loc.start.line}`))
```

We can't just use `applyCheck` as the handler for `Identifier` because `walk.simple` wouldn't know how to call it. This is a (very simple) example of the **Adapter** design pattern: we write a function or class to connect the code we want to call to the already-written code that is going to call it.

The output for the same sample program as before is:

```
x at line 6
y at line 7
```

The exercises will ask why the parameter `x` doesn't show up as a violation of our rule that variables' names must be at least four characters long.

14.4 How does the AST walker work?

The AST walker uses the Visitor pattern, but how does it actually work? We can build our own by defining a class with methods that walk the tree, take action depending on the kind of node, and then go through the children of that node (if any). The user can then derive a class of their own from this and override the set of action methods they're interested in.

One key difference between our implementation and `acorn-walk`'s is that our methods don't need to take `state` as a parameter because it's contained in the object that they're part of. That simplifies the methods—one less parameter—but it does mean that anyone who wants to use our visitor has to derive a class, which is a bit more complicated than writing a function. This tradeoff is a sign that managing state is part of the problem's **intrinsic complexity**: we can move it around, but we can't get rid of it.

The other difference between our visitor and `acorn-walk` is that our class uses **dynamic lookup** (a form of introspection) to look up a method with the same name as the node type in the object. While we normally refer to a particular method of an object using `object.method`, we can also look them up by asking for `object[name]` in the same way that we would look up any other property of any other object. Our completed class looks like this:

```
class Walker {
  // Construct a new AST tree walker.
  constructor (ast) {
    this.ast = ast
```

```
  }

  // Walk the tree.
  walk (accumulator) {
    this.stack = []
    this._walk(this.ast, accumulator)
    return accumulator
  }

  // Act on node and then on children.
  _walk (node, accumulator) {
    if (node && (typeof node === 'object') && ('type' in node)) {
      this._doNode(node, accumulator)
      this._doChildren(node, accumulator)
    }
  }

  // Handle a single node by lookup.
  _doNode (node, accumulator) {
    if (node.type in this) {
      this[node.type](node, accumulator)
    }
  }

  // Recurse for anything interesting within the node.
  _doChildren (node, accumulator) {
    this.stack.push(node)
    for (const key in node) {
      if (Array.isArray(node[key])) {
        node[key].forEach(child => {
          this._walk(child, accumulator)
        })
      } else if (typeof node[key] === 'object') {
        this._walk(node[key], accumulator)
      }
    }
    this.stack.pop(node)
  }

  // Is the current node a child of some other type of node?
  _childOf (nodeTypes) {
    return this.stack &&
      nodeTypes.includes(this.stack.slice(-1)[0].type)
  }
}
```

The code we need to use it is:

```
import acorn from 'acorn'


// Walk to accumulate variable and parameter definitions.
class VariableWalker extends Walker {
  Identifier (node, accumulator) {
    if (this._childOf(['ArrowFunctionExpression',
      'VariableDeclarator'])) {
      accumulator.push(node.name)
    }
  }
}
```

```
// Test.
const program = `const value = 2

const double = (x) => {
  const y = 2 * x
  return y
}

const result = double(value)
console.log(result)
`

const ast = acorn.parse(program, { locations: true })
const walker = new VariableWalker(ast)
const accumulator = []
walker.walk(accumulator)
console.log('definitions are', accumulator)
```

and its output is:

```
definitions are [ 'value', 'double', 'x', 'y', 'result' ]
```

We think this approach to implementing the Visitor pattern is easier to understand and extend than one that relies on callbacks, but that could just be a reflection of our background and experience. As with code style, the most important thing is consistency: if we implement Visitor using classes in one place, we should implement it that way everywhere.

14.5 How else could the AST walker work?

A third approach to this problem uses the **Iterator** design pattern. Instead of taking the computation to the nodes, an iterator returns the elements of a structure for processing (Figure 14.3). One way to think about it is that Visitor encapsulates recursion, while Iterator turns everything into a loop.

We can implement the Iterator pattern in JavaScript using **generator functions**. If we declare a function using `function *` (with an asterisk) instead of `function` then we can use the `yield` keyword to return a value and suspend processing to be resumed later. The result of `yield` is a two-part structure with a value and a flag showing whether or not processing is done:

```
function * threeWords () {
  yield 'first'
  yield 'second'
  yield 'third'
}

const gen = threeWords()

console.log(gen.next())
console.log(gen.next())
console.log(gen.next())
console.log(gen.next())
```

```
{ value: 'first', done: false }
{ value: 'second', done: false }
```

```
{ value: 'third', done: false }
{ value: undefined, done: true }
```

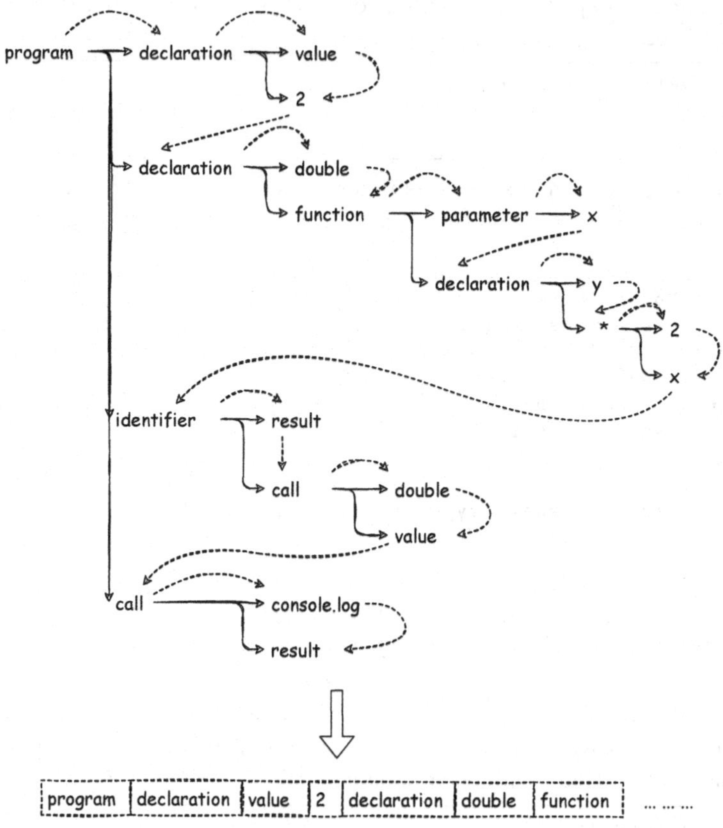

Figure 14.3: Finding nodes in the tree using the Iterator pattern.

As another example, this generator takes a string and produces its vowels one by one:

```
function * getVowels (text) {
  for (const char of text) {
    if ('AEIOUaeiou'.includes(char)) {
      yield char
    }
  }
}

const test = 'this is a test'
const gen = getVowels(test)
let current = gen.next()
while (!current.done) {
  console.log(current.value)
  current = gen.next()
}
```

```
i
i
a
e
```

A generator function doesn't actually generate anything; instead, it creates an object that we can then ask for values repeatedly. This gives us a way to have several generators in play at the same time.

Instead of a `while` loop it is much more common to use `for...of`, which knows how to work with generators:

```
for (const vowel of getVowels(test)) {
  console.log(vowel)
}
```

Finally, just as `function *` says "this function is a generator", `yield *` says "yield the values from a nested generator one by one". We can use it to walk irregular structures like nested arrays:

```
function * getNodes (here) {
  if (typeof here === 'string') {
    yield here
  } else if (Array.isArray(here)) {
    for (const child of here) {
      yield * getNodes(child)
    }
  } else {
    throw new Error(`unknown type "${typeof here}"`)
  }
}

const nested = ['first', ['second', 'third']]
for (const value of getNodes(nested)) {
  console.log(value)
}
```

Let's use generators to count the number of expressions of various types in a program. The generator function that visits each node is:

```
function * getNodes (node) {
  if (node && (typeof node === 'object') && ('type' in node)) {
    yield node
    for (const key in node) {
      if (Array.isArray(node[key])) {
        for (const child of node[key]) {
          yield * getNodes(child)
        }
      } else if (typeof node[key] === 'object') {
        yield * getNodes(node[key])
      }
    }
  }
}
```

and the program that uses it is:

```
const ast = acorn.parse(program, { locations: true })
const result = {}
for (const node of getNodes(ast)) {
  if (node.type === 'BinaryExpression') {
    if (node.operator in result) {
      result[node.operator] += 1
    } else {
      result[node.operator] = 1
    }
  }
```

```
}
console.log('counts are', result)
```

When we run it with our usual test program as input, we get:

```
counts are { '*': 2, '+': 1 }
```

Generators are a clean solution to many hard problems, but we find it more difficult to check variable identifiers using generators than using the class-based Visitor approach because we want to accumulate violations to report later. Again, this could be a reflection of what we're used to rather than anything intrinsic; as with coding style, the most important thing is to be consistent.

14.6 What other kinds of analysis can we do?

As one final example, consider the problem of keeping track of which methods are defined where in a deeply nested class hierarchy. (This problem comes up in some of the later chapters in this book: we wrote so many classes that incrementally extended their predecessors for pedagogical purposes that we lost track of what was defined where.) To create a table of method definitions, we first need to find the ancestors of the last class in the hierarchy:

```
import assert from 'assert'
import acorn from 'acorn'
import fs from 'fs'
import path from 'path'
import walk from 'acorn-walk'

class FindAncestors {
  find (dirname, filename, className) {
    return this.traceAncestry(dirname, filename, className, [])
  }

  traceAncestry (dirname, filename, className, accum) {
    const fullPath = path.join(dirname, filename)
    const program = fs.readFileSync(fullPath, 'utf-8')
    const options = { locations: true, sourceType: 'module' }
    const ast = acorn.parse(program, options)
    const classDef = this.findClassDef(filename, ast, className)
    accum.push({ filename, className, classDef })
    const ancestorName = this.getAncestor(classDef)
    if (ancestorName === null) {
      return accum
    }
    const ancestorFile = this.findImport(filename, ast, ancestorName)
    return this.traceAncestry(dirname, ancestorFile, ancestorName, accum)
  }

}

export default FindAncestors
```

Finding class definitions is a straightforward extension of what we have already done:

```
  findClassDef (filename, ast, className) {
    const state = []
    walk.simple(ast, {
      ClassDeclaration: (node, state) => {
        if ((node.id.type === 'Identifier') &&
            (node.id.name === className)) {
          state.push(node)
        }
      }
    }, null, state)
    assert(state.length === 1,
      `No definition for ${className} in ${filename}`)
    return state[0]
  }
```

To test this code, we start with the last of these three short files:

```
class Upper {
  constructor () {
    this.name = 'upper'
  }

  report () {
    console.log(this.modify(this.name))
  }

  modify (text) {
    return text.toUpperCase()
  }
}

module.exports = Upper
```

```
import Upper from './upper.js'

class Middle extends Upper {
  constructor () {
    super()
    this.range = 'middle'
  }

  modify (text) {
    return `** ${super.modify(text)} **`
  }
}

export default Middle
```

```
import Middle from './middle.js'

class Lower extends Middle {
  report () {
    console.log(this.additional())
  }

  additional () {
    return 'lower'
  }
}
```

```
export default Lower
```

```
Lower in lower.js
Middle in ./middle.js
Upper in ./upper.js
```

Good: we can recover the chain of inheritance. Finding method definitions is also straightforward:

```
import FindAncestors from './find-ancestors.js'

class FindMethods extends FindAncestors {
  find (dirname, filename, className) {
    const classes = super.find(dirname, filename, className)
    classes.forEach(record => {
      record.methods = this.findMethods(record.classDef)
    })
    return classes
  }

  findMethods (classDef) {
    return classDef.body.body
      .filter(item => item.type === 'MethodDefinition')
      .map(item => {
        if (item.kind === 'constructor') {
          return 'constructor'
        } else if (item.kind === 'method') {
          return item.key.name
        } else {
          return null
        }
      })
      .filter(item => item !== null)
  }
}

export default FindMethods
```

And finally, we can print a **Markdown**-formatted table showing which methods are defined in which class:

```
| method | Upper | Middle | Lower |
| ---- | ---- | ---- | ---- |
| additional | . | . | X |
| constructor | X | X | . |
| modify | X | X | . |
| report | X | . | X |
```

which renders as:

method	Upper	Middle	Lower
additional	.	.	X
constructor	X	X	.
modify	X	X	.
report	X	.	X

This may seem rather pointless for our toy example, but it proves its worth when we are looking at something like the virtual machine we will build in Chapter 19, which has a more complex method definition table:

method	Base	Interactive	Test	Exit
clear	.	X	.	.
constructor	X	X	X	.
exit	.	X	.	X
getCommand	.	X	.	.
handle	.	X	.	.
help	.	X	.	.
input	.	X	X	.
interact	.	X	.	.
list	.	X	.	.
message	X	.	X	.
next	.	X	.	.
print	.	X	.	.
run	.	X	.	.
setTester	.	.	X	.
setVM	X	.	.	.
stop	.	X	.	.
variables	.	X	.	.

14.7 Exercises

Function length

Derive a class from `Walker` that reports the length in lines of each function defined in the code being checked.

Expression depth

Derive a class from `Walker` that reports how deep each top-level expression in the source code is. For example, the depth of `1 + 2 * 3` is 2, while the depth of `max(1 + 2 + 3)` is 3 (one level for the function call, one for the first addition, and one for the nested addition).

Downward and upward

Modify `Walker` so that users can specify one action to take at a node on the way down the tree and a separate action to take on the way up. (Hint: require users to specify `Nodename_downward` and/or `Nodename_upward` methods in their class, then use string concatenation to construct method names while traversing the tree.)

Aggregating across files

Create a command-line program called `sniff.js` that checks for style violations in any number of source files. The first command-line argument to `sniff.js` must be a JavaScript source file that exports a class derived from `Walker` called `Check` that implements the checks the user wants. The other command-line arguments must be the names of JavaScript source files to be checked:

```
node sniff.js my-check.js source-1.js source-2.js
```

Finding assertions

Write a program `find-assertions.js` that finds all calls to `assert` or `assert.something` and prints the assertion message (if any).

Finding a missing parameter

1. Why doesn't the parameter `x` show up as a rule violation in the example where we check name lengths?
2. Modify the example so that it does.

Finding nested indexes

Write a tool that finds places where nested indexing is used, i.e., where the program contains expressions like `arr[table[i]]`.

Dynamic lookup

1. Write a function `dynamicExecution` that takes an object, the name of a method, and zero or more parameters as arguments and calls that method on that object:

   ```
   dynamicExecution(obj, 'meth', 1, 'a')
   // same as obj.meth(1, 'a')
   ```

2. What *doesn't* this work for?

Generators and arrays

1. Write a generator that takes a two-dimensional table represented as an array of arrays and returns the values in **column-major** order.
2. Write another generator that takes a similar table and returns the values in **row-major** order.

Generators and identifiers

Rewrite the tool to check identifier lengths using a generator.

15

Code Generator

Terms defined: **byte code, code coverage (in testing), compiler, Decorator pattern, macro, nested function, two hard problems in computer science**

We've been writing tests since Chapter 4, but how much of our code do they actually check? One way to find out is to use a **code coverage** tool like Istanbul[1] that watches a program while it executes and keeps track of which lines have run and which haven't. Making sure that each line is tested at least once doesn't guarantee that the code is bug-free, but any code that *isn't* run shouldn't be trusted.

Our code coverage tool will keep track of which functions have and haven't been called. Rather than rewriting Node[2] to keep track of this for us, we will modify the functions themselves by parsing the code with Acorn[3], inserting the instructions we need into the AST, and then turning the AST back into code.

> **Simple usually isn't**
>
> At first glance it would be a lot simpler to use regular expressions to find every line that looks like the start of a function definition and insert a line right after each one to record the information we want. Of course, some people split function headers across several lines if they have lots of parameters, and there might be things that look like function definitions embedded in comments or strings. It doesn't take long before our simple solution turns into a poorly-implemented parser for a subset of JavaScript that no-one else understands. Using a full-blown parser and working with the AST is almost always less work.

15.1 How can we replace a function with another function?

The first thing we need is a way to wrap up an arbitrary function call. If we declare a function in JavaScript with a parameter like `...args`, all of the "extra" arguments in the call that don't line up with regular parameters are stuffed into the variable `args` (Figure 15.1). We can also call a function by putting values in a variable and using `func(...var)` to spread those values out. There's nothing special about the names `args` and `vars`: what matters is the ellipsis ...

We can use `...args` to capture all of the arguments to a function call and forward them to another function. Let's start by creating functions with a varying number of parameters that run to completion or throw an exception, then run them to make sure they do what we want:

---

[1] https://istanbul.js.org/
[2] https://nodejs.org/en/
[3] https://github.com/acornjs/acorn

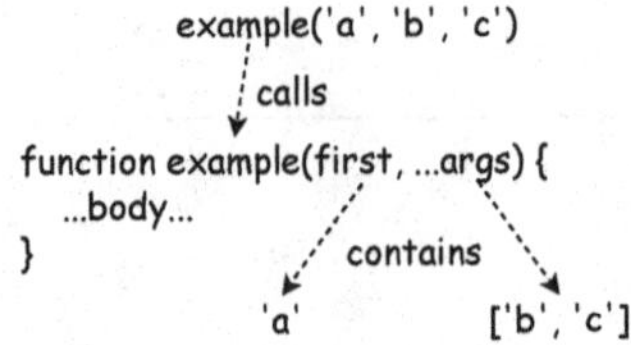

Figure 15.1: Using ...args to capture and spread parameters.

```
let zero = () => console.log('zero')
let one = (first) => console.log(`one(${first})`)
let two = (first, second) => console.log(`two(${first}, ${second})`)

let error = () => {
  console.log('error')
  throw new Error('from error')
  console.log('should not reach this')
}

const runAll = (title) => {
  console.log(title)
  zero()
  one(1)
  two(1, 2)
  try {
    error()
  } catch (error) {
    console.log(`caught ${error} as expected`)
  }
  console.log()
}

runAll('first time')
```

We can now write a function that takes a function as an input and creates a new function that handles all of the errors in the original function:

```
const replace = (func) => {
  return (...args) => {
    console.log('before')
    try {
      const result = func(...args)
      console.log('after')
      return result
    } catch (error) {
      console.log('error')
      throw error
    }
  }
}

zero = replace(zero)
one = replace(one)
two = replace(two)
error = replace(error)

runAll('second time')
```

Let's try it out:

```
first time
zero
one(1)
two(1, 2)
error
caught Error: from error as expected

second time
before
zero
after
before
one(1)
after
before
two(1, 2)
after
before
error
error
caught Error: from error as expected
```

This is an example of the **Decorator** design pattern. A decorator is a function whose job is to modify the behavior of other functions in some general ways. Decorators are built in to some languages (like Python[4]), and we can add them in most others as we have done here.

15.2 How can we generate JavaScript?

We could use a decorator to replace every function in our program with one that keeps track of whether or not it was called, but it would be tedious to apply the decorator to every one of our functions by hand. What we really want is a way to do this automatically for everything, and for that we need to parse and generate code.

Other ways to do it

A third way to achieve what we want is to let the system turn code into runnable instructions and then modify those instructions. This approach is often used in compiled languages like Java[5], where the **byte code** produced by the **compiler** is saved in files in order to be run. We can't do this here because Node compiles and runs code in a single step.

Our tool will parse the JavaScript with Acorn to create an AST, modify the AST, and then use a library called Escodegen[6] to turn the AST back into JavaScript. To start, let's look at the AST for a simple function definition, which is 75 lines of pretty-printed JSON:

```
import acorn from 'acorn'
```

[4]https://www.python.org/
[5]https://en.wikipedia.org/wiki/Java_(programming_language)
[6]https://github.com/estools/escodegen/

```
const text = `const func = (param) => {
  return param + 1
}`

const ast = acorn.parse(text, { sourceType: 'module' })
console.log(JSON.stringify(ast, null, 2))
```


```
{
  "type": "Program",
  "start": 0,
  "end": 46,
  "body": [
    {
      "type": "VariableDeclaration",
      "start": 0,
      "end": 46,
      "declarations": [
        {
          "type": "VariableDeclarator",
          "start": 6,
          "end": 46,
          "id": {
            "type": "Identifier",
            "start": 6,
            "end": 10,
            "name": "func"
          },
          "init": {
            "type": "ArrowFunctionExpression",
            "start": 13,
            "end": 46,
            "id": null,
            "expression": false,
            "generator": false,
            "async": false,
            "params": [
              {
                "type": "Identifier",
                "start": 14,
                "end": 19,
                "name": "param"
              }
            ],
            "body": {
              "type": "BlockStatement",
              "start": 24,
              "end": 46,
              "body": [
                {
                  "type": "ReturnStatement",
                  "start": 28,
                  "end": 44,
                  "argument": {
                    "type": "BinaryExpression",
                    "start": 35,
                    "end": 44,
                    "left": {
                      "type": "Identifier",
                      "start": 35,
                      "end": 40,
```

```
                "name": "param"
              },
              "operator": "+",
              "right": {
                "type": "Literal",
                "start": 43,
                "end": 44,
                "value": 1,
                "raw": "1"
              }
            }
          }
        ]
      }
    }
  }
  ],
  "kind": "const"
  }
 ],
 "sourceType": "module"
}
```

After inspecting a few nodes, we can create some of our own and turn them into code. Here, for example, we have the JSON representation of the expression 40+2:

```
import escodegen from 'escodegen'
const result = escodegen.generate({
  type: 'BinaryExpression',
  operator: '+',
  left: { type: 'Literal', value: 40 },
  right: { type: 'Literal', value: 2 }
})
console.log(result)
```

```
40 + 2
```

15.3 How can we count how often functions are executed?

Our tool will find all the function declaration nodes in the program and insert a node to increment an entry in a global variable called `__counters`. (Prefixing the name with two underscores doesn't guarantee that we won't accidentally clobber a variable in the user's program with the same name, but hopefully it makes that less likely.) Our test case is:

```
const TEXT = `
const funcOuter = (param) => {
  return param + 1
}
const funcInner = (param) => {
  return param + 1
}
for (const i of [1, 3, 5]) {
  funcOuter(funcInner(i) + funcInner(i))
}
`
```

and the main function of our program is:

```
const main = () => {
  const ast = acorn.parse(TEXT, { sourceType: 'module' })

  const allNodes = []
  walk.simple(ast, {
    VariableDeclarator: (node, state) => {
      if (node.init && (node.init.type === 'ArrowFunctionExpression')) {
        state.push(node)
      }
    }
  }, null, allNodes)

  const names = {}
  allNodes.forEach(node => insertCounter(names, node))
  console.log(initializeCounters(names))
  console.log(escodegen.generate(ast))
  console.log(reportCounters())
}
```

To insert a count we call `insertCounter` to record the function's name and modify the node:

```
const insertCounter = (names, node) => {
  const name = node.id.name
  names[name] = 0

  const body = node.init.body.body
  const increment =
    acorn.parse(`__counters['${name}'] += 1`, { sourceType: 'module' })
  body.unshift(increment)
}
```

Notice how we don't try to build the nodes by hand, but instead construct the string we need, use Acorn to parse that, and use the result. Doing this saves us from embedding multiple lines of JSON in our program and also ensures that if a newer version of Acorn decides to generate a different AST, our program will do the right thing automatically.

Finally, we need to add a couple of helper functions:

```
const initializeCounters = (names) => {
  const body = Object.keys(names).map(n => `'${n}': 0`).join(',\n')
  return 'const __counters = {\n' + body + '\n}'
}

const reportCounters = () => {
  return 'console.log(__counters)'
}
```

and run it to make sure it all works:

```
const __counters = {
'funcOuter': 0,
'funcInner': 0
}
const funcOuter = param => {
        __counters['funcOuter'] += 1;
    return param + 1;
};
const funcInner = param => {
        __counters['funcInner'] += 1;
```

```
    return param + 1;
};
for (const i of [
        1,
        3,
        5
    ]) {
    funcOuter(funcInner(i) + funcInner(i));
}
console.log(__counters)
```

Too simple to be safe

Our simple approach to naming counters doesn't work if functions can have the same names, which they can if we use modules or **nested functions**. One solution would be to manufacture a label from the function's name and the line number in the source code; another would be to keep track of which functions are nested within which and concatenate their names to produce a unique key. Problems like this are why people say that naming things is one of the **two hard problems** in computer science.

15.4 How can we time function execution?

Now that we have a way to insert code into functions we can use it to do many other things. For example, we can find out how long it takes functions to run by wrapping them up in code that records the start and end time of each call. As before, we find the nodes of interest and decorate them, then stitch the result together with a bit of bookkeeping:

```
const timeFunc = (text) => {
  const ast = acorn.parse(text, { sourceType: 'module' })
  const allNodes = gatherNodes(ast)
  allNodes.forEach(node => wrapFuncDef(node))
  return [
    initializeCounters(allNodes),
    escodegen.generate(ast),
    reportCounters()
  ].join('\n')
}
```

Gathering nodes is straightforward:

```
const gatherNodes = (ast) => {
  const allNodes = []
  walk.simple(ast, {
    VariableDeclarator: (node, state) => {
      if (node.init && (node.init.type === 'ArrowFunctionExpression')) {
        state.push(node)
      }
    }
  }, null, allNodes)
  return allNodes
}
```

as is wrapping the function definition:

```
const wrapFuncDef = (originalAst) => {
  const name = originalAst.id.name
  const wrapperAst = makeWrapperAst(name)
  wrapperAst.init.body.body[0].declarations[0].init = originalAst.init
  originalAst.init = wrapperAst.init
}
```

The only big difference is how we make the wrapper function. We create it with a placeholder for the original function so that we have a spot in the AST to insert the actual code:

```
const timeFunc = (text) => {
  const ast = acorn.parse(text, { sourceType: 'module' })
  const allNodes = gatherNodes(ast)
  allNodes.forEach(node => wrapFuncDef(node))
  return [
    initializeCounters(allNodes),
    escodegen.generate(ast),
    reportCounters()
  ].join('\n')
}
```

Let's run one last test:

```
const __counters = {
'assignment': 0,
'readFile': 0
}
const assignment = (...originalArgs) => {
    const originalFunc = range => {
        let j = 0;
        for (let i = 0; i < range; i += 1) {
            j = i;
        }
    };
    const startTime = Date.now();
    try {
        const result = originalFunc(...originalArgs);
        const endTime = Date.now();
        __counters['assignment'] += endTime - startTime;
        return result;
    } catch (error) {
        const endTime = Date.now();
        __counters['assignment'] += endTime - startTime;
        throw error;
    }
};
const readFile = (...originalArgs) => {
    const originalFunc = (range, filename) => {
        for (let i = 0; i < range; i += 1) {
            fs.readFileSync(filename, 'utf-8');
        }
    };
    const startTime = Date.now();
    try {
        const result = originalFunc(...originalArgs);
        const endTime = Date.now();
        __counters['readFile'] += endTime - startTime;
        return result;
    } catch (error) {
```

```
        const endTime = Date.now();
        __counters['readFile'] += endTime - startTime;
        throw error;
    }
};
const numLoops = 100000;
assignment(numLoops);
readFile(numLoops, 'index.md');
console.log(__counters)
OUTPUT
{ assignment: 1, readFile: 3879 }
```

Source-to-source translation is widely used in JavaScript: tools like Babel[7] use it to transform modern features like `async` and `await` (Chapter 3) into code that older browsers can understand. The technique is so powerful that it is built into languages like Scheme, which allow programmers to add new syntax to the language by defining **macros**. Depending on how carefully they are used, macros can make programs elegant, incomprehensible, or both.

15.5 Exercises

JSON to JavaScript

Write a tool that uses Escodegen[8] to translate simple expressions written in JSON into runnable JavaScript. For example, the tool should translate:

```
['+', 3, ['*', 5, 'a']]
```

into:

```
3 + (5 * a)
```

JavaScript to HTML

Write a function that takes nested JavaScript function calls for generating HTML like this:

```
div(h1('title'), p('explanation'))
```

and turns them into HTML like this:

```
<div><h1>title</h1><p>explanation</p></div>
```

Handling modules

Modify the code that counts the number of times a function is called to handle functions with the same name from different modules.

[7]https://babeljs.io/
[8]https://github.com/estools/escodegen/

Tracking calls

Write a decorator that takes a function as its argument and returns a new function that behaves exactly the same way except that it keeps track of who called it.

1. The program contains a stack where decorated functions push and pop their names as they are called and as they exit.
2. Each time a function is called it adds a record to an array to record its name and the name at the top of the stack (i.e., the most-recently-called decorated function).

Counting classical function definitions

Modify the code generator to handle functions declared with the `function` keyword as well as functions declared using `=>`.

Recording input file size

1. Write a program that replaces all calls to `fs.readFileSync` with calls to `readFileSyncCount`.
2. Write the function `readFileSyncCount` to read and return a file using `fs.readFileSync` but to also record the file's name and size in bytes.
3. Write a third function `reportInputFileSizes` that reports what files were read and how large they were.
4. Write tests for these functions using Mocha and `mock-fs`.

Checking argument types

Write a tool that modifies functions to check the types of their arguments at run-time.

1. Each function is replaced by a function that passes all of its arguments to `checkArgs` along with the function's name, then continues with the function's original operation.
2. The first time `checkArgs` is called for a particular function it records the actual types of the arguments.
3. On subsequent calls, it checks that the argument types match those of the first call and throws an exception if they do not.

Two-dimensional arrays

The function `make2D` takes a row length and one or more values and creates a two-dimensional array from those values:

```
make2D(2, 'a', 'b', 'c', 'd')
// produces [['a', 'b'], ['c', 'd']]
```

Write a function that searches code to find calls to `make2D` and replaces them with inline arrays-of-arrays. This function only has to work for calls with a fixed row length, i.e., it does *not* have to handle `make2D(N, 'a', 'b')`.

From require to import

Write a function that searches code for simple calls to `require` and replaces them with calls to `import`. This function only needs to work for the simplest case; for example, if the input is:

```
const name = require('module')
```

then the output is:

```
import name from 'module'
```

Removing empty constructors

Write a function that removes empty constructors from class definitions. For example, if the input is:

```
class Example {
  constructor () {
  }

  someMethod () {
    console.log('some method')
  }
}
```

then the output should be:

```
class Example {
  someMethod () {
    console.log('some method')
  }
}
```

16

Documentation Generator

Terms defined: **accumulator**, **block comment**, **deprecation**, **doc comment**, **line comment**, **slug**

Many programmers believe they're more likely to write documentation and keep it up to date if it is close to the code. Tools that extract specially-formatted comments from code and turn them into documentation have been around since at least the 1980s; many are used for JavaScript, including JSDoc[1] and ESDoc[2]. This chapter will use what we learned in Chapter 15 about parsing source code to build a simple documentation generator of our own.

16.1 How can we extract documentation comments?

We will use Acorn[3] once again to parse our source files. This time we will use the parser's `onComment` option, giving it an array to fill in. For the moment we won't bother to assign the AST produced by parsing to a variable because we are just interested in the comments:

```
import fs from 'fs'
import acorn from 'acorn'

const text = fs.readFileSync(process.argv[2], 'utf-8')
const options = {
  sourceType: 'module',
  locations: true,
  onComment: []
}
acorn.parse(text, options)
console.log(JSON.stringify(options.onComment, null, 2))
```

```
// double-slash comment
/* slash-star comment */
```

```
[
  {
    "type": "Line",
    "value": " double-slash comment",
    "start": 0,
    "end": 23,
    "loc": {
      "start": {
        "line": 1,
        "column": 0
      },
```

[1] https://jsdoc.app/
[2] https://esdoc.org/
[3] https://github.com/acornjs/acorn

```
      "end": {
        "line": 1,
        "column": 23
      }
    }
  },
  {
    "type": "Block",
    "value": " slash-star comment ",
    "start": 24,
    "end": 48,
    "loc": {
      "start": {
        "line": 2,
        "column": 0
      },
      "end": {
        "line": 2,
        "column": 24
      }
    }
  }
]
```

There is more information here than we need, so let's slim down the JSON that we extract:

```
import fs from 'fs'
import acorn from 'acorn'

const text = fs.readFileSync(process.argv[2], 'utf-8')
const options = {
  sourceType: 'module',
  locations: true,
  onComment: []
}
acorn.parse(text, options)
const subset = options.onComment.map(entry => {
  return {
    type: entry.type,
    value: entry.value,
    start: entry.loc.start.line,
    end: entry.loc.end.line
  }
})
console.log(JSON.stringify(subset, null, 2))
```

```
node extract-comments-subset.js two-kinds-of-comment.js
```

```
[
  {
    "type": "Line",
    "value": " double-slash comment",
    "start": 1,
    "end": 1
  },
  {
    "type": "Block",
    "value": " slash-star comment ",
    "start": 2,
```

```
    "end": 2
  }
]
```

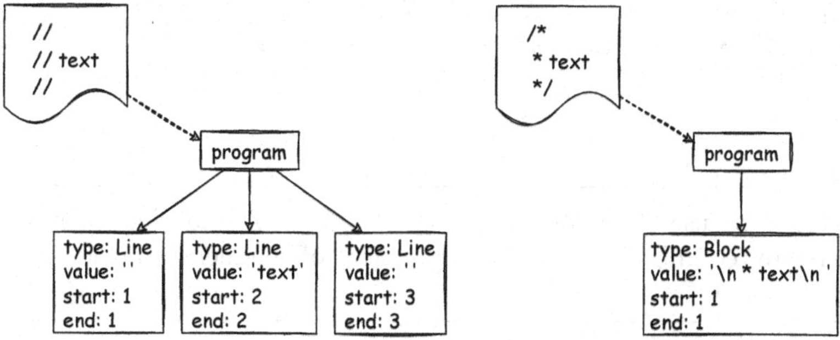

Figure 16.1: How line comments and block comments are distinguished and represented.

Acorn distinguishes two kinds of comments (Figure 16.1). **Line comments** cannot span multiple lines; if one line comment occurs immediately after another, Acorn reports two comments:

```
//
// multi-line double-slash comment
//
```

```
node extract-comments-subset.js multi-line-double-slash-comment.js
```

```
[
  {
    "type": "Line",
    "value": "",
    "start": 1,
    "end": 1
  },
  {
    "type": "Line",
    "value": " multi-line double-slash comment",
    "start": 2,
    "end": 2
  },
  {
    "type": "Line",
    "value": "",
    "start": 3,
    "end": 3
  }
]
```

Block comments, on the other hand, can span any number of lines. We don't need to prefix each line with * but most people do for readability:

```
/*
 * multi-line slash-star comment
 */
```

```
node extract-comments-subset.js multi-line-slash-star-comment.js
```

```
[
  {
    "type": "Block",
    "value": "\n * multi-line slash-star comment\n ",
    "start": 1,
    "end": 3
  }
]
```

By convention, we use block comments that start with /** for documentation. The first two characters are recognized by the parser as "start of comment", so the first character in the extracted text is *:

```
/**
 * doc comment
 */
```

```
[
  {
    "type": "Block",
    "value": "*\n * doc comment\n ",
    "start": 1,
    "end": 3
  }
]
```

16.2 What input will we try to handle?

We will use Markdown[4] for formatting our documentation. The **doc comments** for function definitions look like this:

```
/**
 * # Demonstrate documentation generator.
 */

import util from './util-plain'

/**
 * ## `main`: Main driver.
 */
const main = () => {
  // Parse arguments.
  // Process input stream.
}

/**
 * ## `parseArgs`: Parse command line.
 * - `args` (`string[]`): arguments to parse.
 * - `defaults` (`Object`): default values.
```

[4]https://en.wikipedia.org/wiki/Markdown

```
 *
 * Returns: program configuration object.
 */
const parseArgs = (args, defaults) => {
  // body would go here
}

/**
 * ## `process`: Transform data.
 * - `input` (`stream`): where to read.
 * - `output` (`stream`): where to write.
 * - `op` (`class`): what to do.
 *     Use @BaseProcessor unless told otherwise.
 */
const process = (input, output, op = util.BaseProcessor) => {
  // body would go here
}
```

while the ones for class definitions look like this:

```
/**
 * # Utilities to demonstrate doc generator.
 */

/**
 * ## `BaseProcessor`: General outline.
 */
class BaseProcessor {
  /**
   * ### `constructor`: Build processor.
   */
  constructor () {
    // body would go here
  }

  /**
   * ### `run`: Pass input to output.
   * - `input` (`stream`): where to read.
   * - `output` (`stream`): where to write.
   */
  run (input, output) {
    // body would go here
  }
}

export default BaseProcessor
```

The doc comments are unpleasant at the moment: they repeat the function and method names from the code, we have to create titles ourselves, and we have to remember the back-quotes for formatting code. We will fix some of these problems once we have a basic tool up and running.

The next step in doing that is to translate Markdown into HTML. There are many Markdown parsers in JavaScript; after experimenting with a few, we decided to use `markdown-it`[5] along with the `markdown-it-anchor`[6] extension that creates HTML anchors for headings. The main program gets all the doc comments from all of the input files, converts the Markdown to HTML, and displays that:

[5]https://markdown-it.github.io/

[6]https://www.npmjs.com/package/markdown-it-anchor

```
const STYLE = 'width: 40rem; padding-left: 0.5rem; border: solid;'
const HEAD = `<html><body style="${STYLE}">`
const FOOT = '</body></html>'

const main = () => {
  const allComments = getAllComments(process.argv.slice(2))
  const md = new MarkdownIt({ html: true })
    .use(MarkdownAnchor, { level: 1, slugify: slugify })
  const html = md.render(allComments)
  console.log(HEAD)
  console.log(html)
  console.log(FOOT)
}
```

To get all the comments, we extract comments from all the files, remove the leading * characters (which aren't part of the documentation), and then join the results after stripping off extraneous blanks:

```
const getAllComments = (allFilenames) => {
  return allFilenames
    .map(filename => {
      const comments = extractComments(filename)
      return { filename, comments }
    })
    .map(({ filename, comments }) => {
      comments = comments.map(comment => removePrefix(comment))
      return { filename, comments }
    })
    .map(({ filename, comments }) => {
      const combined = comments
        .map(comment => comment.stripped)
        .join('\n\n')
      return `# ${filename}\n\n${combined}`
    })
    .join('\n\n')
}
```

Extracting the comments from a single file is done as before:

```
const extractComments = (filename) => {
  const text = fs.readFileSync(filename, 'utf-8')
  const options = {
    sourceType: 'module',
    locations: true,
    onComment: []
  }
  acorn.parse(text, options)
  const subset = options.onComment
    .filter(entry => entry.type === 'Block')
    .map(entry => {
      return {
        type: entry.type,
        value: entry.value,
        start: entry.start,
        end: entry.end
      }
    })
  return subset
}
```

and removing the prefix * characters is a matter of splitting the text into lines, removing the leading spaces and asterisks, and putting the lines back together:

```
const removePrefix = (comment) => {
  comment.stripped = comment.value
    .split('\n')
    .slice(0, -1)
    .map(line => line.replace(/^ *\/?\* */, ''))
    .map(line => line.replace('*/', ''))
    .join('\n')
    .trim()
  return comment
}
```

One thing that isn't in this file (because we're going to use it in later versions) is the function `slugify`. A **slug** is a short string that identifies a header or a web page; the name comes from the era of newspapers, where a slug was a short name used to identify an article while it was in production. Our `slugify` function strips unnecessary characters out of a title, adds hyphens, and generally makes it something you might see in a URL:

```
const slugify = (text) => {
  return encodeURIComponent(
    text.split(' ')[0]
      .replace(/.js$/, '')
      .trim()
      .toLowerCase()
      .replace(/[^ \w]/g, '')
      .replace(/\s+/g, '-')
  )
}

export default slugify
```

Let's run this generator and see what it produces (Figure 16.3 and Figure 16.2):

```
node process-plain.js example-plain.js util-plain.js
```

```
<html><body style="width: 40rem; padding-left: 0.5rem; border: solid;">
<h1 id="exampleplain">example-plain.js</h1>
<h1 id="demonstrate">Demonstrate documentation generator.</h1>
<h2 id="main"><code>main</code>: Main driver.</h2>
<h2 id="parseargs"><code>parseArgs</code>: Parse command line.</h2>
<ul>
<li><code>args</code> (<code>string[]</code>): arguments to parse.</li>
<li><code>defaults</code> (<code>Object</code>): default values.</li>
</ul>
<p>Returns: program configuration object.</p>
<h2 id="process"><code>process</code>: Transform data.</h2>
<ul>
<li><code>input</code> (<code>stream</code>): where to read.</li>
<li><code>output</code> (<code>stream</code>): where to write.</li>
<li><code>op</code> (<code>class</code>): what to do.
Use @BaseProcessor unless told otherwise.</li>
</ul>
<h1 id="utilplain">util-plain.js</h1>
<h1 id="utilities">Utilities to demonstrate doc generator.</h1>
<h2 id="baseprocessor"><code>BaseProcessor</code>: General outline.</h2>
<h3 id="constructor"><code>constructor</code>: Build processor.</h3>
<h3 id="run"><code>run</code>: Pass input to output.</h3>
<ul>
```

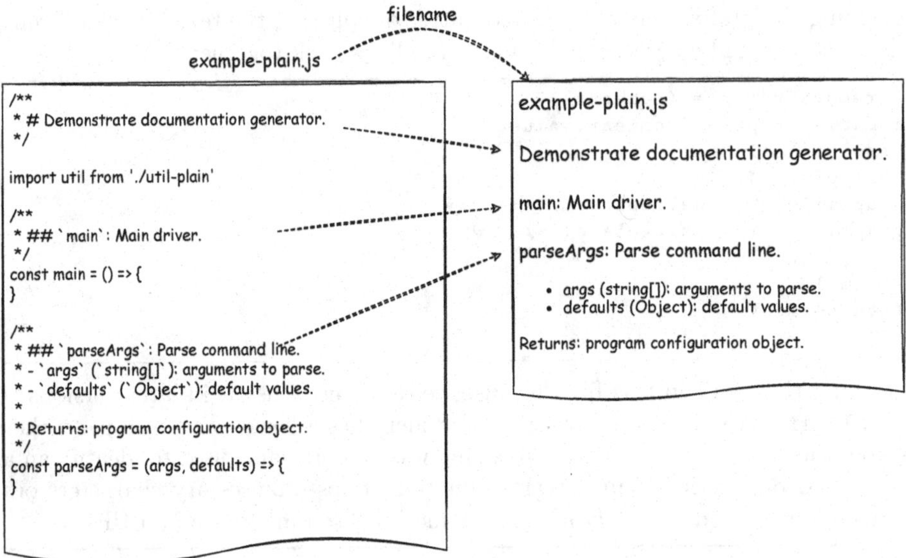

Figure 16.2: How comments in code map to documentation in HTML.

```
<li><code>input</code> (<code>stream</code>): where to read.</li>
<li><code>output</code> (<code>stream</code>): where to write.</li>
</ul>

</body></html>
```

It works, but there is a double **h1** header for each file (the filename and the title comment), the anchor IDs are hard to read, there are no cross-references, and so on. Some of the visual issues can be resolved with CSS, and we can change our input format to make processing easier as long as it also makes authoring easier. However, anything that is written twice will eventually be wrong in one place or another, so our first priority is to remove duplication.

16.3 How can we avoid duplicating names?

If a comment is the first thing in a file, we want to use it as title text; this will save us having to write an explicit level-1 title in a comment. For each other comment, we can extract the name of the function or method from the node on the line immediately following the doc comment. This allows us to write much tidier comments:

```
/**
 * Overall file header.
 */

/**
 * Double the input.
 */
const double = (x) => 2 * x

/**
 * Triple the input.
```

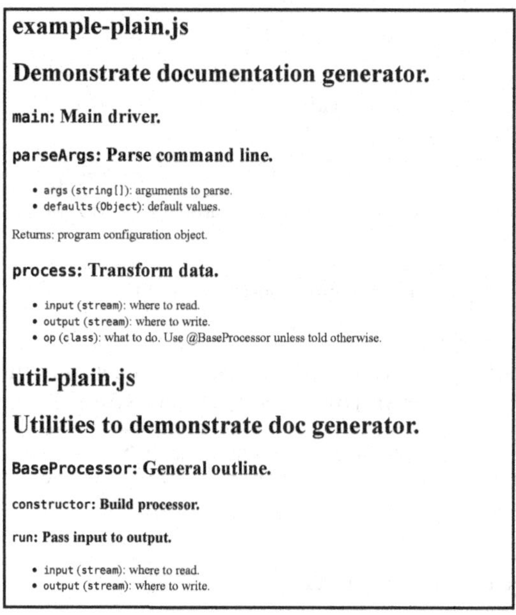

Figure 16.3: The page produced by the documentation generator.

```
 */
function triple (x) {
  return 3 * x
}

/**
 * Define a class.
 */
class Example {
  /**
   * Method description.
   */
  someMethod () {
  }
}
```

To extract and display information from nodes immediately following doc comments we must find all the block comments, record the last line of each, and then search the AST to find nodes that are on lines immediately following any of those trailing comment lines. (We will assume for now that there are no blank lines between the comment and the start of the class or function.) The main program finds the comments as usual, creates a set containing the line numbers we are looking for, then searches for the nodes we want:

```
const main = () => {
  const options = {
    sourceType: 'module',
    locations: true,
    onComment: []
  }
  const text = fs.readFileSync(process.argv[2], 'utf-8')
  const ast = acorn.parse(text, options)
  const comments = options.onComment
    .filter(entry => entry.type === 'Block')
```

```
    .map(entry => {
      return {
        value: entry.value,
        start: entry.loc.start.line,
        end: entry.loc.end.line
      }
    })
  const targets = new Set(comments.map(comment => comment.end + 1))
  const nodes = []
  findFollowing(ast, targets, nodes)
  console.log(nodes.map(node => condense(node)))
}
```

The recursive search is straightforward as well—we delete line numbers from the target set and add nodes to the **accumulator** as we find matches:

```
const findFollowing = (node, targets, accum) => {
  if ((!node) || (typeof node !== 'object') || (!('type' in node))) {
    return
  }

  if (targets.has(node.loc.start.line)) {
    accum.push(node)
    targets.delete(node.loc.start.line)
  }

  for (const key in node) {
    if (Array.isArray(node[key])) {
      node[key].forEach(child => findFollowing(child, targets, accum))
    } else if (typeof node[key] === 'object') {
      findFollowing(node[key], targets, accum)
    }
  }
}
```

Finally, we use a function called `condense` to get the name we want out of the AST:

```
const condense = (node) => {
  const result = {
    type: node.type,
    start: node.loc.start.line
  }
  switch (node.type) {
    case 'VariableDeclaration':
      result.name = node.declarations[0].id.name
      break
    case 'FunctionDeclaration':
      result.name = node.id.name
      break
    case 'ClassDeclaration':
      result.name = node.id.name
      break
    case 'MethodDefinition':
      result.name = node.key.name
      break
    default:
      assert.fail(`Unknown node type ${node.type}`)
      break
  }
  return result
}
```

We need this because we get a different structure with:

```
const name = function() => {
}
```

than we get with:

```
function name() {
}
```

When we run this on our test case we get:

```
[
  { type: 'VariableDeclaration', start: 8, name: 'double' },
  { type: 'FunctionDeclaration', start: 13, name: 'triple' },
  { type: 'ClassDeclaration', start: 20, name: 'Example' },
  { type: 'MethodDefinition', start: 24, name: 'someMethod' }
]
```

We can use this to create better output (Figure 16.4):

```
import MarkdownIt from 'markdown-it'
import MarkdownAnchor from 'markdown-it-anchor'

import getComments from './get-comments.js'
import getDefinitions from './get-definitions.js'
import fillIn from './fill-in.js'
import slugify from './slugify.js'

const STYLE = 'width: 40rem; padding-left: 0.5rem; border: solid;'
const HEAD = `<html><body style="${STYLE}">`
const FOOT = '</body></html>'

const main = () => {
  const filenames = process.argv.slice(2)
  const allComments = getComments(filenames)
  const allDefinitions = getDefinitions(filenames)
  const combined = []
  for (const [filename, comments] of allComments) {
    const definitions = allDefinitions.get(filename)
    const text = fillIn(filename, comments, definitions)
    combined.push(text)
  }
  const md = new MarkdownIt({ html: true })
    .use(MarkdownAnchor, { level: 1, slugify: slugify })
  const html = md.render(combined.join('\n\n'))
  console.log(HEAD)
  console.log(html)
  console.log(FOOT)
}

main()
```

```
<html><body style="width: 40rem; padding-left: 0.5rem; border: solid;">
<h1 id="fillinheadersinput">fill-in-headers-input.js</h1>
<p>Demonstrate documentation generator.</p>
<h2 id="main">main</h2>
<p>Main driver.</p>
<h2 id="parseargs">parseArgs</h2>
<p>Parse command-line arguments.</p>
<ul>
```

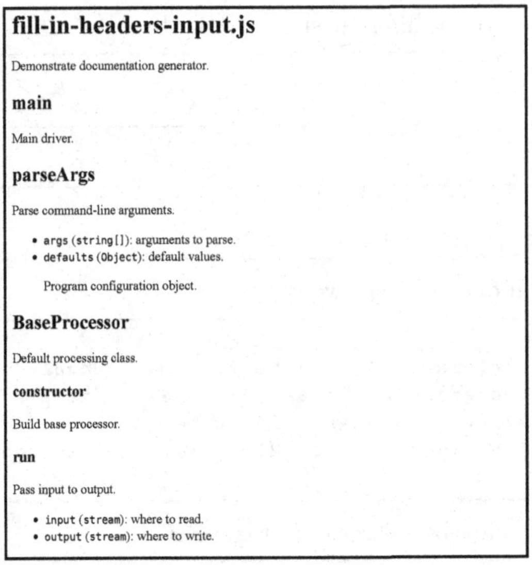

fill-in-headers-input.js

Demonstrate documentation generator.

main

Main driver.

parseArgs

Parse command-line arguments.

- `args` (`string[]`): arguments to parse.
- `defaults` (`Object`): default values.

> Program configuration object.

BaseProcessor

Default processing class.

constructor

Build base processor.

run

Pass input to output.

- `input` (`stream`): where to read.
- `output` (`stream`): where to write.

Figure 16.4: Filling in headers when generating documentation.

```
<li><code>args</code> (<code>string[]</code>): arguments to parse.</li>
<li><code>defaults</code> (<code>Object</code>): default values.</li>
</ul>
<blockquote>
<p>Program configuration object.</p>
</blockquote>
<h2 id="baseprocessor">BaseProcessor</h2>
<p>Default processing class.</p>
<h3 id="constructor">constructor</h3>
<p>Build base processor.</p>
<h3 id="run">run</h3>
<p>Pass input to output.</p>
<ul>
<li><code>input</code> (<code>stream</code>): where to read.</li>
<li><code>output</code> (<code>stream</code>): where to write.</li>
</ul>

</body></html>
```

16.4 Code is Data

We haven't made this point explicitly in a while, so we will repeat it here: code is just another kind of data, and we can process it just like we would process any other data. Parsing code to produce an AST is no different from parsing HTML to produce DOM; in both cases we are simply transforming a textual representation that's easy for people to author into a data structure that's easy for a program to manipulate. Pulling things out of that data to create a report is no different from pulling numbers out of a hospital database to report monthly vaccination rates.

Treating code as data enables us to do routine programming tasks with a single command, which in turn gives us more time to think about the tasks that we can't (yet) automate. Doing this is the foundation of a tool-based approach to software engineering; as the mathematician Alfred North Whitehead once wrote, "Civilization advances by extending the number of important operations which we can perform without thinking about them."

16.5 Exercises

Building an index

Modify the documentation generator to produce an alphabetical index of all classes and methods found. Index entries should be hyperlinks to the documentation for the corresponding item.

Documenting exceptions

Extend the documentation generator to allow people to document the exceptions that a function throws.

Deprecation warning

Add a feature to the documentation generator to allow authors to mark functions and methods as **deprecation** (i.e., to indicate that while they still exist, they should not be used because they are being phased out).

Usage examples

Enhance the documentation generator so that if a horizontal rule `---` appears in a documentation comment, the text following is typeset as usage example. (A doc comment may contain several usage examples.)

Unit testing

Write unit tests for the documentation generator using Mocha.

Summarizing functions

Modify the documentation generator so that line comments inside a function that use `//*` are formatted as a bullet list in the documentation for that function.

Cross referencing

Modify the documentation generator so that the documentation for one class or function can include Markdown links to other classes or functions.

Data types

Modify the documentation generator to allow authors to define new data types in the same way as JSDoc[7].

Inline parameter documentation

Some documentation generators put the documentation for a parameter on the same line as the parameter:

```
/**
 * Transform data.
 */
function process(
  input,  /*- {stream} where to read */
  output, /*- {stream} where to write */
  op      /*- {Operation} what to do */
){
  // body would go here
}
```

Modify the documentation generator to handle this.

Tests as documentation

The doctest[8] library for Python allows programmers to embed unit tests as documentation in their programs. Write a tool that:

1. Finds functions that start with a block comment.

2. Extracts the code and output from those blocks comments and turns them into assertions.

For example, given this input:

```
const findIncreasing = (values) => {
  /**
   * > findIncreasing([])
   * []
   * > findIncreasing([1])
   * [1]
   * > findIncreasing([1, 2])
   * [1, 2]
   * > findIncreasing([2, 1])
   * [2]
   */
}
```

the tool would produce:

```
assert.deepStrictEqual(findIncreasing([]), [])
assert.deepStrictEqual(findIncreasing([1]), [1])
assert.deepStrictEqual(findIncreasing([1, 2]), [1, 2])
assert.deepStrictEqual(findIncreasing([2, 1]), [2])
```

[7]https://jsdoc.app/
[8]https://docs.python.org/3/library/doctest.html

17

Module Bundler

Terms defined: **entry point**, **module bundler**, **transitive closure**

JavaScript was designed in a hurry 25 years ago to make web pages interactive. Nobody realized it would become so popular, so it didn't include support for things that large programs need. One of those things was a way to turn a set of source files into a single file so that browsers could load what they needed with one request.

A **module bundler** finds all the files that an application depends on and combines them into a single loadable file (Figure 17.1). This file is much more efficient to load: it's the same number of bytes but just one network request. (See Table 2.1 for a reminder of why this is important.) Bundling files also tests that dependencies actually resolve so that the application has at least a chance of being able to run.

Bundling requires an **entry point**, i.e., a place to start searching for dependencies. Given that, it finds all dependencies, combines them into one file, and ensures they can find each other correctly once loaded. The sections below go through these steps one by one.

17.1 What will we use as test cases?

Our first test case is a single file that doesn't require anything:

```
const main = () => {
  console.log('in main')
}

module.exports = main
```

```
in main
```

For our second test, `main.js` requires `other.js`:

```
const other = require('./other')

const main = () => {
  console.log(other('main'))
}

module.exports = main
```

and `other.js` doesn't require anything:

```
const other = require('./other')

const main = () => {
  console.log(other('main'))
}

module.exports = main
```

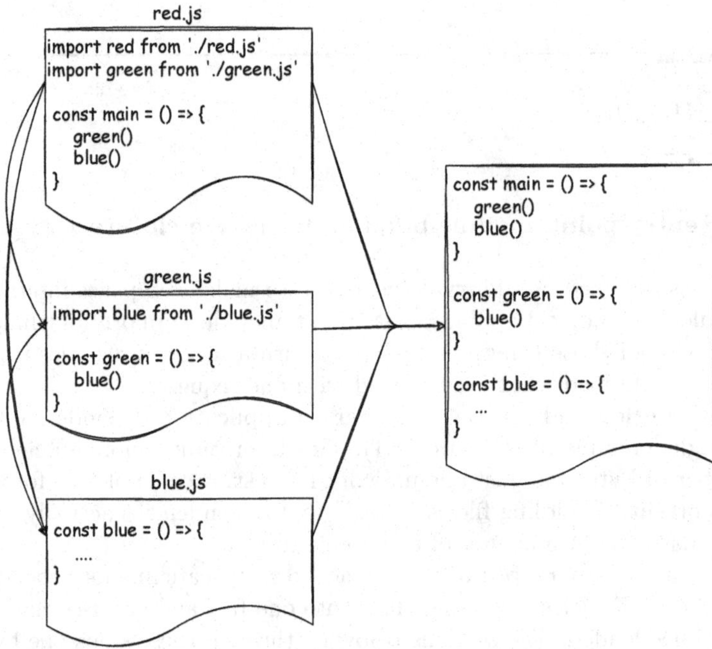

Figure 17.1: Combining multiple modules into one.

The output we expect is:

```
other called from main
```

> **Why require?**
>
> Our tests cases use the old-style `require` function and assign things that are to be visible outside the module to `module.exports` rather than using `import` and `export`. We tried writing the chapter using the latter, but kept stumbling over whether we were talking about `import` in Node's module loader or the `import` we were building. This kind of confusion is common when building programming tools; we hope that splitting terminology as we have will help.

Our third test case has multiple inclusions in multiple directories and is shown in Figure 17.2:

- `./main` requires all four of the files below.
- `./top-left` doesn't require anything.
- `./top-right` requires `top-left` and `bottom-right`.
- `./subdir/bottom-left` also requires `top-left` and `bottom-right`.
- `./subdir/bottom-right` doesn't require anything.

The main program is:

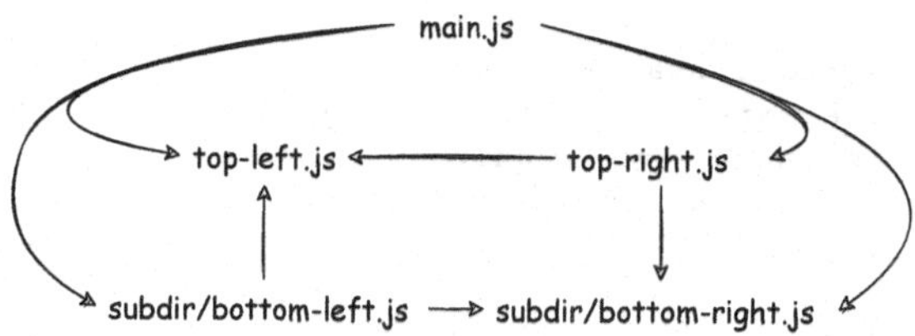

Figure 17.2: Dependencies in large module bundler test case.

```
// main.js

const topLeft = require('./top-left')
const topRight = require('./top-right')
const bottomLeft = require('./subdir/bottom-left')
const bottomRight = require('./subdir/bottom-right')

const main = () => {
  const functions = [topLeft, topRight, bottomLeft, bottomRight]
  functions.forEach(func => {
    console.log(`${func('main')}`)
  })
}

module.exports = main
```

and the other four files use `require` and `module.exports` to get what they need. The output we expect is:

```
topLeft from main
topRight from main with topLeft from topRight and bottomRight from \
 topRight
bottomLeft from main with topLeft from bottomLeft and bottomRight from \
 bottomLeft
bottomRight from main
```

We do not handle circular dependencies because `require` itself doesn't (Chapter 13).

17.2 How can we find dependencies?

To get all the dependencies for one source file, we parse it and extract all of the calls to `require`. The code to do this is relatively straightforward given what we know about Acorn[1]:

```
import acorn from 'acorn'
import fs from 'fs'
import walk from 'acorn-walk'

const getRequires = (filename) => {
  const entryPointFile = filename
  const text = fs.readFileSync(entryPointFile, 'utf-8')
  const ast = acorn.parse(text)
  const requires = []
```

[1]https://github.com/acornjs/acorn

```
  walk.simple(ast, {
    CallExpression: (node, state) => {
      if ((node.callee.type === 'Identifier') &&
          (node.callee.name === 'require')) {
        state.push(node.arguments[0].value)
      }
    }
  }, null, requires)
  return requires
}

export default getRequires
```

```
import getRequires from './get-requires.js'

const result = getRequires(process.argv[2])
console.log(result)
```

```
node test-get-requires.js simple/main.js
```

```
[ './other' ]
```

An unsolvable problem

The dependency finder shown above gives the right answer for reasonable JavaScript programs, but not all JavaScript is reasonable. Suppose creates an alias for `require` and uses that to load other files:

```
const req = require
const weWillMissThis = req('./other-file')
```

We could try to trace variable assignments to catch cases like these, but someone could still fool us by writing this:

```
const clever = eval(`require`)
const weWillMissThisToo = clever('./other-file')
```

There is no general solution to this problem other than running the code to see what it does. If you would like to understand why not, and learn about a pivotal moment in the history of computing, we highly recommend [Petzold2008].

To get all of the dependencies a bundle needs we need to find the **transitive closure** of the entry point's dependencies, i.e., the requirements of the requirements and so on recursively. Our algorithm for doing this uses two sets: `pending`, which contains the things we haven't looked at yet, and `seen`, which contains the things we have (Figure 17.3). `pending` initially contains the entry point file and `seen` is initially empty. We keep taking items from `pending` until it is empty. If the current thing is already in `seen` we do nothing; otherwise we get its dependencies and add them to either `seen` or `pending`.

Finding dependencies is complicated by the fact that we can load something under different names, such as `./subdir/bottom-left` from `main` but `./bottom-left` from `./subdir/bottom-right`. As with the module loader in Chapter 13, we use absolute paths as unique identifiers. Our code is also complicated by the fact that JavaScript's `Set` class doesn't have an equivalent of `Array.pop`, so we will actually maintain the "set" of pending items as a list. The resulting code is:

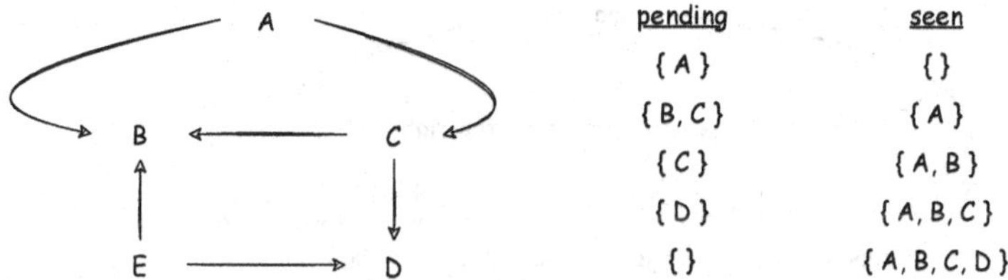

Figure 17.3: Implementing transitive closure using two sets.

```
import path from 'path'

import getRequires from './get-requires.js'

const transitiveClosure = (entryPointPath) => {
  const pending = [path.resolve(entryPointPath)]
  const filenames = new Set()
  while (pending.length > 0) {
    const candidate = path.resolve(pending.pop())
    if (filenames.has(candidate)) {
      continue
    }
    filenames.add(candidate)
    const candidateDir = path.dirname(candidate)
    getRequires(candidate)
      .map(raw => path.resolve(path.join(candidateDir, `${raw}.js`)))
      .filter(cooked => !filenames.has(cooked))
      .forEach(cooked => pending.push(cooked))
  }
  return [...filenames]
}

export default transitiveClosure
```

```
import transitiveClosure from './transitive-closure-only.js'

const result = transitiveClosure(process.argv[2])
console.log(JSON.stringify(result, null, 2))
```

```
node test-transitive-closure-only.js full/main.js
```

```
[
  "/u/stjs/module-bundler/full/main.js",
  "/u/stjs/module-bundler/full/subdir/bottom-right.js",
  "/u/stjs/module-bundler/full/subdir/bottom-left.js",
  "/u/stjs/module-bundler/full/top-left.js",
  "/u/stjs/module-bundler/full/top-right.js"
]
```

This works, but it isn't keeping track of the mapping from required names within files to absolute paths, so when one of the files in our bundle tries to access something, we might not know what it's after. The fix is to modify transitive closure to construct and return a two-level structure. The primary keys are the absolute paths to the files being required, while sub-keys are the paths they refer to when loading things (Figure 17.4).

Adding this takes our transitive closure code from 23 lines to 28 lines:

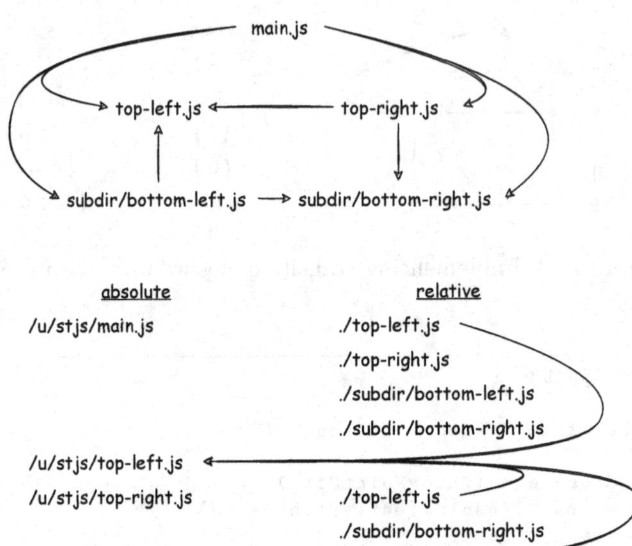

Figure 17.4: Data structure used to map names to absolute paths.

```
import path from 'path'
import getRequires from './get-requires.js'

const transitiveClosure = (entryPointPath) => {
  const mapping = {}
  const pending = [path.resolve(entryPointPath)]
  const filenames = new Set()
  while (pending.length > 0) {
    const candidate = path.resolve(pending.pop())
    if (filenames.has(candidate)) {
      continue
    }
    filenames.add(candidate)
    mapping[candidate] = {}
    const candidateDir = path.dirname(candidate)
    getRequires(candidate)
      .map(raw => {
        mapping[candidate][raw] =
          path.resolve(path.join(candidateDir, `${raw}.js`))
        return mapping[candidate][raw]
      })
      .filter(cooked => cooked !== null)
      .forEach(cooked => pending.push(cooked))
  }
  return mapping
}

export default transitiveClosure
```

```
import transitiveClosure from './transitive-closure.js'

const result = transitiveClosure(process.argv[2])
console.log(JSON.stringify(result, null, 2))
```

```
node test-transitive-closure.js full/main.js
```

```
{
  "/u/stjs/module-bundler/full/main.js": {
    "./top-left": "/u/stjs/module-bundler/full/top-left.js",
    "./top-right": "/u/stjs/module-bundler/full/top-right.js",
    "./subdir/bottom-left": \
    "/u/stjs/module-bundler/full/subdir/bottom-left.js",
    "./subdir/bottom-right": \
    "/u/stjs/module-bundler/full/subdir/bottom-right.js"
  },
  "/u/stjs/module-bundler/full/subdir/bottom-right.js": {},
  "/u/stjs/module-bundler/full/subdir/bottom-left.js": {
    "../top-left": "/u/stjs/module-bundler/full/top-left.js",
    "./bottom-right": \
    "/u/stjs/module-bundler/full/subdir/bottom-right.js"
  },
  "/u/stjs/module-bundler/full/top-left.js": {},
  "/u/stjs/module-bundler/full/top-right.js": {
    "./top-left": "/u/stjs/module-bundler/full/top-left.js",
    "./subdir/bottom-right": \
    "/u/stjs/module-bundler/full/subdir/bottom-right.js"
  }
}
```

The real cost, though, is the extra complexity of the data structure: it took a couple of tries to get it right, and it will be harder for the next person to understand than the original. Comprehension and maintenance would be a little easier if we could draw diagrams directly in our source code, but as long as we insist that our programs be stored in a punchcard-compatible format (i.e., as lines of text), that will remain a dream.

17.3 How can we safely combine several files into one?

We now need to combine the files we have found into one while keeping each in its own namespace. We do this using the same method we used in Chapter 13: wrap the source code in an IIFE, giving that IIFE a `module` object to fill in and an implementation of `require` to resolve dependencies *within the bundle*. For example, suppose we have this file:

```
const main = () => {
  console.log('in main')
}

module.exports = main
```

The wrapped version will look like this:

```
const wrapper = (module, require) => {
  const main = () => {
    console.log('in main')
```

```
  }

  module.exports = main
}
```

And we can test it like this:

```
const wrapper = (module, require) => {
  const main = () => {
    console.log('in main')
  }

  module.exports = main
}

const _require = (name) => null
const temp = {}
wrapper(temp, _require)
temp.exports()
```

```
in main
```

We need to do this for multiple files, so we will put these IIFEs in a lookup table that uses the files' absolute paths as its keys. We will also wrap loading in a function so that we don't accidentally step on anyone else's toys:

```
import fs from 'fs'
import path from 'path'

const HEAD = `const initialize = (creators) => {
`

const TAIL = `
}
`

const combineFiles = (allFilenames) => {
  const body = allFilenames
    .map(filename => {
      const key = path.resolve(filename)
      const source = fs.readFileSync(filename, 'utf-8')
      const func = `(module, require) => {${source}}`
      const entry = `creators.set('${key}',\n${func})`
      return `// ${key}\n${entry}\n`
    })
    .join('\n')
  const func = `${HEAD}\n${body}\n${TAIL}`
  return func
}

export default combineFiles
```

Breaking this down, the code in `HEAD` creates a function of no arguments while the code in `TAIL` returns the lookup table from that function. In between, `combineFiles` adds an entry to the lookup table for each file (Figure 17.5).

We can test that this works in our two-file case:

```
import combineFiles from './combine-files.js'

console.log(combineFiles(process.argv.slice(2)))
```

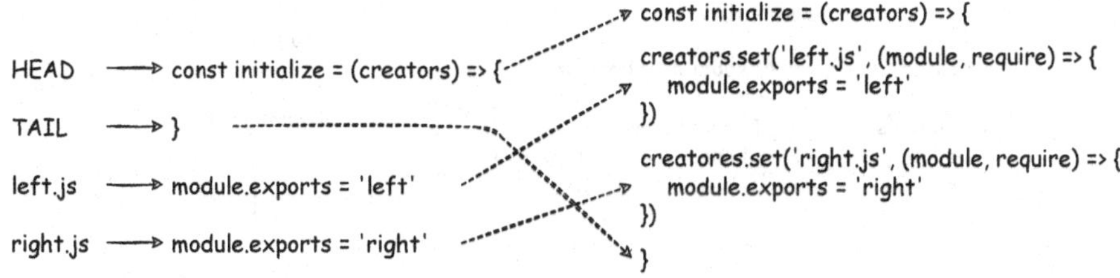

Figure 17.5: Assembling fragments and modules to create a bundle.

```
const initialize = (creators) => {

// /u/stjs/stjs/module-bundler/simple/main.js
creators.set('/u/stjs/stjs/module-bundler/simple/main.js',
(module, require) => {const other = require('./other')

const main = () => {
  console.log(other('main'))
}

module.exports = main
})

// /u/stjs/stjs/module-bundler/simple/other.js
creators.set('/u/stjs/stjs/module-bundler/simple/other.js',
(module, require) => {const other = (caller) => {
  return `other called from ${caller}`
}

module.exports = other
})


}
```

and then load the result and call `initialize`:

```
Map(2) {
  '/u/stjs/module-bundler/simple/main.js' => [Function (anonymous)],
  '/u/stjs/module-bundler/simple/other.js' => [Function (anonymous)]
}
```

17.4 How can files access each other?

The code we have built so far has not created our exports; instead, it has built a lookup table of functions that can create what we asked for. More specifically we have:

- a lookup table from absolute filenames to functions that create module exports;
- a lookup table from the importer's absolute filename to pairs storing the name of the required file as it was written and the required file's absolute filename; and

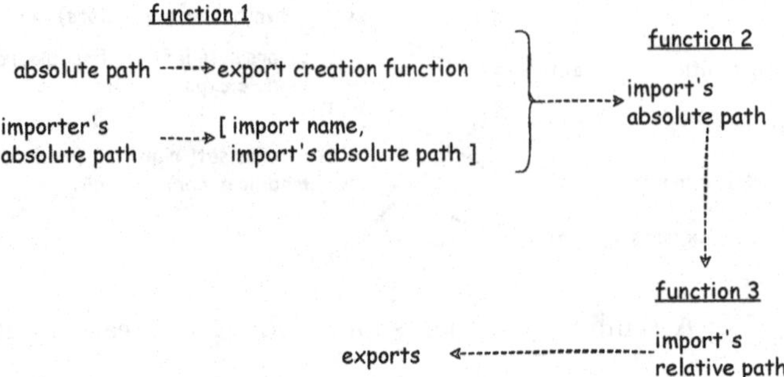

Figure 17.6: A function that returns functions that return functions.

- an entry point.

To turn this into what we want, we must look up the function associated with the entry point and run it, giving it an empty module object and a `require` function that we will describe below, then get the `exports` it has added to that module object. Our replacement for `require` is only allowed to take one argument (because that's all that JavaScript's `require` takes). However, it actually needs four things: the argument to the user's `require` call, the absolute path of the file making the call, and the two lookup tables described above. Those two tables can't be global variables because of possible name collisions: no matter what we call them, the user might have given a variable the same name.

As in Chapter 13 we solve this problem using closures. The result is probably the most difficult code in this book to understand because of its many levels of abstraction. First, we write a function that takes the two tables as arguments and returns a function that takes an absolute path identifying this module. When that function is called, it creates and returns a function that takes a local path inside a module and returns the exports. Each of these wrapping layers remembers more information for us (Figure 17.6), but we won't pretend that it's easy to trace.

We also need a third structure: a cache for the modules we've already loaded. Putting it all together we have:

```
import fs from 'fs'
import path from 'path'

import transitiveClosure from './transitive-closure.js'

const HEAD = `const creators = new Map()
const cache = new Map()

const makeRequire = (absPath) => {
  return (localPath) => {
    const actualKey = translate[absPath][localPath]
    if (!cache.has(actualKey)) {
      const m = {}
      creators.get(actualKey)(m)
      cache.set(actualKey, m.exports)
    }
    return cache.get(actualKey)
  }
}

const initialize = (creators) => {
```

```
`

const TAIL = `
}

initialize(creators)
`

const makeProof = (entryPoint) => `
const start = creators.get('${entryPoint}')
const m = {}
start(m)
m.exports()
`

const createBundle = (entryPoint) => {
  entryPoint = path.resolve(entryPoint)
  const table = transitiveClosure(entryPoint)
  const translate = `const translate = ${JSON.stringify(table, null, 2)}`
  const creators = Object.keys(table).map(filename => makeCreator(filename))
  const proof = makeProof(entryPoint)
  return [
    translate,
    HEAD,
    ...creators,
    TAIL,
    proof
  ].join('\n')
}

const makeCreator = (filename) => {
  const key = path.resolve(filename)
  const source = fs.readFileSync(filename, 'utf-8')
  const func = `(module, require = makeRequire('${key}')) =>\n{${source}}`
  const entry = `creators.set('${key}',\n${func})`
  return `// ${key}\n${entry}\n`
}

export default createBundle
```

This code is hard to read because we have to distinguish what is being printed in the output versus what is being executed right now and because of the levels of nesting needed to capture variables safely. Getting this right took much more time per line of finished code than anything we have seen so far except the promises in Chapter 3. However, it is all intrinsic complexity: anything that does what `require` does is going to be equally convoluted.

To prove that our code works, we will look up the function `main` in the first file and call it. (If we were loading in the browser, we'd capture the exports in a variable for later use.) First, we create the bundled file:

```
echo '
node test-create-bundle.js single/main.js >> bundle-single.js
```

```
const translate = {
  "/u/stjs/stjs/module-bundler/single/main.js": {}
}
const creators = new Map()
const cache = new Map()
```

```
const makeRequire = (absPath) => {
  return (localPath) => {
    const actualKey = translate[absPath][localPath]
    if (!cache.has(actualKey)) {
      const m = {}
      creators.get(actualKey)(m)
      cache.set(actualKey, m.exports)
    }
    return cache.get(actualKey)
  }
}

const initialize = (creators) => {

// /u/stjs/stjs/module-bundler/single/main.js
creators.set('/u/stjs/stjs/module-bundler/single/main.js',
(module, require =
makeRequire('/u/stjs/stjs/module-bundler/single/main.js')) =>
{const main = () => {
  console.log('in main')
}

module.exports = main
})


}

initialize(creators)


const start = creators.get('/u/stjs/stjs/module-bundler/single/main.js')
const m = {}
start(m)
m.exports()
```

and then we run it:

```
in main
```

That was a lot of work to print one line, but what we have should work for other files. The two-file case with `main` and `other` works:

```
const translate = {
  "/u/stjs/stjs/module-bundler/simple/main.js": {
    "./other": "/u/stjs/stjs/module-bundler/simple/other.js"
  },
  "/u/stjs/stjs/module-bundler/simple/other.js": {}
}
const creators = new Map()
const cache = new Map()

const makeRequire = (absPath) => {
  return (localPath) => {
    const actualKey = translate[absPath][localPath]
    if (!cache.has(actualKey)) {
      const m = {}
      creators.get(actualKey)(m)
      cache.set(actualKey, m.exports)
    }
    return cache.get(actualKey)
```

```
  }
}

const initialize = (creators) => {

// /u/stjs/stjs/module-bundler/simple/main.js
creators.set('/u/stjs/stjs/module-bundler/simple/main.js',
(module, require =
makeRequire('/u/stjs/stjs/module-bundler/simple/main.js')) =>
{const other = require('./other')

const main = () => {
  console.log(other('main'))
}

module.exports = main
})

// /u/stjs/stjs/module-bundler/simple/other.js
creators.set('/u/stjs/stjs/module-bundler/simple/other.js',
(module, require =
makeRequire('/u/stjs/stjs/module-bundler/simple/other.js')) =>
{const other = (caller) => {
  return `other called from ${caller}`
}

module.exports = other
})


}

initialize(creators)


const start = creators.get('/u/stjs/stjs/module-bundler/simple/main.js')
const m = {}
start(m)
m.exports()
```

```
other called from main
```

and so does our most complicated test with `main` and four other files:

```
topLeft from main
topRight from main with topLeft from topRight and bottomRight from \
topRight
bottomLeft from main with topLeft from bottomLeft and bottomRight from \
bottomLeft
bottomRight from main
```

17.5 Exercises

Using test-driven development

Suppose we wanted to compress the files being stored by the file backup system in Chapter 5 instead of copying them as-is. What tests would you write before adding this feature in order to ensure that it worked correctly once it was implemented?

Finding `import` dependencies

Modify the dependency finder to work with `import` statements instead of `require` calls.

Track files using hashes

Modify the dependency finder to track files by hashing them instead of relying on paths, so that if exactly the same file is being required from two locations, only one copy is loaded.

Using asynchronous file operations

Modify the dependency finder to use `async` and `await` instead of synchronous file operations.

Unit testing transitive closure

Write unit tests for the tool that finds the transitive closure of files' requirements using Mocha and `mock-fs`. (Rather than parsing JavaScript files in the mock filesystem, have each file contain only a list of the names of the files it depends on.)

Exporting multiple functions

Create test cases for the module bundler in which files export more than one function and fix any bugs in the module bundler that they uncover.

Checking integrity

Write a function that checks the integrity of the data structure returned by the transitive closure routine, i.e., that makes sure every cross-reference resolves correctly.

Logging module loading

1. Write a function called `logLoad` that takes a module name as an argument and prints a message using `console.error` saying that the module has been loaded.

2. Modify the bundle generator to insert calls to this function to report when modules are actually loaded.

Tracing execution

Trace the execution of every function called when the `main` function in the full bundle is called.

Making bundles more readable

Modify the bundle creator to make its output more readable, e.g., by adding comments and indentation. (This does not matter to the computer, but can help debugging.)

18

Package Manager

Terms defined: **backward-compatible**, **combinatorial explosion**, **heuristic**, **manifest**, **patch**, **prune**, **SAT solver**, **scoring function**, **seed**, **semantic versioning**

There is no point building software if you can't install it. Inspired by the Comprehensive TeX Archive Network CTAN[1], most languages now have an online archive from which developers can download packages. Each package typically has a name and one or more version(s); each version may have a list of dependencies, and the package may specify a version or range of versions for each dependency.

Downloading files requires some web programming that is out of scope for this book, while installing those files in the right places uses the systems programming skills of Chapter 2. The piece we are missing is a way to figure out exactly what versions of different packages to install in order to create a consistent setup. If packages A and B require different versions of C, it might not be possible to use A and B together. On the other hand, if each one requires a range of versions of C and those ranges overlap, we might be able to find a combination that works—at least, until we try to install packages D and E.

We *could* install every package's dependencies separately with it; the disk space wouldn't be much of an obstacle, but loading dozens of copies of the same package into the browser would slow applications down. This chapter therefore explores how to find a workable installation or prove that there isn't one. It is based in part on this tutorial[2] by Maël Nison[3].

Satisfiability

What we are trying to do is find a version for each package that makes the assertion "P is compatible with all its dependencies" true for every package P. The general-purpose tools for doing this are called **SAT solvers** because they determine whether there is some assignment of values that satisfies the claim (i.e., makes it true). Finding a solution can be extremely hard in the general case, so most SAT solvers use heuristics to try to reduce the work.

18.1 What is semantic versioning?

Most software projects use **semantic versioning** for software releases. Each version number consists of three integers X.Y.Z, where X is the major version, Y is the minor version, and Z is the **patch** number. (The full specification[4] allows for more fields, but we will ignore them in this tutorial.)

[1] https://www.ctan.org/
[2] https://classic.yarnpkg.com/blog/2017/07/11/lets-dev-a-package-manager/
[3] https://arcanis.github.io/
[4] https://semver.org/

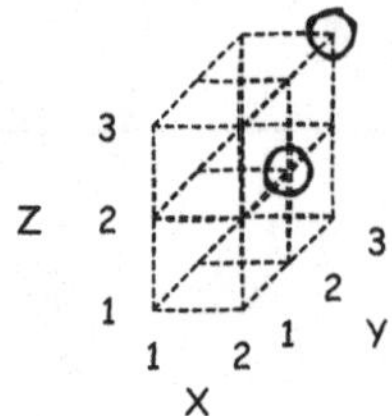

Figure 18.1: Finding allowable combinations of package versions.

A package's authors increment its major version number every time something changes in a way that makes the package incompatible with previous versions. For example, if they add a required parameter to a function, then code built for the old version will fail or behave unpredictably with the new one. The minor version number is incremented when new functionality is **backward-compatible**—i.e., it won't break any existing code—and the patch number is changed for backward-compatible bug fixes that don't add any new features.

The notation for specifying a project's dependencies looks a lot like arithmetic: `>= 1.2.3` means "any version from 1.2.3 onward", `< 4` means "any version before 4.anything", and `1.0 - 3.1` means "any version in the specified range (including patches)". Note that version 2.1 is greater than version 1.99: no matter how large a minor version number becomes, it never spills over into the major version number in the way that minutes add up to hours or months add up to years.

It isn't hard to write a few simple comparisons for semantic version identifiers, but getting all the different cases right is almost as tricky as handling dates and times correctly, so we will rely on the `semver`[5] module. `semver.valid('1.2.3')` checks that `1.2.3` is a valid version identifier, while `semver.satisfies('2.2', '1.0 - 3.1')` checks that its first argument is compatible with the range specified in its second.

18.2 How can we find a consistent set of packages?

Imagine that each package we need is represented as an axis on a multi-dimensional grid, with its versions as the tick marks (Figure 18.1). Each point on the grid is a possible combination of package versions. We can block out regions of this grid using the constraints on the package versions; whatever points are left when we're done represent legal combinations.

For example, suppose we have the set of requirements shown in Table 18.1. There are 18 possible configurations (2 for X $\times$ 3 for Y $\times$ 3 for Z) but 16 are excluded by various incompatibilities. Of the two remaining possibilities, X/2 + Y/3 + Z/3 is strictly greater than X/2 + Y/2 + Z/2, so we would probably choose the former (Table 18.2). If we wound up with A/1 + B/2 versus A/2 + B/1, we would need to add rules for resolving ties.

Reproducibility

No matter what kind of software you build, a given set of inputs should always produce the same output; if they don't, testing is much more difficult (or impossible)

[5] https://www.npmjs.com/package/semver

[Taschuk2017]. There may not be a strong reason to prefer one mutually-compatible set of packages over another, but a package manager should still resolve the ambiguity the same way every time. It may not be what everyone wants, but at least they will be unhappy for the same reasons everywhere. This is why NPM has both `package.json` and a `package-lock.json` files: the former is written by the user and specifies what they *want*, while the latter is created by the package manager and specifies exactly what they *got*. If you want to reproduce someone else's setup for debugging purposes, you should install what is described in the latter file.

Package	Requires
X/1	Y/1-2
X/1	Z/1
X/2	Y/2-3
X/2	Z/1-2
Y/1	Z/2
Y/2	Z/2-3
Y/3	Z/3
Z/1	
Z/2	
Z/3	

Table 18.1: Example package dependencies.

X	Y	Z	Excluded
1	1	1	Y/1 - Z/1
1	1	2	X/1 - Z/2
1	1	3	X/1 - Z/3
1	2	1	Y/2 - Z/1
1	2	2	X/1 - Z/2
1	2	3	X/1 - Z/3
1	3	1	X/1 - Y/3
1	3	2	X/1 - Y/3
1	3	3	X/1 - Y/3
2	1	1	X/2 - Y/1
2	1	2	X/2 - Y/1
2	1	3	X/2 - Y/1
2	2	1	Y/2 - Z/1
2	2	2	
2	2	3	X/2 - Z/3
2	3	1	Y/3 - Z/1
2	3	2	Y/3 - Z/2
2	3	3	X/2 - Z/3

Table 18.2: Result for example package dependencies.

To construct Table 18.1 we find the transitive closure of all packages plus all of their dependencies. We then pick two packages and create a list of their valid pairs. Choosing a third package, we cross off pairs that can't be satisfied to leave triples of legal combinations. We repeat this until all packages are included in our table.

In the worst case this procedure will create a **combinatorial explosion** of possibilities. Smart algorithms will try to add packages to the mix in an order that minimizes the number of new possibilities at each stage, or create pairs and then combine them to create pairs of pairs and so on. Our algorithm will be simpler (and therefore slower), but illustrates the key idea.

18.3 How can we satisfy constraints?

To avoid messing around with parsers, our programs reads a JSON data structure describing the problem; a real package manager would read the **manifests** of the packages in question and construct a similar data structure. We will stick to single-digit version numbers for readability, and will use this as our first test case:

```
{
  "X": {
    "1": {
      "Y": ["1"]
    },
    "2": {
      "Y": ["2"]
    }
  },
  "Y": {
    "1": {},
    "2": {}
  }
}
```

Comments

If you ever design a data format, please include a standard way for people to add comments, because they will always want to. YAML has this, but JSON and CSV don't.

To check if a combination of specific versions of packages is compatible with a manifest, we add each package to our active list in turn and look for violations. If there aren't any more packages to add and we haven't found a violation, then what we have must be a legal configuration.

```
import configStr from './config-str.js'

const sweep = (manifest) => {
  const names = Object.keys(manifest)
  const result = []
  recurse(manifest, names, {}, result)
}

const recurse = (manifest, names, config, result) => {
  if (names.length === 0) {
    if (allows(manifest, config)) {
      result.push({ ...config })
    }
```

```
  } else {
    const next = names[0]
    const rest = names.slice(1)
    for (const version in manifest[next]) {
      config[next] = version
      recurse(manifest, rest, config, result)
    }
  }
}


export default sweep
```

The simplest way to find configurations is to sweep over all possibilities. For debugging purposes, our function prints possibilities as it goes:

```
const allows = (manifest, config) => {
  for (const [leftN, leftV] of Object.entries(config)) {
    const requirements = manifest[leftN][leftV]
    for (const [rightN, rightVAll] of Object.entries(requirements)) {
      if (!rightVAll.includes(config[rightN])) {
        const title = configStr(config)
        const missing = config[rightN]
        console.log(`${title} @ ${leftN}/${leftV} ${rightN}/${missing}`)
        return false
      }
    }
  }
  console.log(configStr(config))
  return true
}
```

If we run this program on the two-package example shown earlier, we get this output:

```
node driver.js ./sweep.js double-chained.json
```

```
{X:1 Y:1}
{X:1 Y:2} @ X/1 Y/2
{X:2 Y:1} @ X/2 Y/1
{X:2 Y:2}
```

When we run it on our triple-package example, we get this:

```
node driver.js ./sweep.js triple.json
```

```
{X:1 Y:1 Z:1} @ Y/1 Z/1
{X:1 Y:1 Z:2} @ X/1 Z/2
{X:1 Y:1 Z:3} @ X/1 Z/3
{X:1 Y:2 Z:1} @ Y/2 Z/1
{X:1 Y:2 Z:2} @ X/1 Z/2
{X:1 Y:2 Z:3} @ X/1 Z/3
{X:1 Y:3 Z:1} @ X/1 Y/3
{X:1 Y:3 Z:2} @ X/1 Y/3
{X:1 Y:3 Z:3} @ X/1 Y/3
{X:2 Y:1 Z:1} @ X/2 Y/1
{X:2 Y:1 Z:2} @ X/2 Y/1
{X:2 Y:1 Z:3} @ X/2 Y/1
{X:2 Y:2 Z:1} @ Y/2 Z/1
{X:2 Y:2 Z:2}
{X:2 Y:2 Z:3} @ X/2 Z/3
```

```
{X:2 Y:3 Z:1} @ Y/3 Z/1
{X:2 Y:3 Z:2} @ Y/3 Z/2
{X:2 Y:3 Z:3} @ X/2 Z/3
```

This works, but it is doing a lot of unnecessary work. If we sort the output by the case that caught the exclusion, it turns out that 9 of the 17 exclusions are redundant rediscovery of a previously known problem (Table 18.3).

Excluded	X	Y	Z
X/1 - Y/3	1	3	1
...	1	3	2
...	1	3	3
X/1 - Z/2	1	1	2
...	1	2	2
X/1 - Z/3	1	1	3
...	1	2	3
X/2 - Y/1	2	1	1
...	2	1	2
...	2	1	3
X/2 - Z/3	2	2	3
...	2	3	3
Y/1 - Z/1	1	1	1
Y/2 - Z/1	1	2	1
...	2	2	1
Y/3 - Z/1	2	3	1
...	2	3	2
	2	2	2

Table 18.3: Package exclusions.

18.4 How can we do less work?

We can make this more efficient by **pruning** the search tree as we go along (Figure 18.2). After all, if we know that X and Y are incompatible, there is no need to check Z as well.

This version of the program collects possible solutions and displays them at the end. It only keeps checking a partial solution if what it has found so far looks good:

```
import configStr from './config-str.js'

const prune = (manifest) => {
  const names = Object.keys(manifest)
  const result = []
  recurse(manifest, names, {}, result)
  for (const config of result) {
    console.log(configStr(config))
  }
}

const recurse = (manifest, names, config, result) => {
  if (names.length === 0) {
    result.push({ ...config })
```

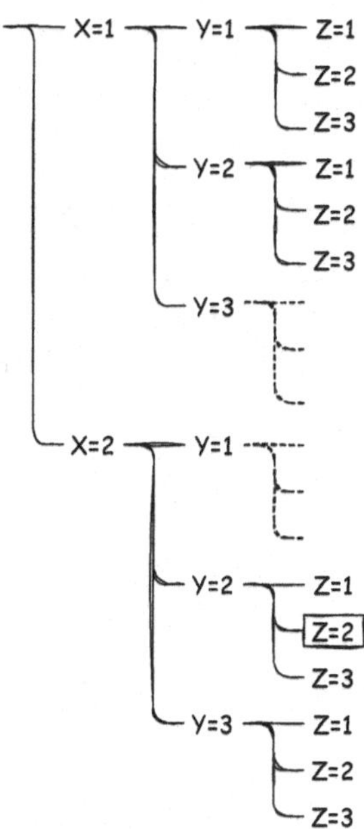

Figure 18.2: Pruning options in the search tree to reduce work.

```
  } else {
    const next = names[0]
    const rest = names.slice(1)
    for (const version in manifest[next]) {
      config[next] = version
      if (compatible(manifest, config)) {
        recurse(manifest, rest, config, result)
      }
      delete config[next]
    }
  }
}


const report = (config, leftN, leftV, rightN, rightV) => {
  const title = configStr(config)
  console.log(`${title} @ ${leftN}/${leftV} ${rightN}/${rightV}`)
}

export default prune
```

The `compatible` function checks to see if adding something will leave us with a consistent configuration:

```
const compatible = (manifest, config) => {
  for (const [leftN, leftV] of Object.entries(config)) {
    const leftR = manifest[leftN][leftV]
    for (const [rightN, rightV] of Object.entries(config)) {
      if ((rightN in leftR) && (!leftR[rightN].includes(rightV))) {
        report(config, leftN, leftV, rightN, rightV)
        return false
      }
      const rightR = manifest[rightN][rightV]
      if ((leftN in rightR) && (!rightR[leftN].includes(leftV))) {
```

```
        report(config, leftN, leftV, rightN, rightV)
        return false
      }
    }
  }
  return true
}
```

Checking as we go gets us from 18 complete solutions to 11. One is workable and two are incomplete—they represent 6 possible complete solutions that we didn't need to finish:

```
{X:1 Y:1 Z:1} @ Y/1 Z/1
{X:1 Y:1 Z:2} @ X/1 Z/2
{X:1 Y:1 Z:3} @ X/1 Z/3
{X:1 Y:2 Z:1} @ Y/2 Z/1
{X:1 Y:2 Z:2} @ X/1 Z/2
{X:1 Y:2 Z:3} @ X/1 Z/3
{X:1 Y:3} @ X/1 Y/3
{X:2 Y:1} @ X/2 Y/1
{X:2 Y:2 Z:1} @ Y/2 Z/1
{X:2 Y:2 Z:3} @ X/2 Z/3
{X:2 Y:3 Z:1} @ Y/3 Z/1
{X:2 Y:3 Z:2} @ Y/3 Z/2
{X:2 Y:3 Z:3} @ X/2 Z/3
{X:2 Y:2 Z:2}
```

Another way to look at the work is the number of steps in the search. The full search had $18 \times 3 = 54$ steps. Pruning leaves us with $(12 \times 3) + (2 \times 2) = 40$ steps so we have eliminated roughly $1/4$ of the work.

What if we searched in the reverse order?

```
import configStr from './config-str.js'

// [reverse]
const reverse = (manifest) => {
  const names = Object.keys(manifest)
  names.reverse()
  const result = []
  recurse(manifest, names, {}, result)
  for (const config of result) {
    console.log(configStr(config))
  }
}
// [/reverse]

const recurse = (manifest, names, config, result) => {
  if (names.length === 0) {
    result.push({ ...config })
  } else {
    const next = names[0]
    const rest = names.slice(1)
    for (const version in manifest[next]) {
      config[next] = version
      if (compatible(manifest, config)) {
        recurse(manifest, rest, config, result)
      }
      delete config[next]
    }
  }
}
```

```
const compatible = (manifest, config) => {
  for (const [leftN, leftV] of Object.entries(config)) {
    const leftR = manifest[leftN][leftV]
    for (const [rightN, rightV] of Object.entries(config)) {
      if ((rightN in leftR) && (!leftR[rightN].includes(rightV))) {
        report(config, leftN, leftV, rightN, rightV)
        return false
      }
      const rightR = manifest[rightN][rightV]
      if ((leftN in rightR) && (!rightR[leftN].includes(leftV))) {
        report(config, leftN, leftV, rightN, rightV)
        return false
      }
    }
  }
  return true
}

const report = (config, leftN, leftV, rightN, rightV) => {
  const title = configStr(config)
  console.log(`${title} @ ${leftN}/${leftV} ${rightN}/${rightV}`)
}

export default reverse
```

```
{Z:1 Y:1} @ Z/1 Y/1
{Z:1 Y:2} @ Z/1 Y/2
{Z:1 Y:3} @ Z/1 Y/3
{Z:2 Y:1 X:1} @ Z/2 X/1
{Z:2 Y:1 X:2} @ Y/1 X/2
{Z:2 Y:2 X:1} @ Z/2 X/1
{Z:2 Y:3} @ Z/2 Y/3
{Z:3 Y:1} @ Z/3 Y/1
{Z:3 Y:2 X:1} @ Z/3 X/1
{Z:3 Y:2 X:2} @ Z/3 X/2
{Z:3 Y:3 X:1} @ Z/3 X/1
{Z:3 Y:3 X:2} @ Z/3 X/2
{Z:2 Y:2 X:2}
```

Now we have $(8\times3) + (5\times2) = 34$ steps, i.e., we have eliminated roughly 1/3 of the work. That may not seem like a big difference, but if we go five levels deep at the same rate, it cuts the work in half. There are lots of **heuristics** for searching trees; none are guaranteed to give better performance in every case, but most give better performance in most cases.

What research is for

SAT solvers are like regular expression libraries and random number generators: it is the work of many lifetimes to create ones that are both fast and correct. A lot of computer science researchers devote their careers to highly-specialized topics like this. The debates often seem esoteric to outsiders, and most ideas turn out to be dead ends, but even small improvements in fundamental tools can have a profound impact.

18.5 Exercises

Comparing semantic versions

Write a function that takes an array of semantic version specifiers and sorts them in ascending order. Remember that `2.1` is greater than `1.99`.

Parsing semantic versions

Using the techniques of Chapter 8, write a parser for a subset of the semantic versioning specification[6].

Using scoring functions

Many different combinations of package versions can be mutually compatible. One way to decide which actual combination to install is to create a **scoring function** that measures how good or bad a particular combination is. For example, a function could measure the "distance" between two versions as:

```
const score (X, Y) => {
  if (X.major !== Y.major) {
    return 100 * abs(X.major - Y.major)
  } else if (X.minor !== Y.minor) {
    return 10 * abs(X.minor - Y.minor)
  } else {
    return abs(X.patch - Y.patch)
  }
}
```

1. Implement a working version of this function and use it to measure the total distance between the set of packages found by the solver and the set containing the most recent version of each package.
2. Explain why this doesn't actually solve the original problem.

Using full semantic versions

Modify the constraint solver to use full semantic versions instead of single digits.

Regular releases

Some packages release new versions on a regular cycle, e.g., Version 2021.1 is released on March 1 of 2021, Version 2021.2 is released on September 1 of that year, version 2022.1 is released on March 1 of the following year, and so on.

1. How does this make package management easier?
2. How does it make it more difficult?

[6] https://semver.org/

Writing unit tests

Write unit tests for the constraint solver using Mocha.

Generating test fixtures

Write a function that creates fixtures for testing the constraint solver:

1. Its first argument is an object whose keys are (fake) package names and whose values are integers indicating the number of versions of that package to include in the test set, such as `{'left': 3, 'middle': 2, 'right': 15}`. Its second argument is a **seed** for random number generation.
2. It generates one valid configuration, such as `{'left': 2, 'middle': 2, 'right': 9}`. (This is to ensure that there is at least one installable set of packages.)
3. It then generates random constraints between the packages. (These may or may not result in other installable combinations.) When this is done, it adds constraints so that the valid configuration from the previous step is included.

Searching least first

Rewrite the constraint solver so that it searches packages by looking at those with the fewest available versions first. Does this reduce the amount of work done for the small examples in this chapter? Does it reduce the amount of work done for larger examples?

Using generators

Rewrite the constraint solver to use generators.

Using exclusions

1. Modify the constraint solver so that it uses a list of package exclusions instead of a list of package requirements, i.e., its input tells it that version 1.2 of package Red can *not* work with versions 3.1 and 3.2 of package Green (which implies that Red 1.2 can work with any other versions of Green).
2. Explain why package managers aren't built this way.

19

Virtual Machine

Terms defined: **Application Binary Interface**, **assembler**, **assembly code**, **bitwise operation**, **disassembler**, **instruction pointer**, **instruction set**, **label (address in memory)**, **op code**, **register**, **virtual machine**, **word (of memory)**

Computers don't execute JavaScript directly. Instead, each processor has its own **instruction set**, and a compiler translates high-level languages into those instructions. Compilers often use an intermediate representation called **assembly code** that gives instructions names instead of numbers. To understand more about how JavaScript actually runs, we will simulate a very simple processor with a little bit of memory. If you want to dive deeper, have a look at Bob Nystrom's[1] *Crafting Interpreters*[2]. You may also enjoy Human Resource Machine[3][, which asks you to solve puzzles of increasing difficulty using a processor almost as simple as ours.

19.1 What is the architecture of our virtual machine?

Our **virtual machine** has three parts, which are shown in Figure 19.1 for a program made up of 110 instructions:

1. An **instruction pointer** (IP) that holds the memory address of the next instruction to execute. It is automatically initialized to point at address 0, which is where every program must start. This rule is part of the **Application Binary Interface** (ABI) for our virtual machine.

2. Four **registers** named R0 to R3 that instructions can access directly. There are no memory-to-memory operations in our VM: everything happens in or through registers.

3. 256 **words** of memory, each of which can store a single value. Both the program and its data live in this single block of memory; we chose the size 256 so that each address will fit in a single byte.

The instructions for our VM are 3 bytes long. The **op code** fits into one byte, and each instruction may optionally include one or two single-byte operands. Each operand is a register identifier, a constant, or an address (which is just a constant that identifies a location in memory); since constants have to fit in one byte, the largest number we can represent directly is 256. Table 19.1 uses the letters `r`, `c`, and `a` to indicate instruction format, where `r` indicates a register identifier, `c` indicates a constant, and `a` indicates an address.

[1] http://journal.stuffwithstuff.com/
[2] https://craftinginterpreters.com/
[3] https://tomorrowcorporation.com/humanresourcemachine

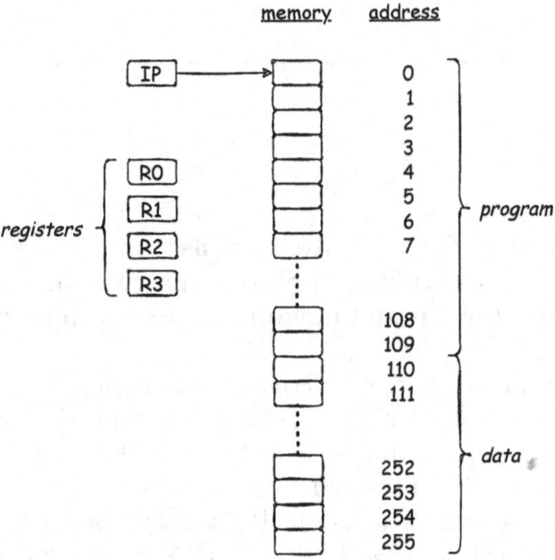

Figure 19.1: Architecture of the virtual machine.

Instruction	Code	Format	Action	Example	Equivalent
`hlt`	1	`--`	Halt program	`hlt`	`process.exit(0)`
`ldc`	2	`rc`	Load immediate	`ldc R0 123`	`R0 := 123`
`ldr`	3	`rr`	Load register	`ldr R0 R1`	`R0 := RAM[R1]`
`cpy`	4	`rr`	Copy register	`cpy R0 R1`	`R0 := R1`
`str`	5	`rr`	Store register	`str R0 R1`	`RAM[R1] := R0`
`add`	6	`rr`	Add	`add R0 R1`	`R0 := R0 + R1`
`sub`	7	`rr`	Subtract	`sub R0 R1`	`R0 := R0 - R1`
`beq`	8	`ra`	Branch if equal	`beq R0 123`	`if (R0 === 0) PC := 123`
`bne`	9	`ra`	Branch if not equal	`bne R0 123`	`if (R0 !== 0) PC := 123`
`prr`	10	`r-`	Print register	`prr R0`	`console.log(R0)`
`prm`	11	`r-`	Print memory	`prm R0`	`console.log(RAM[R0])`

Table 19.1: Virtual machine op codes.

We put our VM's architectural details in a file that can be shared by other components:

```
const OPS = {
  hlt: { code:  1, fmt: '--' }, // Halt program
  ldc: { code:  2, fmt: 'rv' }, // Load immediate
  ldr: { code:  3, fmt: 'rr' }, // Load register
  cpy: { code:  4, fmt: 'rr' }, // Copy register
  str: { code:  5, fmt: 'rr' }, // Store register
  add: { code:  6, fmt: 'rr' }, // Add
  sub: { code:  7, fmt: 'rr' }, // Subtract
  beq: { code:  8, fmt: 'rv' }, // Branch if equal
  bne: { code:  9, fmt: 'rv' }, // Branch if not equal
  prr: { code: 10, fmt: 'r-' }, // Print register
  prm: { code: 11, fmt: 'r-' }  // Print memory
}

const OP_MASK = 0xFF // select a single byte
const OP_SHIFT = 8   // shift up by one byte
const OP_WIDTH = 6   // op width in characters when printing
```

```
const NUM_REG = 4     // number of registers
const RAM_LEN = 256   // number of words in RAM

export {
  OPS,
  OP_MASK,
  OP_SHIFT,
  OP_WIDTH,
  NUM_REG,
  RAM_LEN
}
```

While there isn't a name for this design pattern, putting all the constants that define a system in one file instead of scattering them across multiple files makes them easier to find as well as ensuring consistency.

19.2 How can we execute these instructions?

As in previous chapters, we will split a class that would normally be written in one piece into several parts for exposition. We start by defining a class with an instruction pointer, some registers, and some memory along with a prompt for output:

```
import assert from 'assert'

import {
  OP_MASK,
  OP_SHIFT,
  NUM_REG,
  RAM_LEN
} from './architecture.js'

const COLUMNS = 4
const DIGITS = 8

class VirtualMachineBase {
  constructor () {
    this.ip = 0
    this.reg = Array(NUM_REG)
    this.ram = Array(RAM_LEN)
    this.prompt = '>>'
  }

}

export default VirtualMachineBase
```

A program is just an array of numbers representing instructions. To load one, we copy those numbers into memory and reset the instruction pointer and registers:

```
  initialize (program) {
    assert(program.length <= this.ram.length,
      'Program is too long for memory')
    for (let i = 0; i < this.ram.length; i += 1) {
      if (i < program.length) {
        this.ram[i] = program[i]
```

```
    } else {
      this.ram[i] = 0
    }
  }
  this.ip = 0
  this.reg.fill(0)
}
```

In order to handle the next instruction, the VM gets the value in memory that the instruction pointer currently refers to and moves the instruction pointer on by one address. It then uses **bitwise operations** to extract the op code and operands from the instruction (Figure 19.2):

```
fetch () {
  assert((0 <= this.ip) && (this.ip < RAM_LEN),
    `Program counter ${this.ip} out of range 0..${RAM_LEN}`)
  let instruction = this.ram[this.ip]
  this.ip += 1
  const op = instruction & OP_MASK
  instruction >>= OP_SHIFT
  const arg0 = instruction & OP_MASK
  instruction >>= OP_SHIFT
  const arg1 = instruction & OP_MASK
  return [op, arg0, arg1]
}
```

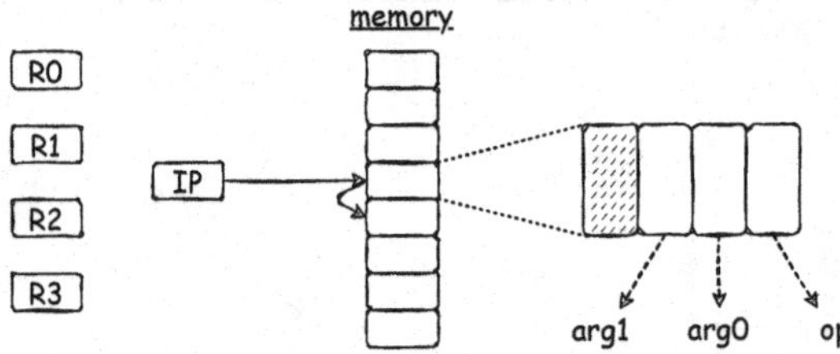

Figure 19.2: Using bitwise operations to unpack instructions.

Semi-realistic

We always unpack two operands regardless of whether the instructions have them or not because this is what a hardware implementation would do. We have also included assertions in our VM to simulate the way that real hardware includes logic to detect illegal instructions and out-of-bound memory addresses.

The next step is to extend our base class with one that has a **run** method. As its name suggests, this runs the program by fetching instructions and executing them until told to stop:

```
import assert from 'assert'

import {
  OPS
} from './architecture.js'

import VirtualMachineBase from './vm-base.js'
```

```
class VirtualMachine extends VirtualMachineBase {
  run () {
    let running = true
    while (running) {
      const [op, arg0, arg1] = this.fetch()
      switch (op) {
        case OPS.hlt.code:
          running = false
          break

        case OPS.ldc.code:
          this.assertIsRegister(arg0, op)
          this.reg[arg0] = arg1
          break


        default:
          assert(false, `Unknown op ${op}`)
          break
      }
    }
  }

  assertIsRegister (reg) {
    assert((0 <= reg) && (reg < this.reg.length),
      `Invalid register ${reg}`)
  }

  assertIsAddress (addr) {
    assert((0 <= addr) && (addr < this.ram.length),
      `Invalid register ${addr}`)
  }
}

export default VirtualMachine
```

Some instructions are very similar to others, so we will only look at three here. The first stores the value of one register in the address held by another register:

```
        case OPS.str.code:
          this.assertIsRegister(arg0, op)
          this.assertIsRegister(arg1, op)
          this.assertIsAddress(this.reg[arg1], op)
          this.ram[this.reg[arg1]] = this.reg[arg0]
          break
```

The first three lines check that the operation is legal; the fourth one uses the value in one register as an address, which is why it has nested array indexing.

Adding the value in one register to the value in another register is simpler:

```
        case OPS.add.code:
          this.assertIsRegister(arg0, op)
          this.assertIsRegister(arg1, op)
          this.reg[arg0] += this.reg[arg1]
          break
```

as is jumping to a fixed address if the value in a register is zero:

```
        case OPS.beq.code:
          this.assertIsRegister(arg0, op)
```

```
        this.assertIsAddress(arg1, op)
        if (this.reg[arg0] === 0) {
          this.ip = arg1
        }
        break
```

19.3 What do assembly programs look like?

We could figure out numerical op codes by hand, and in fact that's what the first programmers[4] did. However, it is much easier to use an **assembler**, which is just a small compiler for a language that very closely represents actual machine instructions.

Each command in our assembly languages matches an instruction in the VM. Here's an assembly language program to print the value stored in R1 and then halt:

```
# Print initial contents of R1.
prr R1
hlt
```

Its numeric representation is:

```
00010a
000001
```

One thing the assembly language has that the instruction set doesn't is **labels on addresses**. The label `loop` doesn't take up any space; instead, it tells the assembler to give the address of the next instruction a name so that we can refer to that address as `@loop` in jump instructions. For example, this program prints the numbers from 0 to 2 (Figure 19.3):

```
# Count up to 3.
# - R0: loop index.
# - R1: loop limit.
ldc R0 0
ldc R1 3
loop:
prr R0
ldc R2 1
add R0 R2
cpy R2 R1
sub R2 R0
bne R2 @loop
hlt
```

```
000002
030102
00000a
010202
020006
010204
000207
020209
000001
```

Let's trace this program's execution (Figure 19.4):

[4] http://eniacprogrammers.org/

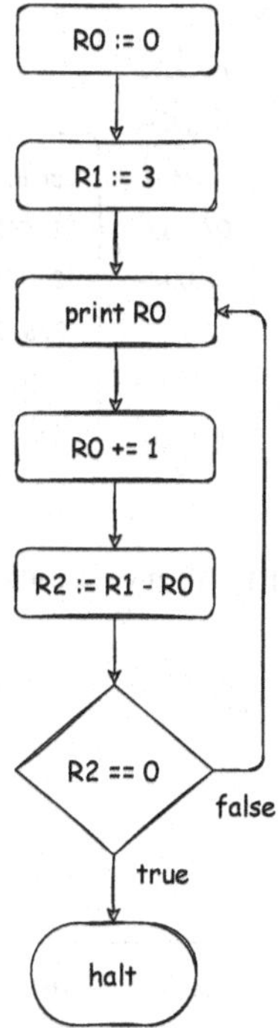

Figure 19.3: Flowchart of assembly language program to count up from 0 to 2.

1. R0 holds the current loop index.
2. R1 holds the loop's upper bound (in this case 3).
3. The loop prints the value of R0 (one instruction).
4. The program adds 1 to R0. This takes two instructions because we can only add register-to-register.
5. It checks to see if we should loop again, which takes three instructions.
6. If the program *doesn't* jump back, it halts.

The implementation of the assembler mirrors the simplicity of assembly language. The main method gets interesting lines, finds the addresses of labels, and turns each remaining line into an instruction:

```
assemble (lines) {
  lines = this.cleanLines(lines)
  const labels = this.findLabels(lines)
  const instructions = lines.filter(line => !this.isLabel(line))
  const compiled = instructions.map(instr => this.compile(instr, labels))
  const program = this.instructionsToText(compiled)
  return program
}

cleanLines (lines) {
  return lines
    .map(line => line.trim())
    .filter(line => line.length > 0)
```

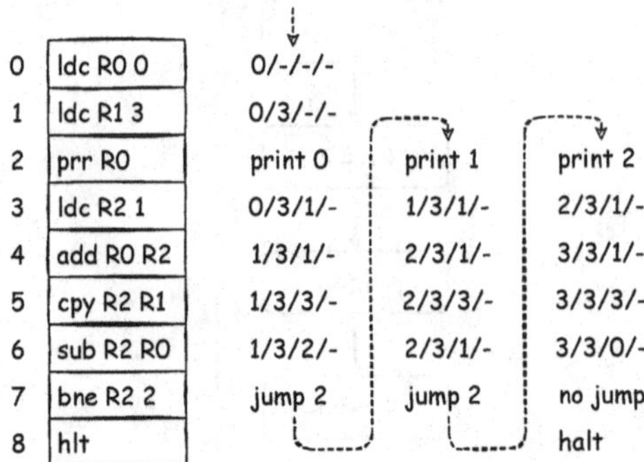

Figure 19.4: Tracing registers and memory values for a simple counting program.

```
      .filter(line => !this.isComment(line))
  }

  isComment (line) {
    return line.startsWith('#')
  }
```

To find labels, we go through the lines one by one and either save the label *or* increment the current address (because labels don't take up space):

```
  findLabels (lines) {
    const result = {}
    let index = 0
    lines.forEach(line => {
      if (this.isLabel(line)) {
        const label = line.slice(0, -1)
        assert(!(label in result),
          `Duplicate label ${label}`)
        result[label] = index
      } else {
        index += 1
      }
    })
    return result
  }

  isLabel (line) {
    return line.endsWith(':')
  }
```

To compile a single instruction we break the line into tokens, look up the format for the operands, and pack them into a single value:

```
  compile (instruction, labels) {
    const [op, ...args] = instruction.split(/\s+/)
    assert(op in OPS,
      `Unknown operation "${op}"`)
    let result = 0
    switch (OPS[op].fmt) {
      case '--':
        result = this.combine(
          OPS[op].code
        )
        break
```

```
      case 'r-':
        result = this.combine(
          this.register(args[0]),
          OPS[op].code
        )
        break
      case 'rr':
        result = this.combine(
          this.register(args[1]),
          this.register(args[0]),
          OPS[op].code
        )
        break
      case 'rv':
        result = this.combine(
          this.value(args[1], labels),
          this.register(args[0]),
          OPS[op].code
        )
        break
      default:
        assert(false,
          `Unknown instruction format ${OPS[op].fmt}`)
    }
    return result
  }
```

Combining op codes and operands into a single value is the reverse of the unpacking done by the virtual machine:

```
combine (...args) {
  assert(args.length > 0,
    'Cannot combine no arguments')
  let result = 0
  for (const a of args) {
    result <<= OP_SHIFT
    result |= a
  }
  return result
}
```

Finally, we need few utility functions:

```
instructionsToText (program) {
  return program.map(op => op.toString(16).padStart(OP_WIDTH, '0'))
}

register (token) {
  assert(token[0] === 'R',
    `Register "${token}" does not start with 'R'`)
  const r = parseInt(token.slice(1))
  assert((0 <= r) && (r < NUM_REG),
    `Illegal register ${token}`)
  return r
}

value (token, labels) {
  if (token[0] !== '@') {
    return parseInt(token)
  }
  const labelName = token.slice(1)
```

```
    assert(labelName in labels,
      `Unknown label "${token}"`)
    return labels[labelName]
  }
```

Let's try assembling a program and display its output, the registers, and the interesting contents of memory. As a test, this program counts up to three:

```
# Count up to 3.
# - R0: loop index.
# - R1: loop limit.
ldc R0 0
ldc R1 3
loop:
prr R0
ldc R2 1
add R0 R2
cpy R2 R1
sub R2 R0
bne R2 @loop
hlt
```

```
>> 0
>> 1
>> 2
R0 = 3
R1 = 3
R2 = 0
R3 = 0
0:   00000002  00030102  0000000a  00010202
4:   00020006  00010204  00000207  00020209
8:   00000001  00000000  00000000  00000000
```

19.4 How can we store data?

It is tedious to write interesting programs when each value needs a unique name. We can do a lot more once we have collections like arrays, so let's add those to our assembler. We don't have to make any changes to the virtual machine, which doesn't care if we think of a bunch of numbers as individuals or elements of an array, but we do need a way to create arrays and refer to them.

We will allocate storage for arrays at the end of the program by using `.data` on a line of its own to mark the start of the data section and then `label: number` to give a region a name and allocate some storage space (Figure 19.5).

This enhancement only requires a few changes to the assembler. First, we need to split the lines into instructions and data allocations:

```
  assemble (lines) {
    lines = this.cleanLines(lines)
    const [toCompile, toAllocate] = this.splitAllocations(lines)
    const labels = this.findLabels(lines)
    const instructions = toCompile.filter(line => !this.isLabel(line))
    const baseOfData = instructions.length
    this.addAllocations(baseOfData, labels, toAllocate)
    const compiled = instructions.map(instr => this.compile(instr, labels))
```

```
    const program = this.instructionsToText(compiled)
    return program
  }
```

```
  splitAllocations (lines) {
    const split = lines.indexOf(DIVIDER)
    if (split === -1) {
      return [lines, []]
    } else {
      return [lines.slice(0, split), lines.slice(split + 1)]
    }
  }
```

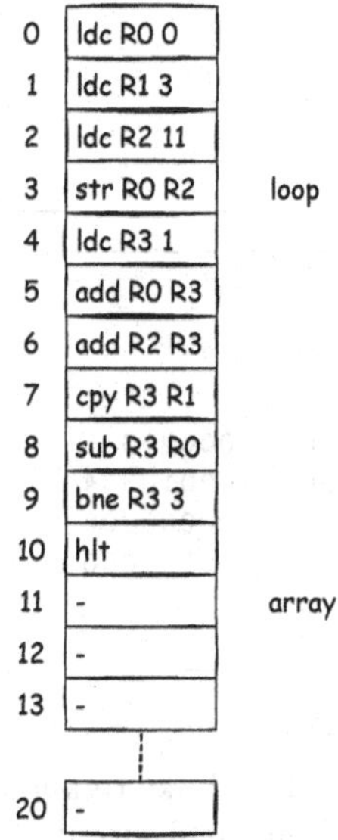

Figure 19.5: Allocating storage for arrays in the virtual machine.

Second, we need to figure out where each allocation lies and create a label accordingly:

```
  addAllocations (baseOfData, labels, toAllocate) {
    toAllocate.forEach(alloc => {
      const fields = alloc.split(':').map(a => a.trim())
      assert(fields.length === 2,
        `Invalid allocation directive "${alloc}"`)
      const [label, numWordsText] = fields
      assert(!(label in labels),
        `Duplicate label "${label}" in data allocation`)
      const numWords = parseInt(numWordsText)
      assert((baseOfData + numWords) < RAM_LEN,
        `Allocation "${label}" requires too much memory`)
      labels[label] = baseOfData
      baseOfData += numWords
    })
  }
```

And that's it: no other changes are needed to either compilation or execution. To test it, let's fill an array with the numbers from 0 to 3:

```
# Count up to 3.
# - R0: loop index.
# - R1: loop limit.
# - R2: array index.
# - R3: temporary.
ldc R0 0
ldc R1 3
ldc R2 @array
loop:
str R0 R2
ldc R3 1
add R0 R3
add R2 R3
cpy R3 R1
sub R3 R0
bne R3 @loop
hlt
.data
array: 10
```

```
R0 = 3
R1 = 3
R2 = 14
R3 = 0
0:   00000002  00030102  000b0202  00020005
4:   00010302  00030006  00030206  00010304
8:   00000307  00030309  00000001  00000000
c:   00000001  00000002  00000000  00000000
```

How does it actually work?

Our VM is just another program. If you'd like to know what happens when instructions finally meet hardware, and how electrical circuits are able to do arithmetic, make decisions, and talk to the world, [Patterson2017] has everything you want to know and more.

19.5 Exercises

Swapping values

Write an assembly language program that swaps the values in R1 and R2 without affecting the values in other registers.

Reversing an array

Write an assembly language program that starts with:

- the base address of an array in one word
- the length of the array N in the next word

- N values immediately thereafter

and reverses the array in place.

Increment and decrement

1. Add instructions `inc` and `dec` that add one to the value of a register and subtract one from the value of a register respectively.

2. Rewrite the examples to use these instructions. How much shorter do they make the programs? How much easier to read?

Using long addresses

1. Modify the virtual machine so that the `ldr` and `str` instructions contain 16-bit addresses rather than 8-bit addresses and increase the virtual machine's memory to 64K words to match.

2. How does this complicate instruction interpretation?

Operating on strings

The C programming language stored character strings as non-zero bytes terminated by a byte containing zero.

1. Write a program that starts with the base address of a string in R1 and finishes with the length of the string (not including the terminator) in the same register.

2. Write a program that starts with the base address of a string in R1 and the base address of some other block of memory in R2 and copies the string to that new location (including the terminator).

3. What happens in each case if the terminator is missing?

Call and return

1. Add another register to the virtual machine called SP ("stack pointer") that is automatically initialized to the *last* address in memory.

2. Add an instruction `psh` (short for "push") that copies a value from a register to the address stored in SP and then subtracts one from SP.

3. Add an instruction `pop` (short for "pop") that adds one to SP and then copies a value from that address into a register.

4. Using these instructions, write a subroutine that evaluates `2x+1` for every value in an array.

Disassembling instructions

A **disassembler** turns machine instructions into assembly code. Write a disassembler for the instruction set used by our virtual machine. (Since the labels for addresses are not stored in machine instructions, disassemblers typically generate labels like `@L001` and `@L002`.)

Linking multiple files

1. Modify the assembler to handle `.include filename` directives.

2. What does your modified assembler do about duplicate label names? How does it prevent infinite includes (i.e., `A.as` includes `B.as` which includes `A.as` again)?

Providing system calls

Modify the virtual machine so that developers can add "system calls" to it.

1. On startup, the virtual machine loads an array of functions defined in a file called `syscalls.js`.

2. The `sys` instruction takes a one-byte constant argument. It looks up the corresponding function and calls it with the values of R0-R3 as parameters and places the result in R0.

Unit testing

1. Write unit tests for the assembler.

2. Once they are working, write unit tests for the virtual machine.

20

Debugger

Terms defined: **breakpoint**, **source map**, **tab completion**, **watchpoint**

We have finally come to another of the topics that sparked this book: how does a debugger work? Debuggers are as much a part of programmers' lives as version control but are taught far less often (in part, we believe, because it's harder to create homework questions for them). In this chapter we will build a simple single-stepping debugger and show one way to test interactive applications (Chapter 4).

20.1 What is our starting point?

We would like to debug a higher-level language than the assembly code of Chapter 19, but we don't want to have to write a parser or wrestle with the ASTs of Chapter 14. As a compromise, we will represent programs as JSON data structures whose elements have the form `[command ...args]`. If the JavaScript version of our program is:

```
const a = [-3, -5, -1, 0, -2, 1, 3, 1]
const b = Array()
let largest = a[0]
let i = 0
while (i < length(a)) {
  if (a[i] > largest) {
    b.push(a[i])
  }
  i += 1
}
i = 0
while (i < length(b)) {
  console.log(b[i])
  i += 1
}
```

then the JSON representation is:

```
[
  ["defA", "a", ["data", -3, -5, -1, 0, -2, 1, 3, 1]],
  ["defA", "b", ["data"]],
  ["defV", "largest", ["getA", "a", ["num", 0]]],
  ["append", "b", ["getV", "largest"]],
  ["defV", "i", ["num", 0]],
  ["loop", ["lt", ["getV", "i"], ["len", "a"]],
    ["test", ["gt", ["getA", "a", ["getV", "i"]], ["getV", "largest"]],
      ["setV", "largest", ["getA", "a", ["getV", "i"]]],
      ["append", "b", ["getV", "largest"]]
    ],
    ["setV", "i", ["add", ["getV", "i"], ["num", 1]]]
  ],
  ["setV", "i", ["num", 0]],
```

```
  ["loop", ["lt", ["getV", "i"], ["len", "b"]],
    ["print", ["getA", "b", ["getV", "i"]]],
    ["setV", "i", ["add", ["getV", "i"], ["num", 1]]]
  ]
]
```

Our virtual machine is structured like the one in Chapter 19. A real system would parse a program to create JSON, then translate JSON into assembly code, then assemble that to create machine instructions. Again, to keep things simple we will execute a program by removing comments and blank lines and then running commands by looking up the command name's and calling that method:

```
import assert from 'assert'

class VirtualMachineBase {
  constructor (program) {
    this.program = this.compile(program)
    this.prefix = '>>'
  }

  compile (lines) {
    const text = lines
      .map(line => line.trim())
      .filter(line => (line.length > 0) && !line.startsWith('//'))
      .join('\n')
    return JSON.parse(text)
  }

  run () {
    this.env = {}
    this.runAll(this.program)
  }

  runAll (commands) {
    commands.forEach(command => this.exec(command))
  }

  exec (command) {
    const [op, ...args] = command
    assert(op in this,
      `Unknown op "${op}"`)
    return this[op](args)
  }

}

export default VirtualMachineBase
```

Remember, functions and methods are just another kind of data, so if an object has a method called "meth", the expression this["meth"] looks it up and this["meth"](args) calls it. If "meth" is stored in a variable called name, then this[name](args) will do exactly the same thing.

The method in our VM that defines a new variable with an initial value looks like this:

```
  defV (args) {
    this.checkOp('defV', 2, args)
    const [name, value] = args
    this.env[name] = this.exec(value)
  }
```

while the one that adds two values looks like this:

```
add (args) {
  this.checkOp('add', 2, args)
  const left = this.exec(args[0])
  const right = this.exec(args[1])
  return left + right
}
```

Running a `while` loop is:

```
loop (args) {
  this.checkBody('loop', 1, args)
  const body = args.slice(1)
  while (this.exec(args[0])) {
    this.runAll(body)
  }
}
```

and checking that a variable name refers to an array is:

```
checkArray (op, name) {
  this.checkName(op, name)
  const array = this.env[name]
  assert(Array.isArray(array),
    `Variable "${name}" used in "${op}" is not array`)
}
```

The other operations are similar to these.

20.2 How can we make a tracing debugger?

The next thing we need in our debugger is a **source map** that keeps track of where in the source file each instruction came from. Since JSON is a subset of JavaScript, we could get line numbers by parsing our programs with Acorn[1]. However, we would then have to scrape the information we want for this example out of the AST. Since this chapter is supposed to be about debugging, not parsing, we will instead cheat and add a line number to each interesting statement by hand so that our program looks like this:

```
[
  [1, "defA", "a", ["data", -3, -5, -1, 0, -2, 1, 3, 1]],
  [2, "defA", "b", ["data"]],
  [3, "defV", "largest", ["getA", "a", ["num", 0]]],
  [4, "append", "b", ["getV", "largest"]],
  [5, "defV", "i", ["num", 0]],
  [6, "loop", ["lt", ["getV", "i"], ["len", "a"]],
   [7, "test", ["gt", ["getA", "a", ["getV", "i"]], ["getV", "largest"]],
    [8, "setV", "largest", ["getA", "a", ["getV", "i"]]],
    [9, "append", "b", ["getV", "largest"]]
   ],
   [11, "setV", "i", ["add", ["getV", "i"], ["num", 1]]]
  ],
  [13, "setV", "i", ["num", 0]],
  [14, "loop", ["lt", ["getV", "i"], ["len", "b"]],
```

[1]https://github.com/acornjs/acorn

```
    [15, "print", ["getA", "b", ["getV", "i"]]],
    [16, "setV", "i", ["add", ["getV", "i"], ["num", 1]]]
  ]
]
```

Building the source map from that is simple; for now, we just modify `exec` to ignore the line number:

```
import assert from 'assert'

import VirtualMachineBase from './vm-base.js'

class VirtualMachineSourceMap extends VirtualMachineBase {
  compile (lines) {
    const original = super.compile(lines)
    this.sourceMap = {}
    const result = original.map(command => this.transform(command))
    return result
  }

  transform (node) {
    if (!Array.isArray(node)) {
      return node
    }
    if (Array.length === 0) {
      return []
    }
    const [first, ...rest] = node
    if (typeof first !== 'number') {
      return [first, null, ...rest.map(arg => this.transform(arg))]
    }
    const [op, ...args] = rest
    this.sourceMap[first] =
      [op, first, ...args.map(arg => this.transform(arg))]
    return this.sourceMap[first]
  }

  exec (command) {
    const [op, lineNum, ...args] = command
    assert(op in this,
      `Unknown op "${op}"`)
    return this[op](args)
  }
}

export default VirtualMachineSourceMap
```

It's not really cheating

We said that adding line numbers by hand was cheating, but it isn't. What we're actually doing is deferring a problem until we're sure we need to solve it. If our approach is clumsy or fails outright because of some aspect of design we didn't foresee, there will have been no point handling line numbers the "right" way. A good rule for software design is to tackle the thing you're least sure about first, using temporary code in place of what you think you'll eventually need.

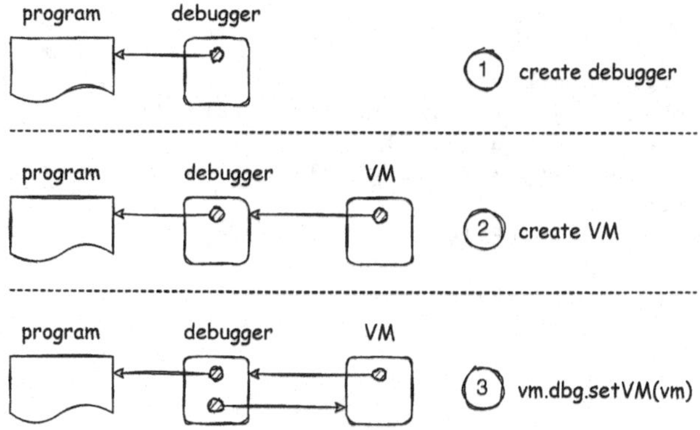

Figure 20.1: Two-step initialization of mutually-dependent objects.

The next step is to modify the VM's **exec** method so that it executes a callback function for each significant operation (where "significant" means "we bothered to record its line number"). Since we're not sure what our debugger is going to need, we give this callback the environment holding the current set of variables, the line number, and the operation being performed:

```
import assert from 'assert'

import VirtualMachineSourceMap from './vm-source-map.js'

class VirtualMachineCallback extends VirtualMachineSourceMap {
  constructor (program, dbg) {
    super(program)
    this.dbg = dbg
    this.dbg.setVM(this)
  }

  exec (command) {
    const [op, lineNum, ...args] = command
    this.dbg.handle(this.env, lineNum, op)
    assert(op in this,
      `Unknown op "${op}"`)
    return this[op](args, lineNum)
  }

  message (prefix, val) {
    this.dbg.message(`${prefix} ${val}`)
  }
}

export default VirtualMachineCallback
```

We also modify the VM's constructor to record the debugger and give it a reference to the virtual machine (Figure 20.1). We have to connect the two objects explicitly because each one needs a reference to the other, but one of them has to be created first. "A gets B then B tells A about itself" is a common pattern; we will look at other ways to manage it in the exercises.

To run the program, we create a debugger object and pass it to the VM's constructor:

```
import assert from 'assert'

import readSource from './read-source.js'
```

```
const main = () => {
  assert(process.argv.length === 5,
    'Usage: run-debugger.js ./vm ./debugger input|-')
  const VM = require(process.argv[2])
  const Debugger = require(process.argv[3])
  const inFile = process.argv[4]
  const lines = readSource(inFile)
  const dbg = new Debugger()
  const vm = new VM(lines, dbg)
  vm.run()
}

main()
```

A simple debugger just traces interesting statements as they run:

```
import DebuggerBase from './debugger-base.js'

class DebuggerTrace extends DebuggerBase {
  handle (env, lineNum, op) {
    if (lineNum !== null) {
      console.log(`${lineNum} / ${op}: ${JSON.stringify(env)}`)
    }
  }
}

export default DebuggerTrace
```

Let's try it on a program that adds the numbers in an array:

```
// const a = [-5, 1, 3]
// const total = 0
// let i = 0
// while (i < length(a)) {
//   total += a[i]
//   i += 1
// }
// console.log(total)

[
  [1, "defA", "a", ["data", -5, 1, 3]],
  [2, "defV", "total", ["num", 0]],
  [3, "defV", "i", ["num", 0]],
  [4, "loop", ["lt", ["getV", "i"], ["len", "a"]],
    [5, "setV", "total",
      ["add", ["getV", "total"], ["getA", "a", ["getV", "i"]]]
    ],
    [8, "setV", "i", ["add", ["getV", "i"], ["num", 1]]]
  ],
  [10, "print", ["getV", "total"]]
]
```

```
1 / defA: {}
2 / defV: {"a":[-5,1,3]}
3 / defV: {"a":[-5,1,3],"total":0}
4 / loop: {"a":[-5,1,3],"total":0,"i":0}
5 / setV: {"a":[-5,1,3],"total":0,"i":0}
8 / setV: {"a":[-5,1,3],"total":-5,"i":0}
5 / setV: {"a":[-5,1,3],"total":-5,"i":1}
8 / setV: {"a":[-5,1,3],"total":-4,"i":1}
```

```
5 / setV: {"a":[-5,1,3],"total":-4,"i":2}
8 / setV: {"a":[-5,1,3],"total":-1,"i":2}
10 / print: {"a":[-5,1,3],"total":-1,"i":3}
>> -1
```

20.3 How can we make the debugger interactive?

What we have built so far is an always-on `print` statement. To turn it into an interactive debugger, we will use the `prompt-sync`[2] module to manage user input with the following set of commands:

- `?` or `help` to list commands.
- `clear #` to clear a **breakpoint** at a numbered line.
- `list` to list lines and breakpoints.
- `next` to go forward one line.
- `print name` to show a variable while at a breakpoint.
- `run` to run to the next breakpoint.
- `stop #` to break at a numbered line.
- `variables` to list all variable names.
- `exit` to exit immediately.

When the virtual machine calls the debugger, the debugger first checks if it is on a numbered line. If it isn't, it hands control back to the VM. Otherwise, if we are single-stepping or this line is a breakpoint, the debugger takes over. Its overall structure is:

```
import prompt from 'prompt-sync'

import DebuggerBase from './debugger-base.js'

const PROMPT_OPTIONS = { sigint: true }

class DebuggerInteractive extends DebuggerBase {
  constructor () {
    super()
    this.singleStep = true
    this.breakpoints = new Set()
    this.lookup = {
      '?': 'help',
      c: 'clear',
      l: 'list',
      n: 'next',
      p: 'print',
      r: 'run',
      s: 'stop',
      v: 'variables',
```

[2] https://www.npmjs.com/package/prompt-sync

```
      x: 'exit'
    }
  }

  handle (env, lineNum, op) {
    if (lineNum === null) {
      return
    }
    if (this.singleStep) {
      this.singleStep = false
      this.interact(env, lineNum, op)
    } else if (this.breakpoints.has(lineNum)) {
      this.interact(env, lineNum, op)
    }
  }

}

export default DebuggerInteractive
```

It interacts with users by lookup up a command and invoking the corresponding method, just as the VM does:

```
  interact (env, lineNum, op) {
    let interacting = true
    while (interacting) {
      const command = this.getCommand(env, lineNum, op)
      if (command.length === 0) {
        continue
      }
      const [cmd, ...args] = command
      if (cmd in this) {
        interacting = this[cmd](env, lineNum, op, args)
      } else if (cmd in this.lookup) {
        interacting = this[this.lookup[cmd]](env, lineNum, op, args)
      } else {
        this.message(`unknown command ${command} (use '?' for help)`)
      }
    }
  }

  getCommand (env, lineNum, op) {
    const options = Object.keys(this.lookup).sort().join('')
    const display = `[${lineNum} ${options}] `
    return this.input(display)
      .split(/\s+/)
      .map(s => s.trim())
      .filter(s => s.length > 0)
  }

  input (display) {
    return prompt(PROMPT_OPTIONS)(display)
  }
```

Learning as we go

We didn't originally put the input and output in methods that could be overridden, but realized later we needed to do this to make the debugger testable. Rather than coming back and rewriting this, we have done it here.

With this structure in place, the command handlers are pretty straightforward. For example, this method moves us to the next line:

```
next (env, lineNum, op, args) {
  this.singleStep = true
  return false
}
```

while this one prints the value of a variable:

```
print (env, lineNum, op, args) {
  if (args.length !== 1) {
    this.message('p[rint] requires one variable name')
  } else if (!(args[0] in env)) {
    this.message(`unknown variable name "${args[0]}"`)
  } else {
    this.message(JSON.stringify(env[args[0]]))
  }
  return true
}
```

After using this for a few moments, though we realized that we needed to change the signature of the `loop` method. We want to stop the loop each time it runs, and need to know where we are. We didn't allow for this in the base class, and we don't want to have to change every method, so we take advantage of the fact that JavaScript ignores any extra arguments passed to a method:

```
import VirtualMachineCallback from './vm-callback.js'

class VirtualMachineInteractive extends VirtualMachineCallback {
  loop (args, lineNum) {
    this.checkBody('loop', 1, args)
    const body = args.slice(1)
    while (this.exec(args[0])) {
      this.dbg.handle(this.env, lineNum, 'loop')
      this.runAll(body)
    }
  }
}

export default VirtualMachineInteractive
```

This is sloppy, but it works; we will tidy it up in the exercises.

20.4 How can we test an interactive application?

How can we test an interactive application like a debugger? The answer is, "By making it non-interactive." Like many tools over the past 30 years, our approach is based on a program

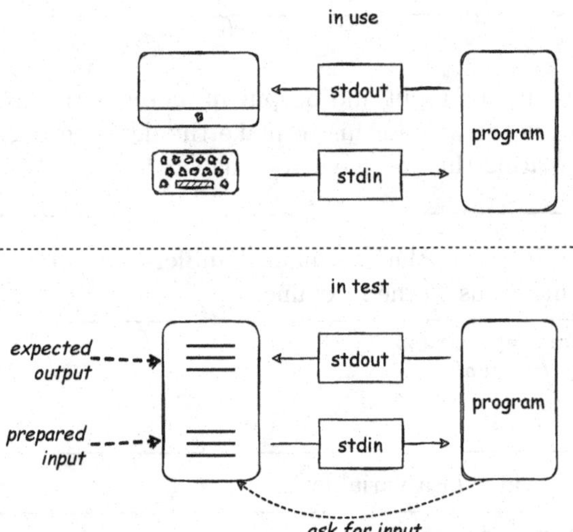

Figure 20.2: Replacing input and output to test interactive applications.

called Expect[3]. Our library replaces the input and output functions of the application being tested with callbacks, then provides input when asked and checks output when it is given (Figure 20.2).

The results look like this:

```
describe('interactive debugger', () => {
  it('runs and prints', (done) => {
    setup('print-0.json')
      .get('[1 ?clnprsvx] ')
      .send('r')
      .get('>> 0')
      .run()
    done()
  })

  it('breaks and resumes', (done) => {
    setup('print-3.json')
      .get('[1 ?clnprsvx] ')
      .send('s 3')
      .get('[1 ?clnprsvx] ')
      .send('r')
      .get('>> 0')
      .get('>> 1')
      .get('[3 ?clnprsvx] ')
      .send('x')
      .run()
    done()
  })
})
```

Our Expect class may be short, but it is hard to understand because it is so abstract:

```
import assert from 'assert'

class Expect {
```

[3]https://en.wikipedia.org/wiki/Expect

```
  constructor (subject, start) {
    this.start = start
    this.steps = []
    subject.setTester(this)
  }

  send (text) {
    this.steps.push({ op: 'toSystem', arg: text })
    return this
  }

  get (text) {
    this.steps.push({ op: 'fromSystem', arg: text })
    return this
  }

  run () {
    this.start()
    assert.strictEqual(this.steps.length, 0,
      'Extra steps at end of test')
  }

  toSystem () {
    return this.next('toSystem')
  }

  fromSystem (actual) {
    const expected = this.next('fromSystem')
    assert.strictEqual(expected, actual,
      `Expected "${expected}" got "${actual}"`)
  }

  next (kind) {
    assert(this.steps.length > 0,
      'Unexpected end of steps')
    assert.strictEqual(this.steps[0].op, kind,
      `Expected ${kind}, got "${this.steps[0].op}"`)
    const text = this.steps[0].arg
    this.steps = this.steps.slice(1)
    return text
  }
}

export default Expect
```

Piece-by-piece:

- `subject` is the thing being tested.
- `start` is a callback to start the system running. It gives control to the subject, which then calls back into the test framework for input and output.
- `get` and `send` store things to be given to the subject and to be checked against its output. Both methods return `this` so that we can chain calls together.
- `run` starts the system and checks that all expected interactions have been used up when testing is done.
- `toSystem` and `fromSystem` use `next` to get the next test record, check its type, and return the string.

Let's modify the debugger to use the tester, keeping in mind that the prompt counts as an output (and yes, we forgot this in the first version):

```
import DebuggerInteractive from './debugger-interactive.js'

class DebuggerTest extends DebuggerInteractive {
  constructor () {
    super()
    this.tester = null
  }

  setTester (tester) {
    this.tester = tester
  }

  input (display) {
    this.tester.fromSystem(display)
    return this.tester.toSystem()
  }

  message (m) {
    this.tester.fromSystem(m)
  }
}

export default DebuggerTest
```

Again, we can't pass the tester as a constructor parameter because of initialization order, so we write a `setup` function to make sure everything is connected the right way:

```
import Expect from '../expect.js'
import VM from '../vm-interactive.js'
import Debugger from '../debugger-test.js'
import readSource from '../read-source.js'

const setup = (filename) => {
  const lines = readSource(path.join('debugger/test', filename))
  const dbg = new Debugger()
  const vm = new VM(lines, dbg)
  return new Expect(dbg, () => vm.run())
}
```

Let's try running our tests:

```
npm run test -- -g 'interactive debugger'
```

```
> stjs@1.0.0 test /u/stjs
> mocha */test/test-*.js "-g" "interactive debugger"


  interactive debugger
    ✓ runs and prints
```

That works—or does it? Why is only one test shown, and doesn't the summary appear? After a bit of digging, we realize that the debugger's `exit` command calls `process.exit` when the simulated program ends, so the whole program including the VM, debugger, and test framework stops immediately *before* the promises that contain the tests have run.

We could fix this by modifying the debugger callback to return an indication of whether or not execution should continue, then modify the VM to pay attention to that flag. However, this approach becomes very complicated when we have deeply-nested calls to `exec`, which will happen with loops and conditionals.

A better alternative is to use an exception for control flow. We can define our own kind of exception as an empty class: it doesn't need any data because we are only using it to get a typed object:

```
class HaltException {
}

export default HaltException
```

Next, we modify the debugger to throw this exception when asked to exit:

```
import HaltException from './halt-exception.js'
import DebuggerTest from './debugger-test.js'

class DebuggerExit extends DebuggerTest {
  exit (env, lineNum, op, args) {
    throw new HaltException()
  }
}

export default DebuggerExit
```

And finally we modify the VM to finish cleanly if this exception is thrown, but re-throw any other kind of exception:

```
import HaltException from './halt-exception.js'
import VirtualMachineInteractive from './vm-interactive.js'

class VirtualMachineExit extends VirtualMachineInteractive {
  run () {
    this.env = {}
    try {
      this.runAll(this.program)
    } catch (exc) {
      if (exc instanceof HaltException) {
        return
      }
      throw exc
    }
  }
}

export default VirtualMachineExit
```

With these changes in place, we are finally able to test our interactive debugger:

```
npm run test -- -g 'exitable debugger'
```

```
> stjs@1.0.0 test /u/stjs
> mocha */test/test-*.js "-g" "exitable debugger"


  exitable debugger
    ✓ runs and prints
    ✓ breaks and resumes


  2 passing (7ms)
```

20.5 Exercises

Implementing tab completion

Read the documentation for `prompt-sync` and then implement **tab completion** for the debugger.

Modifying variables while running

Add a `set` command that sets the value of a variable to a new value in a running program. How do you handle setting array elements?

Making output more readable

Modify the tracing debugger so that the statements inside loops and conditionals are indented for easier reading.

Better loops

Our solution for handling loops is sloppy; fix it.

Using a flag to continue execution

Modify the debugger and virtual machine to use a "continue executing" flag rather than throwing an exception when execution should end. Which approach is easier to understand? Which will be easier to extend in the future?

Numbering lines

Write a tool that takes a JSON program representation *without* statement numbers and produces one that numbers all of the interesting statements for debugging purposes. Use whatever definition of "interesting" you think would be most useful.

Looping around again

Implement a "next loop iteration" command that runs the program until it reaches the current point in the next iteration of the current loop.

Looking up objects

Rather than having some objects call `setXYZ` methods in other objects, it is common practice to use a lookup table for mutual dependencies:

1. Every object initializes calls `table.set(name, this)` in its constructor.

2. Whenever object A needs the instance of object B, it calls `table.lookup('B')`. It does *not* store the result in a member variable.

   Modify the virtual machine and debugger to use this pattern.

Watching for variable changes

Modify the debugger and virtual machine to implement **watchpoints** that halt the program whenever the value of a variable changes.

Translating JSON to assembler

Write a tool that translates the JSON program representation into the assembly code of Chapter 19. To simplify things, increase the number of registers so that there is always storage for intermediate results when doing arithmetic.

21

Conclusion

We have come a long way since we listed the contents of a directory in Chapter 2. Saving files in version control, making sure code meets style rules, debugging it and bundling it (hopefully in that order)—programmers do these things every day, and we hope that understanding how they work will help you do them better.

We also hope that your journey won't stop here. If you would like to add a chapter to this book or translate it into another programming language, human language, or both, your help would be very welcome: please see the introduction in Chapter 1 and the contributors' guide in Appendix C for more information.

> We shape our tools, and thereafter our tools shape us.
> — Marshall McLuhan

A

License

All of the written material is made available under the Creative Commons - Attribution - NonCommercial 4.0 International license (CC-BY-NC-4.0), while the software is made available under the Hippocratic License.

Writing

This is a human-readable summary of (and not a substitute for) the license. For the full legal text of this license, please see https://creativecommons.org/licenses/by-nc/4.0/legalcode[1].

All of this site is made available under the terms of the Creative Commons Attribution - NonCommercial 4.0 license. You are free to:

- **Share** — copy and redistribute the material in any medium or format
- **Adapt** — remix, transform, and build upon the material

The licensor cannot revoke these freedoms as long as you follow the license terms.

Under the following terms:

- **Attribution** — You must give appropriate credit, provide a link to the license, and indicate if changes were made. You may do so in any reasonable manner, but not in any way that suggests the licensor endorses you or your use.
- **NonCommercial** — You may not use the material for commercial purposes.
- **No additional restrictions** — You may not apply legal terms or technological measures that legally restrict others from doing anything the license permits.

Notices:

You do not have to comply with the license for elements of the material in the public domain or where your use is permitted by an applicable exception or limitation.

No warranties are given. The license may not give you all of the permissions necessary for your intended use. For example, other rights such as publicity, privacy, or moral rights may limit how you use the material.

Software

Licensor hereby grants permission by this license ("License"), free of charge, to any person or entity (the "Licensee") obtaining a copy of this software and associated documentation files

[1] https://creativecommons.org/licenses/by-nc/4.0/legalcode

(the "Software"), to deal in the Software without restriction, including without limitation the rights to use, copy, modify, merge, publish, distribute, sublicense, and/or sell copies of the Software, and to permit persons to whom the Software is furnished to do so, subject to the following conditions:

- The above copyright notice and this License or a subsequent version published on the Hippocratic License Website[2] shall be included in all copies or substantial portions of the Software. Licensee has the option of following the terms and conditions either of the above numbered version of this License or of any subsequent version published on the Hippocratic License Website.
- Compliance with Human Rights Laws and Human Rights Principles:
    1. Human Rights Laws. The Software shall not be used by any person or entity for any systems, activities, or other uses that violate any applicable laws, regulations, or rules that protect human, civil, labor, privacy, political, environmental, security, economic, due process, or similar rights (the "Human Rights Laws"). Where the Human Rights Laws of more than one jurisdiction are applicable to the use of the Software, the Human Rights Laws that are most protective of the individuals or groups harmed shall apply.
    2. Human Rights Principles. Licensee is advised to consult the articles of the United Nations Universal Declaration of Human Rights[3] and the United Nations Global Compact[4] that define recognized principles of international human rights (the "Human Rights Principles"). It is Licensor's express intent that all use of the Software be consistent with Human Rights Principles. If Licensor receives notification or otherwise learns of an alleged violation of any Human Rights Principles relating to Licensee's use of the Software, Licensor may in its discretion and without obligation (i) (a) notify Licensee of such allegation and (b) allow Licensee 90 days from notification under (i)(a) to investigate and respond to Licensor regarding the allegation and (ii) (a) after the earlier of 90 days from notification under (i)(a), or Licensee's response under (i)(b), notify Licensee of License termination and (b) allow Licensee an additional 90 days from notification under (ii)(a) to cease use of the Software.
    3. Indemnity. Licensee shall hold harmless and indemnify Licensor against all losses, damages, liabilities, deficiencies, claims, actions, judgments, settlements, interest, awards, penalties, fines, costs, or expenses of whatever kind, including Licensor's reasonable attorneys' fees, arising out of or relating to Licensee's non-compliance with this License or use of the Software in violation of Human Rights Laws or Human Rights Principles.
- Enforceability: If any portion or provision of this License is determined to be invalid, illegal, or unenforceable by a court of competent jurisdiction, then such invalidity, illegality, or unenforceability shall not affect any other term or provision of this License or invalidate or render unenforceable such term or provision in any other jurisdiction. Upon a determination that any term or provision is invalid, illegal, or unenforceable, to the extent permitted by applicable law, the court may modify this License to affect the original intent of the parties as closely as possible. The section headings are for convenience only and are not intended to affect the construction or interpretation of this License. Any rule of construction to the effect that ambiguities are to be resolved against the drafting party shall not apply in interpreting this License. The language in this License shall be interpreted as to its fair meaning and not strictly for or against any party.

[2]https://firstdonoharm.dev/

[3]https://www.un.org/en/universal-declaration-human-rights/

[4]https://www.unglobalcompact.org/what-is-gc/mission/principles

THE SOFTWARE IS PROVIDED "AS IS", WITHOUT WARRANTY OF ANY KIND, EXPRESS OR IMPLIED, INCLUDING BUT NOT LIMITED TO THE WARRANTIES OF MERCHANTABILITY, FITNESS FOR A PARTICULAR PURPOSE AND NONINFRINGEMENT. IN NO EVENT SHALL THE AUTHORS OR COPYRIGHT HOLDERS BE LIABLE FOR ANY CLAIM, DAMAGES OR OTHER LIABILITY, WHETHER IN AN ACTION OF CONTRACT, TORT OR OTHERWISE, ARISING FROM, OUT OF OR IN CONNECTION WITH THE SOFTWARE OR THE USE OR OTHER DEALINGS IN THE SOFTWARE.

The Hippocratic License is an Ethical Source license[5].

[5]https://ethicalsource.dev

B

Code of Conduct

In the interest of fostering an open and welcoming environment, we as contributors and maintainers pledge to making participation in our project and our community a harassment-free experience for everyone, regardless of age, body size, disability, ethnicity, gender identity and expression, level of experience, education, socioeconomic status, nationality, personal appearance, race, religion, or sexual identity and orientation.

Our Standards

Examples of behavior that contributes to creating a positive environment include:

- using welcoming and inclusive language,
- being respectful of differing viewpoints and experiences,
- gracefully accepting constructive criticism,
- focusing on what is best for the community, and
- showing empathy towards other community members.

Examples of unacceptable behavior by participants include:

- the use of sexualized language or imagery and unwelcome sexual attention or advances,
- trolling, insulting/derogatory comments, and personal or political attacks,
- public or private harassment,
- publishing others' private information, such as a physical or electronic address, without explicit permission, and
- other conduct which could reasonably be considered inappropriate in a professional setting

Our Responsibilities

Project maintainers are responsible for clarifying the standards of acceptable behavior and are expected to take appropriate and fair corrective action in response to any instances of unacceptable behavior.

Project maintainers have the right and responsibility to remove, edit, or reject comments, commits, code, wiki edits, issues, and other contributions that are not aligned to this Code of Conduct, or to ban temporarily or permanently any contributor for other behaviors that they deem inappropriate, threatening, offensive, or harmful.

Scope

This Code of Conduct applies both within project spaces and in public spaces when an individual is representing the project or its community. Examples of representing a project or community include using an official project email address, posting via an official social media account, or acting as an appointed representative at an online or offline event. Representation of a project may be further defined and clarified by project maintainers.

Enforcement

Instances of abusive, harassing, or otherwise unacceptable behavior may be reported by emailing the project team. All complaints will be reviewed and investigated and will result in a response that is deemed necessary and appropriate to the circumstances. The project team is obligated to maintain confidentiality with regard to the reporter of an incident. Further details of specific enforcement policies may be posted separately.

Project maintainers who do not follow or enforce the Code of Conduct in good faith may face temporary or permanent repercussions as determined by other members of the project's leadership.

Attribution

This Code of Conduct is adapted from the Contributor Covenant[1] version 1.4.

[1] https://www.contributor-covenant.org/

C

Contributing

Contributions are very welcome; please contact us by email or by filing an issue on this site. All contributors must abide by our Code of Conduct.

Making Decisions

This project uses Martha's Rules[1] for consensus decision making:

1. Before each meeting, anyone who wishes may sponsor a proposal by filing an issue in the GitHub repository tagged "proposal". People must file proposals at least 24 hours before a meeting in order for them to be considered at that meeting, and must include:
    - a one-line summary (the subject line of the issue)
    - the full text of the proposal
    - any required background information
    - pros and cons
    - possible alternatives
2. A quorum is established in a meeting if half or more of voting members are present.
3. Once a person has sponsored a proposal, they are responsible for it. The group may not discuss or vote on the issue unless the sponsor or their delegate is present. The sponsor is also responsible for presenting the item to the group.
4. After the sponsor presents the proposal, a "sense" vote is cast for the proposal before any discussion:
    - Who likes the proposal?
    - Who can live with the proposal?
    - Who is uncomfortable with the proposal?
5. If everyone likes or can live with the proposal, it passes immediately.
6. If most of the group is uncomfortable with the proposal, it is postponed for further rework by the sponsor.
7. Otherwise, members who are uncomfortable can briefly state their objections. A timer is then set for a brief discussion moderated by the facilitator. After 10 minutes or when no one has anything further to add (whichever comes first), the facilitator calls for a yes-or-no vote on the question: "Should we implement this decision over the stated objections?" If a majority votes "yes" the proposal is implemented. Otherwise, the proposal is returned to the sponsor for further work.

[1] https://journals.sagepub.com/doi/10.1177/088610998600100206

Formatting

This material uses Ivy[2] with some custom extensions. Run `make` in the root directory to get a list of available commands. Some of these rely on scripts in the `./bin/` directory. Please see our Git repository[3] for up-to-date instructions.

[2]https://www.dmulholl.com/docs/ivy/dev/
[3]https://github.com/gvwilson/sdxjs/

D

Bibliography

[Binkley2012] Dave Binkley, Marcia Davis, Dawn Lawrie, Jonathan I. Maletic, Christopher Morrell, and Bonita Sharif. "The Impact of Identifier Style on Effort and Comprehension". In: *ESE* 18.2 (2012). DOI: `10.1007/s10664-012-9201-4`.

[Brand1995] Stewart Brand. *How Buildings Learn: What Happens After They're Built.* Penguin USA, 1995. ISBN: 978-0140139969.

[Brown2016] Amy Brown and Michael DiBernardo, eds. *500 Lines or Less: Experienced Programmers Solve Interesting Problems.* Lulu, 2016. ISBN: 978-1329871274.

[Brown2011] Amy Brown and Greg Wilson, eds. *The Architecture of Open Source Applications: Elegance, Evolution, and a Few Fearless Hacks.* Lulu, 2011. ISBN: 978-1257638017.

[Brown2012] Amy Brown and Greg Wilson, eds. *The Architecture of Open Source Applications: Structure, Scale, and a Few More Fearless Hacks.* Lulu, 2012. ISBN: 978-0201103427.

[Casciaro2020] Mario Casciaro and Luciano Mammino. *Node.js Design Patterns.* Packt, 2020. ISBN: 978-1839214110.

[Conery2021] Rob Conery. *The Imposter's Handbook: A CS Primer for Self-Taught Developers.* Independently published, 2021. ISBN: 978-8708185266.

[Davis2018] Ashley Davis. *Data Wrangling with JavaScript.* Manning, 2018. ISBN: 978-1617294846.

[Feathers2004] Michael C. Feathers. *Working Effectively with Legacy Code.* Prentice-Hall, 2004. ISBN: 978-0131177055.

[Fucci2017] Davide Fucci, Hakan Erdogmus, Burak Turhan, Markku Oivo, and Natalia Juristo. "A Dissection of the Test-Driven Development Process: Does It Really Matter to Test-First or to Test-Last?" In: *TSE* 43.7 (July 2017). DOI: `10.1109/tse.2016.2616877`.

[Fucci2016] Davide Fucci, Giuseppe Scanniello, Simone Romano, Martin Shepperd, Boyce Sigweni, Fernando Uyaguari, Burak Turhan, Natalia Juristo, and Markku Oivo. "An External Replication on the Effects of Test-driven Development Using a Multi-site Blind Analysis Approach". In: *Proc. ESEM'16.* ACM Press, 2016. DOI: `10.1145/2961111.2962592`.

[Gregg2020] Brendan Gregg. *Systems Performance: Enterprise and the Cloud.* Pearson, 2020. ISBN: 978-0136820154.

[Johnson2019] John Johnson, Sergio Lubo, Nishitha Yedla, Jairo Aponte, and Bonita Sharif. "An Empirical Study Assessing Source Code Readability in Comprehension". In: *Proc. ICSME'19.* 2019. DOI: `10.1109/ICSME.2019.00085`.

[Kernighan1983] Brian W. Kernighan and Rob Pike. *The Unix Programming Environment.* Prentice-Hall, 1983. ISBN: 978-0139376818.

[Kernighan1979] Brian W. Kernighan and P. J. Plauger. *The Elements of Programming Style*. McGraw-Hill, 1979. ISBN: 978-0070342071.

[Kernighan1981] Brian W. Kernighan and P. J. Plauger. *Software Tools in Pascal*. Addison-Wesley Professional, 1981. ISBN: 978-0201103427.

[Kernighan1988] Brian W. Kernighan and Dennis M. Ritchie. *The C Programming Language*. Prentice-Hall, 1988. ISBN: 978-0131103627.

[Kohavi2020] Ron Kohavi, Diane Tang, and Ya Xu. *Trustworthy Online Controlled Experiments: A Practical Guide to A/B Testing*. Cambridge University Press, 2020. ISBN: 978-1108724265.

[Meszaros2007] Gerard Meszaros. *xUnit Test Patterns: Refactoring Test Code*. Addison-Wesley, 2007. ISBN: 978-0131495050.

[Oram2007] Andy Oram and Greg Wilson, eds. *Beautiful Code: Leading Programmers Explain How They Think*. O'Reilly, 2007. ISBN: 978-0596510046.

[Osmani2017] Addy Osmani. *Learning JavaScript Design Patterns*. 2017. URL: `https://addyosmani.com/resources/essentialjsdesignpatterns/book/`.

[Patterson2017] David A. Patterson and John L. Hennessy. *Computer Organization and Design: The Hardware/Software Interface*. Morgan Kaufmann, 2017. ISBN: 978-0128122754.

[Petre2016] Marian Petre and André van der Hoek. *Software Design Decoded: 66 Ways Experts Think*. MIT Press, 2016. ISBN: 978-0262035187.

[Petzold2008] Charles Petzold. *The Annotated Turing*. Wiley, 2008. ISBN: 978-0470229057.

[Schon1984] Donald A. Schon. *The Reflective Practitioner: How Professionals Think in Action*. Basic Books, 1984. ISBN: 978-0465068784.

[Smith2011] Peter Smith. *Software Build Systems: Principles and Experience*. Addison-Wesley Professional, 2011. ISBN: 978-0134185965.

[Taschuk2017] Morgan Taschuk and Greg Wilson. "Ten Simple Rules for Making Research Software More Robust". In: *PLoS Comp Bio* 13.4 (Apr. 2017). DOI: `10.1371/journal.pcbi.1005412`.

[Tudose2020] Cătălin Tudose. *JUnit in Action*. Manning, 2020. ISBN: 978-1617297045.

E

Glossary

absolute error: The absolute value of the difference between the observed and the correct value. Absolute error is usually less useful than **relative error**.

absolute path: A path that points to the same location in the **filesystem** regardless of where it is evaluated. An absolute path is the equivalent of latitude and longitude in geography.

abstract method: In **object-oriented programming**, a **method** that is defined but not implemented. Programmers will define an abstract method in a **parent class** to specify operations that **child classes** must provide.

abstract syntax tree (AST): A deeply nested data structure, or **tree**, that represents the structure of a program. For example, the AST might have a **node** representing a `while` loop with one **child** representing the loop condition and another representing the **loop body**.

accidental complexity: The extra (avoidable) complexity introduced by poor design choices. The term is used in contrast with **intrinsic complexity**.

accumulator: A variable that collects and/or combines many values. For example, if a program sums the values in an array by adding them all to a variable called `result`, then `result` is the accumulator.

actual result (of test): The value generated by running code in a test. If this matches the **expected result**, the test **passes**; if the two are different, the test **fails**.

Adapter pattern: A **design pattern** that rearranges parameters, provides extra values, or does other work so that one function can be called by another.

alias: A second or subsequent reference to the same object. Aliases are useful, but increase the **cognitive load** on readers who have to remember that all these names refer to the same thing.

anonymous function: A function that has not been assigned a name. Anonymous functions are usually quite short, and are usually defined where they are used, e.g., as callbacks. In Python, these are called lambda functions and are created through use of the lambda reserved word.

Application Binary Interface (ABI): The low-level layout that a piece of software must have to work on a particular kind of machine.

Application Programming Interface (API): A set of functions provided by a software library or web service that other software can call.

argument: A value passed to a function when it is called.

ASCII: A standard way to represent the characters commonly used in the Western European languages as 7- or 8-bit integers, now largely superceded by **Unicode**.

assembler: A **compiler** that translates software written in **assembly code** into machine instructions.

assembly code: A low-level programming language whose statements correspond closely to the actual **instruction set** of a particular kind of processor.

assertion: A **Boolean** expression that must be true at a certain point in a program. Assertions may be built into the language (e.g., Python's `assert` statement) or provided as functions (as with Node's `assert` library).

associative array: See **dictionary**.

asynchronous: Not happening at the same time. In programming, an asynchronous operation is one that runs independently of another, or that starts at one time and ends at another.

attribute: A name-value pair associated with an object, used to store metadata about the object such as an array's dimensions.

automatic variable: A variable that is automatically given a value in a **build rule**. For example, Make automatically assigns the name of a rule's **target** to the automatic variable `$@`. Automatic variables are frequently used when writing **pattern rules**.

backward-compatible: A property of a system that enables interoperability with an older legacy system, or with input designed for such a system.

bare object: An object that isn't an instance of any particular class.

base class: In **object-oriented programming**, a **class** from which other classes are derived.

binary: A system which can have one of two possible states, often represented as 0 and 1 or true and false.

bit: A single binary digit (0 or 1).

bitwise operation: An operation that manipulates individual bits in memory. Common bitwise operations include `and`, `or`, `not`, and `xor`.

block comment: A **comment** that spans multiple lines. Block comments may be marked with special start and end symbols, like `/*` and `*/` in C and its descendents, or each line may be prefixed with a marker like `#`.

Boolean: Relating to a variable or data type that can have either a logical value of true or false. Named for George Boole, a 19th century mathematician.

breadth first: To go through a nested data structure such as a **tree** by exploring all of one level, then going on to the next level and so on, or to explore a problem by examining the first step of each possible solution, and then trying the next step for each.

breakpoint: An instruction to a debugger telling it to suspend execution whenever a specific point in the program (such as a particular line) is reached.

bug: A missing or undesirable **feature** of a piece of software.

build manager: A program that keeps track of how files depend on one another and runs commands to update any files that are out-of-date. Build managers were invented to **compile** only those parts of programs that had changed, but are now often used to implement workflows in which plots depend on results files, which in turn depend on raw data files or configuration files.

build recipe: The part of a **build rule** that describes how to update something that has fallen out-of-date.

build rule: A specification for a **build manager** that describes how some files depend on others and what to do if those files are out-of-date.

build target: The file(s) that a **build rule** will update if they are out-of-date compared to their **dependencies**.

byte code: A set of instructions designed to be executed efficiently by an **interpreter**.

cache: Something that stores copies of data so that future requests for it can be satisfied more quickly. The CPU in a computer uses a hardware cache to hold recently-accessed values; many programs rely on a software cache to reduce network traffic and latency. Figuring out when something in a cache is out-of-date and should be replaced is one of the **two hard problems in computer science**.

caching: To save a copy of some data in a local **cache** to make future access faster.

call stack: A data structure that stores information about the active subroutines executed.

callback function: A function A that is passed to another function B so that B can call it at some later point. Callbacks can be used **synchronously**, as in generic functions like `map` that invoke a callback function once for each element in a collection, or **asynchronously**, as in a **client** that runs a callback when a **response** is received in answer to a **request**.

Cascading Style Sheets (CSS): A way to control the appearance of HTML. CSS is typically used to specify fonts, colors, and layout.

catch (an exception): To handle an error or other unexpected event represented by an **exception**.

Chain of Responsibility pattern: A **design pattern** in which each **object** either handles a request or passes it on to another object.

character encoding: A specification of how characters are stored as bytes. The most commonly-used encoding today is **UTF-8**.

child (in a tree): A **node** in a **tree** that is below another node (called the **parent**).

child class: In **object-oriented programming**, a **class** derived from another class (called the **parent class**).

circular dependency: A situation in which X depends on Y and Y depends on X, either directly or indirectly. If there is a circular dependency, then the **dependency graph** is not **acyclic**.

class: In **object-oriented programming**, a structure that combines data and operations (called **methods**). The program then uses a **constructor** to create an **object** with those properties and methods. Programmers generally put generic or reusable behavior in **parent classes**, and more detailed or specific behavior in **child classes**.

client: A program such as a web browser that gets data from a **server** and displays it to, or interacts with, users. The term is used more generally to refer to any program A that makes requests of another program B. A single program can be both a client and a server.

closure: A set of variables defined in the same **scope** whose existence has been preserved after that scope has ended.

code coverage (in testing): How much of a **library** or program is executed when tests run. This is normally reported as a percentage of lines of code.

cognitive load: The amount of working memory needed to accomplish a set of simultaneous tasks.

collision: A situation in which a program tries to store two items in the same location in memory. For example, a collision occurs when a **hash function** generates the same **hash code** for two different items.

column-major storage: Storing each column of a two-dimensional array as one block of memory so that elements in the same row are far apart.

combinatorial explosion: The exponential growth in the size of a problem or the time required to solve it that arises when all possible combinations of a set of items must be searched.

comma-separated values (CSV): A text format for tabular data in which each **record** is one row and **fields** are separated by commas. There are many minor variations, particularly around quoting of **strings**.

command-line argument: A filename or control flag given to a command-line program when it is run.

command-line interface (CLI): A user interface that relies solely on text for commands and output, typically running in a **shell**.

comment: Text written in a script that is not treated as code to be run, but rather as text that describes what the code is doing. These are usually short notes, often beginning with a # (in many programming languages).

compile: To translate textual source into another form. Programs in **compiled languages** are translated into machine instructions for a computer to run, and **Markdown** is usually translated into **HTML** for display.

compiled language: Originally, a language such as C or Fortran that is translated into machine instructions for execution. Languages such as Java are also compiled before execution, but into **byte code** instead of machine instructions, while **interpreted languages** like JavaScript are compiled to byte code on the fly.

compiler: An application that translates programs written in some languages into machine instructions or **byte code**.

confirmation bias: The tendency for someone to look for evidence that they are right rather than searching for reasons why they might be wrong.

console: A computer terminal where a user may enter commands, or a program, such as a shell that simulates such a device.

constructor: A function that creates an **object** of a particular **class**.

Coordinated Universal Time (UTC): The standard time against which all others are defined. UTC is the time at longitude 0°, and is not adjusted for daylight savings. **Timestamps** are often reported in UTC so that they will be the same no matter what timezone the computer is in.

corner case: Another name for an **edge case**.

coupling: The degree of interaction between two **classes**, **modules**, or other software components. If a system's components are **loosely coupled**, changes to one are unlikely to affect others. If they are **tightly coupled**, then any change requires other changes elsewhere, which complicates maintenance and evolution.

cryptographic hash function: A **hash function** that produces an apparently-random value for any input.

current working directory: The **folder** or **directory** location in which the program operates. Any action taken by the program occurs relative to this directory.

cycle (in a graph): A set of links in a graph that leads from a node back to itself.

data frame: A two-dimensional data structure for storing tabular data in memory. Rows represent **records** and columns represent **fields**.

data migration: Moving data from one location or format to another. The term refers to translating data from an old format to a newer one.

Decorator pattern: A **design pattern** in which a function adds additional features to another function or a **class** after its initial definition. Decorators are a feature of Python and can be implemented in most other languages as well.

defensive programming: A set of programming practices that assumes mistakes will happen and either reports or corrects them, such as inserting **assertions** to report situations that are not ever supposed to occur.

dependency: See **prerequisite**.

dependency graph: A **directed graph** showing how things depend on one another, such as the files to be updated by a **build manager**. If the dependency graph is not **acyclic**, the dependencies cannot be resolved.

deprecation: To indicate that while a function, method, or class exists, its use is no longer recommended (for example, because it is going to be phased out in a future release).

depth-first: A search algorithm that explores one possibility all the way to its conclusion before moving on to the next.

derived class: In **object-oriented programming**, a class that is a direct or indirect extension of a **base class**.

design by contract: A style of designing software in which functions specify the **pre-conditions** that must be true in order for them to run and the **post-conditions** they guarantee will be true when they return. A function can then be replaced by one with weaker pre-conditions (i.e., it accepts a wider set of input) and/or stronger post-conditions (i.e., it produces a smaller range of output) without breaking anything else.

design pattern: A recurring pattern in software design that is specific enough to be worth naming, but not so specific that a single best implementation can be provided by a **library**.

destructuring assignment: Unpacking values from data structures and assigning them to multiple variables in a single statement.

dictionary: A data structure that allows items to be looked up by value, sometimes called an **associative array**. Dictionaries are often implemented using **hash tables**.

directed acyclic graph (DAG): A **directed graph** which does not contain any loops (i.e., it is not possible to reach a **node** from itself by following edges).

directed graph: A **graph** whose **edges** have directions.

directory: A structure in a **filesystem** that contains references to other structures, such as files and other directories.

disassembler: A program that translates machine instructions into **assembly code** or some other higher-level language.

doc comment: A documentation comment ("doc comment" for short) is a specially-formatted comment containing documentation about a piece of code that is embedded in the code itself.

Document Object Model (DOM): A standard, in-memory representation of **HTML** and **XML**. Each **element** is stored as a **node** in a **tree** with a set of named **attributes**; contained elements are **child nodes**.

driver: A program that runs other programs, or a function that drives all of the other functions in a program.

dynamic loading: To **import** a **module** into the memory of a program while it is already running. Most **interpreted languages** use dynamic loading, and provide tools so that programs can find and load modules dynamically to configure themselves.

dynamic lookup: To find a function or a property of an **object** by name while a program is running. For example, instead of getting a specific property of an object using `obj.name`, a program might use `obj[someVariable]`, where `someVariable` could hold `"name"` or some other property name.

dynamic scoping: To find the value of a variable by looking at what is on the **call stack** at the moment the lookup is done. Almost all programming languages use **lexical-scoping** instead, since it is more predictable.

eager matching: Matching as much as possible, as early as possible.

easy mode: A term borrowed from gaming meaning to do something with obstacles or difficulties simplified or removed, often for practice purposes.

edge: A connection between two **nodes** in a **graph**. An edge may have data associated with it, such as a name or distance.

edge case: A problem that only comes up under unusual circumstances or when a system is pushed to its limits; also sometimes called a **corner case**. Programs intended for widespread use have to handle edge cases, but doing so can make them much more complicated.

element: A named component in an **HTML** or **XML** document. Elements are usually written `<name>...</name>`, where "..." represents the content of the element. Elements often have **attributes**.

encapsulate: To store data inside some kind of structure so that it is only accessible through that structure.

entry point: Where a program begins executing.

environment: A structure that stores a set of variable names and the values they refer to.

error (in a test): Signalled when something goes wrong in a **unit test** itself rather than in the system being tested. In this case, we do not know anything about the correctness of the system.

error handling: What a program does to detect and correct for errors. Examples include printing a message and using a default configuration if the user-specified configuration cannot be found.

event loop: A mechanism for managing concurrent activities in a program. Tasks are represented as items in a queue; the event loop repeatedly takes an item from the front of the queue and runs it, adding any other tasks it generates to the back of the queue to run later.

exception: An object that stores information about an error or other unusual event in a program. One part of a program will create and **raise an exception** to signal that something unexpected has happened; another part will **catch** it.

exception handler: A piece of code that deals with an **exception** after it is **caught**, e.g., by recording a message, retrying the operation that failed, or performing an alternate operation.

expected result (of test): The value that a piece of software is supposed to produce when tested in a certain way, or the state in which it is supposed to leave the system.

exploratory programming: A software development methodology in which requirements emerge or change as the software is being written, often in response to results from early runs.

export: To make something visible outside a **module** so that other parts of a program can **import** it. In most languages a module must export things explicitly in an attempt to avoid **name collision**.

fail (a test): A test fails if the **actual result** does not match the **expected result**.

feature (in software): Some aspect of software that was deliberately designed or built. A **bug** is an undesired feature.

field: A component of a **record** containing a single value. Every record in a database **table** has the same fields.

filename extension: The last part of a filename, usually following the '.' symbol. Filename extensions are commonly used to indicate the type of content in the file, though there is no guarantee that this is correct.

filesystem: The part of the **operating system** that manages how files are stored and retrieved. Also used to refer to all of those files and **directories** or the specific way they are stored (as in "the Unix filesystem").

filter: As a verb, to choose a set of **records** (i.e., rows of a table) based on the values they contain. As a noun, a command-line program that reads lines of text from files or **standard input**, performs some operation on them (such as filtering), and writes to a file or **stdout**.

finite state machine (FSM): A theoretical model of computing consisting of a directed graph whose nodes represent the states of the computation and whose arcs show how to move from one state to another. Every **regular expression** corresponds to a finite state machine.

fixed-width (of strings): A set of character strings that have the same length. Databases often used fixed-width strings to make storage and access more efficient; short strings are **padded** up to the required length and long strings are truncated.

fixture: The thing on which a test is run, such as the **parameters** to the function being tested or the file being processed.

fluent interface: A style of object-oriented programming in which methods return objects so that other methods can immediately be called.

folder: Another term for a **directory**.

garbage collection: The process of identifying memory that has been allocated but is no longer in use and reclaiming it to be re-used.

generator function: A function whose state is automatically saved when it returns a value so that execution can be restarted from that point the next time it is called. One example of generator functions use is to produce streams of values that can be processed by `for` loops.

generic function: A collection of functions with similar purpose, each operating on a different class of data.

global variable: A variable defined outside any particular function or **package** namespace, which is therefore visible to all functions.

globbing: To specify a set of filenames using a simplified form of **regular expressions**, such as `*.dat` to mean "all files whose names end in `.dat`". The name is derived from "global".

graph: A plot or a chart that displays data, or a data structure in which **nodes** are connected to one another by **edges**.

greedy algorithm: An algorithm that consumes as much input as possible, as early as possible.

handler: A **callback function** responsible for handling some particular event, such as the user clicking on a button or new data being received from a file.

hash code: A value generated by a **hash function**. Good hash codes have the same properties as random numbers in order to reduce the frequency of **collisions**.

hash function: A function that turns arbitrary data into a bit array, or a **key**, of a fixed size. Hash functions are used to determine where data should be stored in a **hash table**.

hash table: A data structure that calculates a pseudo-random key (location) for each value passed to it and stores the value in that location. Hash tables enable fast lookup for arbitrary data. This occurs at the cost of extra memory because hash tables must always be larger than the amount of information they need to store, to avoid the possibility of data collisions, when the hash function returns the same key for two different values.

header file: In C and C++, a file that defines constants and function **signatures** but does not contain runnable code. Header files tell the including file what is defined in other files so that the compiler can generate correct code.

heterogeneous: Containing mixed data types. For example, an array in Javascript can contain a mix of numbers, character strings, and values of other types.

heuristic: A rule or guideline that isn't guaranteed to produce the desired result, but usually does.

homogeneous: Containing a single data type. For example, a **vector** must be homogeneous: its values must all be numeric, logical, etc.

HTTP request: A message sent from a **client** to a **server** using the **HTTP protocol** asking for data. A request usually asks for a web page, image, or other data.

HTTP response: A reply sent from a **server** to a **client** using the **HTTP protocol** in response to a **request**. The response usually contains a web page, image, or data.

HyperText Markup Language (HTML): The standard **markup language** used for web pages. HTML is represented in memory using **DOM** (Digital Object Model).

HyperText Transfer Protocol (HTTP): The standard **protocol** for data transfer on the World-Wide Web. HTTP defines the format of **requests** and **responses**, the meanings of standard error codes, and other features.

idiomatic: To use a language in the same way as a fluent or native speaker. Programs are called idiomatic if they use the language the way that proficient programmers use it.

immediately-invoked function expression (IIFE): A function that is invoked once at the point where it is defined. IIFEs are typically used to create a **scope** to hide some function or variable definitions.

immutable: Data that cannot be changed after being created. Immutable data is easier to think about, particularly if data structures are shared between several tasks, but may result in higher memory requirements.

import: To bring things from a **module** into a program for use. In most languages a program can only import things that the module explicitly **exports**.

index (in a database): An auxiliary data structure in a database used to speed up search for some entries. An index increases memory and disk requirements but reduces search time.

inner function: A function defined inside another (outer) function. Creating and returning inner functions is a way to create **closures**.

instance: An **object** of a particular **class**.

instruction pointer: A special **register** in a processor that stores the address of the next instruction to execute.

instruction set: The basic operations that a particular processor can execute directly.

interpreted language: A high-level language that is not executed directly by the computer, but instead is run by an **interpreter** that translates program instructions into machine commands on the fly.

interpreter: A program whose job it is to run programs written in a high-level **interpreted language**. Interpreters can run interactively, but may also execute commands saved in a file.

intrinsic complexity: The unavoidable complexity inherent in a problem that any solution must deal with. The term is used in contrast with **accidental complexity**.

introspection: Having a program examine itself as it is running; common examples are to determine the specific class of a generic object or to get the fields of an object when they are not known in advance.

ISO date format: An international standard for formatting dates. While the full standard is complex, the most common form is `YYYY-MM-DD`, i.e., a four-digit year, a two-digit month, and a two-digit day, separated by hyphens.

Iterator pattern: A **design pattern** in which a temporary **object** or **generator function** produces each value from a collection in turn for processing. This pattern hides the differences between different kinds of data structures so that everything can be processed using loops.

JavaScript Object Notation (JSON): A way to represent data by combining basic values like numbers and character strings in **lists** and **key/value** structures. The acronym stands for "JavaScript Object Notation"; unlike better-defined standards like **XML**, it is unencumbered by a syntax for comments or ways to define a **schema**.

join: An operation that combines two **tables**, typically by matching **keys** from one with keys from another.

key: A **field** or combination of fields whose value(s) uniquely identify a **record** within a **table** or dataset. Keys are often used to select specific records and in **joins**.

label (address in memory): A human-readable name given to a particular location in memory when writing programs in **assembly code**.

layout engine: A piece of software that decides where to place text, images, and other elements on a page.

lazy matching: Matching as little as possible while still finding a valid match.

Least Recently Used cache (LRU cache): A **cache** that discards items that have not been used recently in order to limit memory requirements.

lexical scoping: To look up the value associated with a name according to the textual structure of a program. Most programming languages use lexical scoping instead of **dynamic scoping** because the latter is less predictable.

library: An installable collection of software, also often called a **module** or **package**.

lifecycle: The steps that something is allowed or required to go through. The lifecycle of an **object** runs from its **construction** through the operations it can or must perform before it is destroyed.

line comment: A **comment** in a program that spans part of a single line, as opposed to a **block comment** that may span multiple lines.

link (a program): To combine separately **compiled** modules into a single runnable program.

linter: A program that checks for common problems in software, such as violations of indentation rules or variable naming conventions. The name comes from the first tool of its kind, called `lint`.

Liskov Substitution Principle: A design rule stating that it should be possible to replace objects in a program with objects of derived classes without breaking the program. **Design by contract** is intended to enforce this rule.

list: A **vector** that can contain values of many different (**heterogeneous**) types.

literal: A representation of a fixed value in a program, such as the digits `123` for the number 123 or the characters `"abc"` for the string containing those three letters.

literate programming: A programming paradigm that mixes prose and code so that explanations and instructions are side by side.

loader: A function whose job is to read files containing runnable code into memory and make that code available to the calling program.

local variable: A variable defined inside a function which is only visible within that function.

log message: A status report or error message written to a file as a program runs.

loop body: The statement or statements executed by a loop.

loosely coupled: Components in a software system are said to be loosely coupled if they are relatively independent of one another, i.e., if any one of them can be changed or replaced without others having to be altered as well.

macro: Originally short for "macro-instruction", an instruction to translate some of the text into a program into other text before using it.

Makefile: A configuration file for the original **build manager**.

manifest: A list that specifies the precise versions of a complete set of libraries or other software components.

Markdown: A **markup language** with a simple syntax intended as a replacement for **HTML**.

markup language: A set of rules for annotating text to define its meaning or how it should be displayed. The markup is usually not displayed, but instead controls how the underlying text is interpreted or shown. **Markdown** and **HTML** are widely-used markup languages for web pages.

method: An implementation of a **generic function** that handles objects of a specific class.

method chaining: A style of object-oriented programming in which an object's methods return that object as their result so that another method can immediately be called, as in `obj.a().b().c()`.

mock object: A simplified replacement for part of a program whose behavior is easy to control and predict. Mock objects are used in **unit tests** to simulate databases, web services, and other complex systems.

module: A reusable software **package**, also often called a **library**.

module bundler: A program that finds all the dependencies of a set of source files and combines them into a single loadable file.

multi-threaded: Capable of performing several operations simultaneously. Multi-threaded programs are usually more efficient than **single-threaded** ones, but also harder to understand and debug.

name collision: The ambiguity that arises when two or more things in a program that have the same name are active at the same time. Most languages use **namespaces** to prevent such collisions.

namespace: A collection of names in a program that exists in isolation from other namespaces. Each function, **object**, **class**, or **module** in a program typically has its own namespace so that references to "X" in one part of a program do not accidentally refer to something called "X" in another part of the program. Scope is a distinct, but related, concept.

nested function: A function that is defined inside another function.

node: An element of a **graph** that is connected to other nodes by **edges**. Nodes typically have data associated with them, such as names or weights.

non-blocking execution: To allow a program to continue running while an operation is in progress. For example, many systems support non-blocking execution for file I/O so that the program can continue doing work while it waits for data to be read from or written to the **filesystem** (which is typically much slower than the CPU).

object: In **object-oriented programming**, a structure that contains the data for a specific instance of a **class**. The operations the object is capable of are defined by the class's **methods**.

object-oriented programming (OOP): A style of programming in which functions and data are bound together in **objects** that only interact with each other through well-defined interfaces.

off-by-one error: A common error in programming in which the program refers to element `i` of a structure when it should refer to element `i-1` or `i+1`, or processes `N` elements when it should process `N-1` or `N+1`.

op code: The numerical code for a particular instruction that a processor can execute.

Open-Closed Principle: A design rule stating that software should be open for extension but closed for modification, i.e., it should be possible to extend functionality without having to rewrite existing code.

operating system: A program that provides a standard interface to whatever hardware it is running on. Theoretically, any program that only interacts with the operating system should run on any computer that operating system runs on.

package: A collection of code, data, and documentation that can be distributed and re-used. Also referred to in some languages as a **library** or **module**.

pad (a string): To add extra characters to a string to make it a required length.

parameter: A variable specified in a function definition that is assigned a value when the function is called.

parent (in a tree): A **node** in a **tree** that is above another node (called a **child**). Every node in a tree except the **root node** has a single parent.

parent class: In **object-oriented programming**, the **class** from which a sub class (called the **child class**) is derived.

parser: A piece of software that translates a textual representation of something into a data structure. For example, a **YAML** parser reads indented text and produces nested lists and objects.

pass (a test): A test passes if the **actual result** matches the **expected result**.

patch: A single file containing a set of changes to a set of files, separated by markers that indicate where each individual change should be applied.

path (in filesystem): A **string** that specifies a location in a **filesystem**. In Unix, the **directories** in a path are joined using `/`.

pattern rule: A generic **build rule** that describes how to update any file whose name matches a pattern. Pattern rules often use **automatic variables** to represent the actual filenames.

pipe: To use the output of one computation as the input for the next, or the connection between the two computations responsible for the data transfer. Pipes were popularized by the **Unix shell**, and are now used in many different programming languages and systems.

pipe (in the Unix shell): The `|` used to make the output of one command the input of the next.

plugin architecture: A style of application design in which the main program loads and runs small independent modules that do the bulk of the work.

polymorphism: Having many different implementations of the same interface. If a set of functions or objects are polymorphic, they can be called interchangeably.

post-condition: Something that is guaranteed to be true after a function runs successfully. Post-conditions are often expressed as **assertions** that are guaranteed to be true of a function's results.

pre-condition: Something that must be true before a function runs in order for it to work correctly. Pre-conditions are often expressed as as **assertions** that must be true of a function's inputs in order for it to run successfully.

precedence: The priority of an operation. For example, multiplication has a higher precedence than addition, so `a+b*c` is read as "the sum of `a` with the product of `b` and `c`".

prerequisite: Something that a **build target** depends on.

process: An **operating system**'s representation of a running program. A process typically has some memory, the identity of the user who is running it, and a set of connections to open files.

promise: A way to represent the result of a delayed or **asynchronous** computation. A promise is a placeholder for a value that will eventually be computed; any attempt to read the value before it is available blocks, while any such attempt after the computation finishes acts like a normal read.

promisification: In JavaScript, the act of wrapping a callback function in a **promise** for uniform asynchronous execution.

protocol: Any standard specifying how two pieces of software interact. A network protocol such as **HTTP** defines the messages that **clients** and **servers** exchange on the World-Wide Web; **object-oriented** programs often define protocols for interactions between **objects** of different **classes**.

prune: To remove branches and nodes from a tree, or to rule out partially-complete solutions when searching for an overall solution in order to reduce work.

pseudo-random number: A value generated in a repeatable way that resembles the true randomness of the universe well enough to fool observers.

pseudo-random number generator (PRNG): A function that can generate **pseudo-random numbers**.

query selector: A pattern that specifies a set of **DOM** nodes. Query selectors are used in **CSS** to specify the elements that rules apply to, or by JavaScript programs to manipulate web pages.

query string: The portion of a **URL** after the question mark ? that specifies extra parameters for the **HTTP request** as name-value pairs.

race condition: A situation in which a result depends on the order in which two or more concurrent operations are carried out.

raise (an exception): To signal that something unexpected or unusual has happened in a program by creating an **exception** and handing it to the **error-handling** system, which then tries to find a point in the program that will **catch** it.

read-eval-print loop (REPL): An interactive program that reads a command typed in by a user, executes it, prints the result, and then waits patiently for the next command. REPLs are often used to explore new ideas, or for debugging.

record: A group of related values that are stored together. A record may be represented as a **tuple** or as a row in a **table**; in the latter case, every record in the table has the same **fields**.

register: A small piece of memory (typically one **word** long) built into a processor that operations can refer to directly.

regular expression: A pattern for matching text, written as text itself. Regular expressions are sometimes called "regexp", "regex", or "RE", and are powerful tools for working with text.

relational database: A database that organizes information into **tables**, each of which has a fixed set of named **fields** (shown as columns) and a variable number of **records** (shown as rows).

relative error: The absolute value of the difference between the actual and correct value divided by the correct value. For example, if the actual value is 9 and the correct value is 10, the relative error is 0.1. Relative error is usually more useful than **absolute error**.

relative path: A path that is interpreted relative to some other location, such as the **current working directory**. A relative path is the equivalent of giving directions using terms like "straight" and "left".

root (in a tree): The **node** in a **tree** of which all other nodes are direct or indirect **children**, or equivalently the only node in the tree that has no **parent**.

row-major storage: Storing each row of a two-dimensional array as one block of memory so that elements in the same column are far apart.

runnable documentation: Statements about code that can be executed to check their correctness, such as **assertions** or **type declarations**.

sandbox: A testing environment that is separate from the production system, or an environment that is only allowed to perform a restricted set of operations for security reasons.

SAT solver: A library or application that determines whether there is an assignment of true and false to a set of **Boolean** variables that makes an expression true (i.e., that satisfies the expression).

schema: A specification of the format of a dataset, including the name, format, and content of each **table**.

scope: The portion of a program within which a definition can be seen and used.

scope creep: Slow but steady increase in a project's goals after the project starts.

scoring function: A function that measures or estimates how good a solution to a problem is.

search path: The list of directories that a program searches to find something. For example, the Unix **shell** uses the search path stored in the `PATH` variable when trying to find a program whose name it has been given.

seed: A value used to initialize a **pseudo-random number generator**.

semantic versioning: A standard for identifying software releases. In the version identifier `major.minor.patch`, `major` changes when a new version of software is incompatible with old versions, `minor` changes when new features are added to an existing version, and `patch` changes when small **bugs** are fixed.

server: Typically, a program such as a database manager or web server that provides data to a **client** upon request.

SHA-1 hash: A **cryptographic hash function** that produces a 160-bit output.

shell: A **command-line interface** that allows a user to interact with the **operating system**, such as Bash (for Unix and MacOS) or PowerShell (for Windows).

shell variable: A variable set and used in the **Unix shell**. Commonly-used shell variables include `HOME` (the user's home directory) and `PATH` (their **search path**).

side effect: A change made by a function while it runs that is visible after the function finishes, such as modifying a **global variable** or writing to a file. Side effects make programs harder for people to understand, since the effects are not necessarily clear at the point in the program where the function is called.

signature: The set of parameters (with types or meaning) that characterize the calling interface of a function or set of functions. Two functions with the same signature can be called interchangeably.

single-threaded: A model of program execution in which only one thing can happen at a time. Single-threaded execution is easier for people to understand, but less efficient than **multi-threaded** execution.

singleton: A set with only one element, or a **class** with only one **instance**.

Singleton pattern: A **design pattern** that creates a **singleton object** to manage some resource or service, such as a database or **cache**. In **object-oriented programming**, the pattern is usually implemented by hiding the **constructor** of the **class** in some way so that it can only be called once.

slug: An abbreviated portion of a page's URL that uniquely identifies it. In the example `https://www.mysite.com/category/post-name`, the slug is `post-name`.

source map: A table used to translate a piece of code back to the lines in the original source.

sparse matrix: A matrix in which most of the values are zero (or some other value). Rather than storing many copies of the same values, programs will often use a special data structure that only stores the "interesting" values.

SQL: The language used for writing queries for a **relational database**. The term was originally an acronym for Structured Query Language.

stack frame: A section of the **call stack** that records details of a single call to a specific function.

stale (in build): To be out-of-date compared to a **prerequisite**. A **build manager**'s job is to find and update things that are stale.

standard error: A predefined communication channel for a **process** typically used to report errors.

standard input: A predefined communication channel for a **process**, typically used to read input from the keyboard or from the previous process in a **pipe**.

standard output: A predefined communication channel for a **process**, typically used to send output to the screen or to the next process in a **pipe**.

static site generator: A software tool that creates HTML pages from templates and content.

stream: A sequential flow of data, such as the **bits** arriving across a network connection or the bytes read from a file.

streaming API: An **API** that processes data in chunks rather than needing to have all of it in memory at once. Streaming APIs usually require **handlers** for events such as "start of data", "next block", and "end of data".

string: A block of text in a program. The term is short for "character string".

string interpolation: The process of inserting text corresponding to specified values into a **string**, usually to make output human-readable.

synchronous: To happen at the same time. In programming, synchronous operations are ones that have to run simultaneously, or complete at the same time.

tab completion: A technique implemented by most **REPLs**, **shells**, and programming editors that completes a command, variable name, filename, or other text when the TAB key is pressed.

table: A set of **records** in a **relational database** or **data frame**.

tagged data: A technique for storing data in a two-part structure, where one part identifies the type and the other part stores the bits making up the value.

Template Method pattern: A **design pattern** in which a **parent class** defines an overall sequence of operations by calling **abstract methods** that **child classes** must then implement. Each child class then behaves in the same general way, but implements the steps differently.

test harness: A program written to test some other program or set of functions, typically to measure their performance.

test runner: A program that finds and runs software tests and reports their results.

test subject: The thing being tested, sometimes also called the system under test (SUT).

test-driven development (TDD): A programming practice in which tests are written before a new feature is added or a **bug** is fixed in order to clarify the goal.

throw (exception): Another term for **raising** an exception.

tightly coupled: Components in a software system are said to be tightly coupled if they depend on each other's internals, so that if one is altered then others have to be altered as well.

Time of check/time of use (ToCToU): A **race condition** in which a process checks the state of something and then operates on it, but some other process might alter that state between the check and the operation.

timestamp: A digital identifier showing the time at which something was created or accessed. Timestamps should use **ISO date format** for portability.

token: An indivisible unit of text for a parser, such as a variable name or a number. Exactly what constitutes a token depends on the language.

topological order: Any ordering of the **nodes** in a **graph** that respects the direction of its **edges**, i.e., if there is an edge from node A to node B, A comes before B in the ordering. There may be many topological orderings of a particular graph.

transitive closure: The set of all **nodes** in a **graph** that are reachable from a starting node, either directly or indirectly.

tree: A **graph** in which every node except the **root** has exactly one **parent**.

tuple: A value that has a fixed number of parts, such as the three color components of a red-green-blue color specification.

Turing Machine: A theoretical model of computation that manipulates symbols on an infinite tape according to a fixed table of rules. Any computation that can be expressed as an algorithm can be done by a Turing Machine.

two hard problems in computer science: Refers to a quote by Phil Karlton: "There are only two hard problems in computer science—cache invalidation and naming things." Many variations add a third problem as a joke, such as **off-by-one errors**.

type declaration: A statement in a program that a variable or value has a particular data type. Languages like Java require type declarations for all variables; they are optional in TypeScript and Python, and not allowed in pure JavaScript.

Unicode: A standard that defines numeric codes for many thousands of characters and symbols. Unicode does not define how those numbers are stored; that is done by standards like **UTF-8**.

Uniform Resource Locator (URL): A unique address on the World-Wide Web. URLs originally identified web pages, but may also represent datasets or database queries, particularly if they include a **query string**.

unit test: A test that exercises one function or feature of a piece of software and produces **pass**, **fail**, or **error**.

UTF-8: A way to store the numeric codes representing **Unicode** characters in memory that is **backward-compatible** with the older **ASCII** standard.

vector: A sequence of values, usually of **homogeneous** type.

version control system: A system for managing changes made to software during its development.

virtual machine: A program that pretends to be a computer. This may seem a bit redundant, but VMs are quick to create and start up, and changes made inside the virtual machine are contained within that VM so we can install new **packages** or run a completely different operating system without affecting the underlying computer.

Visitor pattern: A **design pattern** in which the operation to be done is taken to each element of a data structure in turn. It is usually implemented by having a generator "visitor" that knows how to reach the structure's elements, which is given a function or method to call for each in turn, and that carries out the specific operation.

walk (a tree): To visit each **node** in a **tree** in some order, typically **depth-first** or **breadth-first**.

watchpoint: An instruction for a debugger telling it to suspect execution whenever the value of a variable (or more generally an expression) changes.

well formed: A piece of text that obeys the rules of a formal grammar is said to be well formed.

word (of memory): The unit of memory that a particular processor most naturally works with. While a byte is a fixed size (8 bits), a word may be 16, 32, or 64 bits long depending on the processor.

XML: A set of rules for defining **HTML**-like tags and using them to format documents (typically data). XML was popular in the early 2000s, but its complexity led many programmers to adopt **JSON**, instead.

YAML: Short for "YAML Ain't Markup Language", a way to represent nested data using indentation rather than the parentheses and commas of **JSON**. YAML is often used in configuration files and to define **parameters** for various flavors of **Markdown** documents.

z-buffering: A drawing method that keeps track of the depth of what lies "under" each pixel so that it displays whatever is nearest to the observer.

Index